Experiments in Love

American Society of Missiology
Monograph Series

Series Editor, James R. Krabill

The ASM Monograph Series provides a forum for publishing quality dissertations and studies in the field of missiology. Collaborating with Pickwick Publications—a division of Wipf and Stock Publishers of Eugene, Oregon—the American Society of Missiology selects high quality dissertations and other monographic studies that offer research materials in mission studies for scholars, mission and church leaders, and the academic community at large. The ASM seeks scholarly work for publication in the series that throws light on issues confronting Christian world mission in its cultural, social, historical, biblical, and theological dimensions.

Missiology is an academic field that brings together scholars whose professional training ranges from doctoral-level preparation in areas such as Scripture, history and sociology of religions, anthropology, theology, international relations, interreligious interchange, mission history, inculturation, and church law. The American Society of Missiology, which sponsors this series, is an ecumenical body drawing members from Independent and Ecumenical Protestant, Catholic, Orthodox, and other traditions. Members of the ASM are united by their commitment to reflect on and do scholarly work relating to both mission history and the present-day mission of the church. The ASM Monograph Series aims to publish works of exceptional merit on specialized topics, with particular attention given to work by younger scholars, the dissemination and publication of which is difficult under the economic pressures of standard publishing models.

Persons seeking information about the ASM or the guidelines for having their dissertations considered for publication in the ASM Monograph Series should consult the Society's website—www.asmweb.org.

Members of the ASM Monograph Committee who approved this book are:

Roger Schroeder, Professor of Intercultural Studies and Ministry, Catholic Theological Union

William P. Gregory, Associate Professor of Religious Studies, Clarke University

RECENTLY PUBLISHED IN THE ASM MONOGRAPH SERIES

Rosalia Meza, *Toward a New, Praxis-Oriented Missiology: Rediscovering Paulo Freire's Concept of Conscientizacao and Enhancing Christian Mission as Prophetic Dialogue*

Taylor Walters Denyer, *Decolonizing Mission Partnerships: Evolving Collaboration between United Methodists in North Katanga and the United States of America*

Experiments in Love

An Anabaptist Theology of Risk-Taking in Mission

EMILY RALPH SERVANT

American Society of Missiology Monograph
Series vol. 49

PICKWICK *Publications* • Eugene, Oregon

EXPERIMENTS IN LOVE
An Anabaptist Theology of Risk-Taking in Mission

American Society of Missiology Monograph Series 49

Pickwick Publications
An Imprint of Wipf and Stock Publishers
199 W. 8th Ave., Suite 3
Eugene, OR 97401

www.wipfandstock.com

PAPERBACK ISBN: 978-1-7252-6004-7
HARDCOVER ISBN: 978-1-7252-6005-4
EBOOK ISBN: 978-1-7252-6006-1

Cataloguing-in-Publication data:

Names: Ralph Servant, Emily, author.

Title: Experiments in love : an Anabaptist theology of risk-taking in mission / by Emily Ralph Servant.

Description: Eugene, OR: Pickwick Publications, 2021 | American Society of Missiology Monograph Series 49 | Includes bibliographical references and index.

Identifiers: ISBN 978-1-7252-6004-7 (paperback) | ISBN 978-1-7252-6005-4 (hardcover) | ISBN 978-1-7252-6006-1 (ebook)

Subjects: LCSH: Mennonite Church—Missions. | Risk-taking (Psychology)— Religious aspects—Christianity.

Classification: BV2545.A1 R35 2021 (print) | BV2545.A1 (ebook)

03/10/21

To Ryan and our girls.

Loving you has been the greatest risk of my life.
You are so worth it.
Thank you for making this theology come alive.

Contents

Acknowledgments

THIS BOOK WAS ORIGINALLY written as my doctoral dissertation, completed in 2017 while studying missiology at Cliff College in Derbyshire, England. Thank you to Cliff's staff, faculty, and members of my cohort, whose friendship, insight, and passion for God's mission challenged me to find my voice and pursue the Spirit on this unusual path.

A special thank you to my friend Trevor Hutton, who "taught" me about the Trinity, provided valuable feedback on my chapters, and had faith in me from the day we first met. Thank you to my advisor Stephen Skuce, whose eye for detail pushed me to be perfect and who never let me coast. Thanks for making me laugh and for believing in this project, even though it sometimes verged on crazy.

Thank you to Stephen Kriss and my colleagues in Mosaic Mennonite Conference. Our conference grounded me in a rich history while also sparking a passion for the interconnectedness of mission, interculturalism, and spiritual formation. God's Spirit is moving in our midst and I'm grateful I get to serve alongside all of you.

Thank you to Sherill Hostetter for cheering me on when the world seemed overwhelming and when I couldn't find a place to belong. You reminded me of my calling and gave me courage to keep walking my own path, speaking truth, and trusting the Spirit's work in the chaos.

Thank you to my parents, Jim and Anna Ralph. Mom, you kept this project going when it felt all but impossible. Dad, you are much of the reason that I still love the Church despite everything. Mom and Dad, this book is the fruit of our ministry together and I'm grateful for the ways God has redeemed all the hopes dashed, experiments, and failures, and has brought new life out of the compost. I love you.

Abbreviations

AMBS	Anabaptist Mennonite Biblical Seminary
CGR	Conrad Grebel Review
GAMEO	Global Anabaptist Mennonite Encyclopedia Online
IMS	Institute of Mennonite Studies
JMS	Journal of Mennonite Studies
MC USA	Mennonite Church USA
MMN	Mennonite Mission Network
MPH	Mennonite Publishing House
MQR	Mennonite Quarterly Review
MWC	Mennonite World Conference
MWR	Mennonite World Review

Introduction

"Agape is not a weak, passive love. It is love in action . . . *Agape* is the willingness to go to any length to restore community."

—Martin Luther King Jr., "An Experiment in Love"[1]

LEAVES WERE JUST BEGINNING to change color that fall as I sat across the table from a fellow pastor, discussing his congregation's decision to embark on a "missional journey" the following year. The church was ready to commit money and staff time to exploring what it meant to be more engaged in their neighborhood. Not everyone was comfortable with the idea, however. "How is it," the pastor asked, looking at me across his coffee mug, "that the very businesspeople in our congregations who have taken huge risks to grow their companies are unwilling to take risks with the church?"

His question has echoed in my mind ever since. As a Mennonite pastor and leadership minister[2] in southeastern Pennsylvania and a consultant who works with congregations who are experiencing times of transition or conflict, I have often observed a disconnect between missional impulse and missional action. I grew up the child of a church planter and have been involved in ministry and mission since childhood. I remember the thrill of leading lessons and games for waves of children who rushed to the basement of our home every week to hear about Jesus and to bask in our love. I remember prayer and home group meetings when we expected that

1. King, "Experiment in Love," 20.

2. A "leadership minister" provides accountability, coaching, and support for congregations and pastors on behalf of a middle judicatory.

revival was near and the desire of those gathered to share with one more neighbor or respond to one more need.

I was a soon-to-be high school graduate when we closed down our church plant and moved into the heart of the traditional Mennonite community. Franconia Conference of Mennonite Church USA (MC USA) contained some of the oldest Mennonite congregations in the United States.[3] We soon discovered that, in Franconia, Anabaptism was linked more to the Swiss-German "Pennsylvania Dutch" culture and family heritage than to fiery evangelism and charismatic expectation. It was in Franconia that I first dabbled in official leadership and where I was called, affirmed, and ordained.

Even as a teenager, I had been drawn to passages in Scripture that talk about healing, liberation, and the reconciliation of people to one another and to God through Jesus. Although I matured in my understanding and expression of Anabaptist life and faith, I never lost the zeal of wanting to share that good news with the world—a zeal, I believe, that was rooted in the call to mission of the "Radical Reformation."[4] The actions of the early Anabaptists illustrate the very definition of risk: exposing someone or something of value to danger, harm, or loss.[5] Many Anabaptists lost property, family, and homeland, and some even lost their lives. Others followed in the footsteps of those early Anabaptists, even knowing the risks existed. Their risk-taking, however, was not just for the thrill of it, but for a greater purpose, in "order to achieve a goal":[6] bringing their neighbors to reconciliation with God and others.

In this book, I will explore how risk-taking in the context of mission intentionally puts individuals or congregations in positions of physical, emotional, spiritual,[7] or financial uncertainty for the goal of joining with God in bringing about God's Dream[8] on earth: *shalom*, transformation,

3. For the history of Franconia Conference, see Ruth, *Maintaining*. Franconia Conference is now Mosaic Conference (MosaicMennonites.org).

4. George Williams was the first to use the term "Radical Reformation" in *Spiritual and Anabaptist Writers*.

5. Oxford Dictionary, "Risk."

6. Merriam-Webster Learners Dictionary, "Risk-taking."

7. I define theological or spiritual risk as when Christians believe that a change in belief or practice could result in God's judgment.

8. *Mujerista* theologian Ada María Isasi-Díaz warns that we have come to understand God's kingdom through the lens of patriarchy, elitism, and autocracy and suggests using the phrase "kin-dom" to more closely reflect God's desire for the human family ("Kin-dom of God"). Cherokee theologian Randy Woodley recommends the phrase "Community of Creation" (*Shalom*, 25–40). White feminist Elisabeth Schüssler Fiorenza is concerned that some of these alternatives to "kingdom" language miss

and union with God. All of these risks are birthed out of and motivated by the risk of vulnerable relationship, which is the crucial risk of mission. I have seen how traditional churches have experienced waves of missional impulse but have been unable to follow through with effective missional engagement by taking the risks that mission would require. In response, I argue that only when our congregations rediscover the narrative of a risk-taking God who risked the vulnerability of creating and relating to humanity can we join with God in taking the risk of vulnerable relationship in mission for the sake of love.

Having served as a pastor for a congregation in the farmlands of eastern Pennsylvania, a former mission outpost in Lancaster city, and a newly "converted" Indonesian immigrant congregation in Philadelphia and as leadership minister for both thriving and struggling congregations, these issues are haunting and insistent. I am what anthropologist Ruth Behar calls a "vulnerable observer,"[9] one who is involved in and impacted by the very realities that I observe. As such, I cannot remain entirely objective; reflexivity requires an awareness of my own experiences and biases. My life experiences have shaped how I read and engage with theology, how I see the world, and even how I evaluate what I know to be true. My correlational methodology of liberation (described in chapter 2) requires me to explore my own story and consider my own lens.

I began my life at the lower end of the socioeconomic spectrum. As the daughter of church planters near Philadelphia, we often struggled to make ends meet. At the same time, we were part of a loving church community who, although they had little themselves, would often step in to meet our needs. Both of my parents had college educations and my mother and three out of four grandparents had one or more graduate degree. I received a challenging education that allowed me to enter college with a considerable scholarship, keeping my school loans to a minimum. For the next decade, I often worked up to four jobs at a time, which allowed me to pay off my school loans and pay my way through seminary and doctoral studies without taking out additional loans. Now, my husband and I are settled comfortably in the middle-class, a position that surprises and often discomforts me.

---

the political nature of the original phrase and suggests that talking about the *basileia* ("reigning") of God is more accurate ("To Follow the Vision," 134–5). My concerns reflect these critiques of hierarchy and patriarchy as well as the irrelevance of "kingdom" language in a twenty-first-century democracy. The language of "God's Dream" reflects my narrative method as well as the political subversion of dreaming. This is the kind of dreaming Martin Luther King Jr. linked to the ongoing struggle for freedom: dreaming leads to doing ("I Have a Dream," 219).

9. Behar, *Vulnerable Observer*.

I was raised in an Anabaptist setting outside of the mainstream Swiss-German US-American Mennonite culture. When I became part of the oldest US Mennonite conference as a senior in high school, I found myself on the outside of a tight-knit community of families who were interrelated both biologically and through common history. In the decade that followed, I established relationships and networks that gave me an "in" with this community, helping me to understand them even as my perspectives were often at odds with their historical consciousness. With these learnings, I often became a bridge, helping "insider" and "outsider" Mennonites to understand one another. I worked to foster intercultural[10] worship in our communal gatherings and was stimulated by relationships with people of other ethnicities, through whom I learned much about white privilege and cultural stereotypes. I felt most at home in these communities as someone who never quite fit in with the US-American Mennonite establishment.

After seminary, I was called to the pastoral team of a middle-class congregation in one of the poorest neighborhoods in Lancaster city. Our weekly community meal and food pantry helped me to build relationships with people who represented the beautiful brokenness that was our community; on Sunday mornings, however, most of our (white) congregation drove in from the suburbs. Several of us who did live in the city worked within the poverty of our setting but had the privilege of returning to our safer, working-class neighborhoods at the end of the day. Later, when I became the interim pastor of an immigrant congregation in south Philadelphia, I discovered the additional privilege of mobility that came from owning a car and, even more importantly, having the documentation needed to get a driver's license. Although I was in the minority in my congregation—preaching, teaching, and interacting through interpreters—in our broader culture I speak the dominant language and have a lifetime of experience to understand the quirks of US life.

As a young woman pastor who served for two years in a conservative conference,[11] I experienced the oppression of being forced into "women's roles" in the Church. I looked around at conference events and saw very few people who "looked like me;" I rarely experienced women in positions of leadership. As a woman raised outside of the local geography, I was even more suspect; I did not have the relationships or historical memory to help me fit into the local white Mennonite culture. At the same time, as someone who was ordained in the Church for pastoral ministry, I carried the positional

10. Interculturalism moves beyond multiculturalism by engaging in deep relationships of mutual transformation. See Mosaic Mennonite Conference, "Intercultural."

11. Lancaster Mennonite Conference only approved women's ordination in 2008 (Rutter, "Lancaster Mennonites").

power of pastor. My leadership and ministry gifts had been recognized, called out, and affirmed by the Church. This in itself is a privilege.

It was in this context that I began my research on risk-taking in mission. Halfway through my program, however, I moved to Baltimore, Maryland. Here, in the midst of a majority black city, I am in the minority, but a minority that holds a disproportionate percentage of power, wealth, and education. I am once again on the outskirts in a sea of unfamiliar faces, very few of whom are Anabaptist, yet knowing that my voice carries more weight here, the color of my skin makes me more trustworthy to my white neighbors, and my race and economic status make it possible for my family to choose where we live. In a city known for its government-sanctioned racial profiling and segregated neighborhoods, the means and ability to own one's own house in a safe neighborhood is a privilege. As I learn more about the #BlackLivesMatter movement in the brokenness of Baltimore, I realize that, as a white woman, I do not have to be afraid of the police because of the color of my skin, because I do not possess the right documentation or identification, or because I am in the wrong place at the wrong time.

As a white feminist Anabaptist theologian, I read Scripture through these lenses.[12] I resonate with the thought of liberation theologians because I have faced both freedom and oppression myself. My experience as the child of church planters and as a pastor serving both a mission outpost and an ethnic congregation on the margins of society has given me a passion for mission—but not mission as it has been understood in the past. Those experiences have led me to challenge whether the stories and practices of mission in the Mennonite Church are a reflection of a good and life-giving God. As a leadership minister, I find myself wondering how I and the pastors I serve can shape congregational dynamics of thought and practice so that our congregations are able to take radical risks of vulnerable relationship in mission for the sake of love.

In this book, I will argue that, in contrast to the fiery evangelism and bold risk-taking of the Radical Reformation, today's Mennonite Church has become increasingly risk-averse in local, congregational mission. As we[13] have attempted to encourage mission in the Church, Mennonites have

---

12. See my methodology in chapter 2.

13. Throughout this book, I will use the personal plural when critiquing the current Mennonite Church. In *Disunity in Christ*, sociologist Christena Cleveland suggests that by using inclusive "us" language, we no longer "perceive the problems of other groups in the body of Christ as solely their problems. As newly minted members of us, their problems are now our problems. We can no longer stand at a distance, point our fingers at them and shake our heads in disgust. We must lovingly and wisely engage because to fail to do so would only hurt ourselves" (64).

been "great ecumenical borrowers."[14] When we have worked to identify our unique perspectives, Mennonites have traditionally been prolific in deconstruction (identifying how other traditions are wrong) without being equally imaginative in constructive missional theology. Over the last century, the Mennonite Church has seen a renewed effort to define "Anabaptist" theology as a unique alternative to the mainstream, but these stories have been limited by traditional ways of knowing and understanding the world, the Church, and God. As a result, rather than promoting risk-taking in mission, some of the stories that Mennonites tell about God in our theology, ecclesiology, and missional literature may have undermined the efforts of local and denominational leaders as they have encouraged congregations to make changes and take risks essential to mission.[15]

This book presents a constructive theology of risk-taking in mission from an Anabaptist perspective, expressed through a distinctly christocentric but trinitarian lens, and integrating two areas of study that have been, up to this point, engaged individually—the risk-taking God and missional ecclesiology. This book brings additional contributions to knowledge by developing a correlational methodology of liberation, which engages Anabaptist[16] mission in conversation with both the behavioral and social sciences as well as liberation and feminist theologies. Together, these emphases form a new way of seeing the world, the Church, and God, narrating the story of Anabaptist mission to promote rather than undermine congregational risk-taking.

Although this book necessarily presents the following chapters in a linear fashion, the research and argument it contains resemble more of a spiral, with many of the chapters intricately interrelated, informing and building on chapters that both precede and follow them. As white feminist theologian Letty Russell explains, writing in a spiral that "constantly

14. Shenk, "Developing Missiological Vision," 46.

15. I embarked on this research just before the start of a volatile time in MC USA. Since I began writing my dissertation, the denomination has experienced massive change, reorganization, and the loss of congregational membership in response to theological disagreement over human sexuality. In 2014, after a series of conversations with local pastors and conference leadership, it became clear that growing anxiety around the conflict could result in interviews and survey results being skewed as participants primarily, but not exclusively, reflected on risk-taking through the lens of the sexuality debate. In response to these circumstances, I focused my research on the literature that forms the basis for congregational storytelling and pastoral education. See Schrag, "Year in Review."

16. Throughout this book, I use both the terms "Anabaptist" and "Mennonite." The two are not synonymous; the Mennonite Church is a subset of Anabaptism. When I am specifying my family of Anabaptists, I use the label "Mennonite" in reference to the stream of Anabaptism that later became the "old" Mennonite Church and then MC USA.

returns to basic themes and holds them up to look at them from the angle of new evidence and perspective is part of the action-reflection process." This allows the underlying themes "to come to the fore no matter what theological aspect is being investigated, but each time it is hoped that new insights are added."[17]

In chapter 1, I provide an overview of Mennonite mission in thought and practice. I begin with a historical survey of mission, starting with early Anabaptism in the sixteenth century and following the line through the MC USA denomination. In articulating this story, I identify initial risk-taking behaviors and show how, over time, the early Anabaptist inclination to take risks in evangelism diminished in response to the threat of persecution, offers of security, and the building of an insular, homogenous community. Even when the Mennonite Church began to reengage with mission in the early twentieth century, risk-taking was reserved for isolated individuals who were sent out from the community while congregations were slow to integrate new members from diverse backgrounds. Today's Mennonite Church rarely resembles the community of risk-takers who birthed it. Following the historical survey, I explore the stories that Mennonites have traditionally told about God in theology and missiology. These stories have focused on the work of Jesus and the believer's choice to follow him, neglecting robust understandings of the Father and Spirit, and thus, the Trinity. Mennonite theology and missiology clearly reflect many themes prominent in wider missiological thought; additionally, they emphasize the Messianic nature of Jesus, the call to make disciples who follow Jesus in life and thus willingly submit to the reign of God, the suffering nature of discipleship and mission, the understanding of the Church as a set-apart community witnessing to reconciliation, and the inclusion of peace (*shalom*) as an essential characteristic of the gospel. Not only are images of a risk-taking God absent in these conversations, but the emphasis on following Jesus may undermine congregational leaders in their attempts to promote risk-taking in mission.

If the Mennonite Church wants to experience transformation as risk-takers in mission, we must develop new stories that do not undermine our efforts. In chapter 2, I argue that, in order to change our existing theological and missiological stories, we must dialogue with voices from outside and on the margins of our tradition. I first consider the transformational nature of narrative and the importance of acknowledging and respecting perspective in theological storytelling. Then I explore and define what it means for theology to be "Anabaptist" by establishing the context of Anabaptist biblical interpretation. Based on these Anabaptist values and narrative principles, I

---

17. Russell, *Human Liberation*, 22–23.

articulate a correlational method of liberation designed to facilitate change in the theological stories of the Mennonite Church.

In chapter 3, I apply this correlational method through engagement with the behavioral and social sciences. As very little research has been done on risk in the Church, I develop the practical implications of congregational risk-taking in mission by exploring literature on risk across other disciplines. In conversation with anthropology and psychology, I develop an understanding of vulnerability as the nature of risk, the foundation upon which the other understandings of risk are built. In dialogue with attachment theory in child development, I explore how community provides the courage for risk. In light of creativity research in cultural context, I engage with creativity as an essential energy for risk. In response to the work of researchers in the fields of business and management, I argue that failure is an unavoidable consequence of risk. Finally, as an important overlying principle, I dialogue with philosophers and ethicists to explore love as the ethical barometer of risk. These understandings of risk provide a set of best practices in light of which the existing literature on risk in theology and Mennonite theological and missiological literature can be critiqued.

Literature on risk in the Church is limited. Many missional authors use the term "risk" and describe missional engagement as "risky" but rarely explore what risk-taking looks like in the context of mission; in fact, risk often seems to be assumed rather than examined. In chapter 4, I consider existing literature on risk in theology and missiology, identifying areas of resonance and tension with the best practices of chapter 3. These explorations highlight themes of relationality, sacrifice, love, creativity, vulnerability, and failure. Although these stories provide rich material for continued theological development, they are inadequate in and of themselves to support the efforts of congregations who desire to embrace risk-taking in mission. Chapter 4 reveals how those stories that present a picture of a risk-taking God do not take the final step in applying these insights to relational risk-taking in mission and those stories that do discuss risk-taking in mission do not engage with a risk-taking God. These disparate pieces need to be engaged in conversation with one another and in dialogue with Anabaptist values and with voices on the margins to articulate a new theology of risk-taking for congregations in the Anabaptist tradition.

Chapters 3 and 4 provide a critical foundation for evaluating growing edges for risk-taking in Mennonite theological and missiological literature. In chapter 5, I revisit themes from the history and literature of Mennonite mission that impact both the practice and narrative surrounding mission in contemporary life. I argue that the common stories that dominate Mennonite theology as a result of the Mennonite emphasis on following Jesus in community, such as the divinity of Jesus and the importance of suffering for the faith (especially as illustrated by the martyr stories), mask the vulnerability of ordinary, everyday risk. This risk includes the possibility of being changed—a narrative which Mennonite stories of the pure and separated Church undermine. If the Church is not open to being transformed in our encounters with the "world," then stories of the Spirit's unpredictable work will be limited in their efficacy. If we are unreceptive to the Spirit, we will remain unconnected to the Trinity, a relationship which offers us safety and community for risk-taking. Without this narrative of reunion with God, we are cut off from the source of motivation for risk-taking in mission: God's overflowing love. These stories about God (and, as a result, the Church and mission) weaken our efforts to be transformed into congregations who take the risk of vulnerable relationship for the sake of love.

The final three chapters of this book begin the process of re-storying Anabaptist theology by constructing new narratives around the methodologies and principles discovered in conversation with the behavioral and social sciences, voices from outside and on the margins of the Mennonite Church, and a correlational methodology of liberation. This theology is built upon the story of a God who takes the risk of being radically present to a vulnerable world. By sharing in our vulnerability, Jesus breaks down barriers to the Spirit's energies in and around us, so that we may share together in God's life. Because of God's radical presence with us, we can be radically present to others, taking the risk of vulnerable closeness as an overflow of God's life and love. The nature of the Good News is an invitation to union with God so that we share in God's life of healing, wholeness, and well-being.

Chapter 6 tells the story of creation and humanity, as God risks creating a world in which vulnerability opens up possibilities for both harm and transformation. Into this vulnerability, God the Expression risks becoming the fully human one, embracing the vulnerability of human life without seeking to protect himself by harming other vulnerable people. In his incarnation, Jesus becomes radically present to humans, even to the extent of death. God's motivation for this risk is an all-consuming love built on the foundation of radical presence.

Chapter 7 further explores the incarnation by telling the story of how Jesus depended on God the Energy for his connection to divine power and community. As the fully human one, Jesus needed the Spirit's energy to break down barriers to wholeness and relationship. Through the Spirit's radical presence, Jesus experienced the life of God's Community. This connection to the Community of God formed a "secure base" for Jesus from which to take risks in mission. This same energy is available for the Church, connecting us to the Community of God, and enabling us to be radically, creatively, and vulnerably present with those around us, offering transformation to others and consenting to transformation ourselves.

Chapter 8 tells the story of resurrection, in which God the Source brings life where there is no life. The resurrection of Jesus was not triumphalistic, but a vulnerable redemption, the risk of new life coming from death and suffering. Jesus was sent from the Source and returned to the Source even as he was intimately connected to the Source throughout his life and ministry. In the same way, all of creation was imagined by the Source and is sustained by the Source; God's Dream is that all will be reunited with the Source—the final Judge and Redeemer. Knowing that God can redeem death or failure makes it possible for today's Church to continue to take risks even when confronted by overwhelming evil and hopelessness. Only through the love and creativity of the Source can we experience vulnerable resurrection as we take risks in mission for the sake of love.

As a white female pastor who believes that God loves and desires to work through the Church, I write these chapters as a loving encouragement—and challenge—to both the progressive and evangelical branches of the white Mennonite Church. Although this book is specifically grounded in the Mennonite tradition, the stories it contains and the theology it imagines are not limited to those congregations who claim an Anabaptist heritage. As the Church continues to explore the meaning and purpose of risk-taking in mission in the twenty-first century, may we all find security and courage as we share in the life of God so that our "love might become even more and more rich with knowledge and all kinds of insight" as we are "filled with the fruit of righteousness, which comes from Jesus Christ, in order to give glory and praise to God" (Phil 1:9–11 CEB).

1

Risk-Taking in a Mennonite Context

INTRODUCTION

IN ORDER TO FOCUS this book on an *Anabaptist* theology of risk-taking, I will first engage with the Mennonite experience of mission in practice and thought. The particularities of the Mennonite context require an exploration of the Anabaptist history of mission as a separate stream from generalized evangelical or mainstream mission. While these streams overlap, they come from different sources and thus the resulting narratives that have been passed down through the generations are not identical. Historically, many Anabaptists have treasured their differences from other Christian traditions and stressed stories that emphasize contemporary connections to early Anabaptist heroes.

In this chapter, I provide an overview of Mennonite mission in practice, beginning with early Anabaptism in the sixteenth century and following the historical line through the MC USA denomination. Although Anabaptism was born out of expressions of risky mission, the following overview of mission in the Mennonite Church will show that the evangelical fervor of its beginnings faded with time. The Anabaptist stream that eventually settled in the American colony of Pennsylvania and, nearly 300 years later, became part of MC USA, dabbled in mission as it encountered various mission movements in the nineteenth and twentieth centuries. Now, in the twenty-first century, the denominational leadership has embraced the missional church movement, yet has seen little positive change in its membership to reflect that commitment. Although many of the denomination's congregations that are primarily attended by people of the global majority are committed to local mission, very few of its historic, majority-white congregations appear to be willing to make the changes or to take the risks that mission might require. This lack of evangelical urgency is a far cry from the passionate risk-taking out of which the Anabaptist tradition began.

Following the historical overview, I consider the stories about God that have been traditionally told in Mennonite literature and life and their impact on Mennonite missional ecclesiology.[1] Not only are discussions of risk and images of a risk-taking God largely absent in these conversations, but I will suggest that the unique emphasis on following Jesus may undermine congregational leaders in their attempts to foster cultures of risk-taking in mission, instead promoting responses of suffering, duty, separatism, and a resistance to change.

The following history reflects the dominant stream in the Mennonite Church: it traces the story of Mennonites of European origin through the sixteenth century and into the twenty-first without deeply exploring the experiences of Mennonites of color. This narrative has been the most common one in shaping the self-identity of the established white Mennonite Church. In 1976, Black Mennonite pastor Hubert Brown reflected that every time "I hear the term 'our' forefathers, or 'our' Mennonite heritage I instinctively wonder if I'm included in the term 'our.'"[2] He felt a connection to the spiritual heritage of Anabaptism, but not the Euro-centric culture and racism that accompanied it into the twentieth century. "Yet I can appreciate and understand the special significance of Anabaptism to me," he acknowledged. "I view Anabaptism as a movement, a movement of poor folks, oppressed peoples seeking liberation and the ushering in of God's kingdom for His will to be done on earth as it is in heaven."[3] For Brown, exploring the story of the early Anabaptists and the disintegration of their identities as missionaries and boundary-pushers helps to identify the ways in which today's white Mennonites are not the "heirs of Anabaptism" and, therefore, need to open ourselves up to being transformed by the voices of those on the margins who are.[4]

A RISKY BEGINNING[5]

Today's Mennonite Church traces its roots to sixteenth-century Europe. While Martin Luther and Ulrich Zwingli were establishing their own

1. That is, mission in and as a local congregation (Niemandt, "Trends," 1–2).

2. Brown, *Black and Mennonite*, 78.

3. Brown, *Black and Mennonite*, 91.

4. Brown, *Black and Mennonite*, 93–95.

5. The following two paragraphs reflect the "popular" history of Anabaptism as described in multiple sources, including Dyck, *Introduction*.

forms of State Church in protest of Catholicism, various small groups of dissidents were concerned that these reformers were not taking their critique of the Church to its logical conclusions. These radical reformers agreed with much of the Reformation's theological content but insisted that the theological reformation must be reflected in an ethical and behavioral reformation as well. Followers of Jesus were called to more than just right belief; they were called to a radical expression of right living. Right living demanded an adult decision to walk in the way of Jesus. When adults decided to follow Jesus, they were baptized as a sign of that commitment. Therefore, the dissidents argued, baptism should be reserved for adults only; child baptism was invalid. In response to this practice, the radical reformers were labelled as "Anabaptists" ("re-baptizers"), a designation that qualified them for the death penalty.

Another implication of the adult decision to follow Jesus was the voluntary nature of participation in the Church. According to these radicals, one could not be born into the Church and one was not automatically a member of the Church because of citizenship. Participation in the Church was voluntary and required a real commitment to piety. While Zwingli and Luther continued to utilize a partnership between Church and State for the spreading of the faith, these early Anabaptists began a widespread pattern of evangelization. These men and women had experienced regeneration, an encounter with the Spirit, and deep community; they wanted to share this new life with others.[6] Early Anabaptist leader Menno Simons describes how:

> To this end we preach as much as opportunity and possibility affords, both in day time and by night, in houses and in fields, . . . in prison and bonds, in water, fire and the scaffold, on the gallows, . . . orally and by writing at the risk of possessions and life, as we have done these many years without ceasing. We are not ashamed of the Gospel of the glory of Christ, for we are its living fruit and mightily realize its moving power in our hearts.[7]

In their passion for adult baptism and evangelization, early Anabaptists were deeply influenced by the work of the Rotterdam humanist, Erasmus.[8] In his paraphrase of the Gospel of Matthew, Erasmus declared that the Great Commission was a formula of sorts, clarifying the call of the Church

---

6. Colin Godwin points to five underlying concerns in early Anabaptist mission: adult baptism as the reason for mission, human initiative as the means of mission, the Church as the community in mission, eschatology adding urgency to mission, and social transformation as the result of mission (*Baptizing*).

7. Simons, "Reply," 10.

8. Friesen, *Erasmus*.

to evangelization and discipleship: Jesus had commanded his followers to first make disciples, then to baptize and teach them.[9] This order meant that infant baptism was unacceptable, for how could infants be disciples? Making disciples became a driving impulse for the Anabaptists and they devoted much of their time, energy, and resources to calling their family, friends, and neighbors to join them in following Jesus in life.

This impulse to make disciples was made all the more urgent by a widespread belief that they were living in the end times.[10] This belief was not unique to the Anabaptists, but, rather, pervaded the Reformation scene.[11] What *was* unique to the Anabaptists was how they responded to their eschatological expectations:[12] "in a climate of strong eschatological hope," Anabaptists saw their evangelism as "end-time obedience to the Great Commission."[13]

At first, the early Anabaptists had very little strategy; they simply shared the good news of new and regenerated lives. Mission happened naturally, sometimes through Bible reading and study, in which literate Anabaptists read the scripture to their non-literate friends and neighbors, and house meetings, in which friends gathered their extended networks to hear and respond to the Anabaptist message.[14] Additionally, many converts were won through the witness of Anabaptists "in the fire" who remained faithful despite the threat of death.[15] As a result of these persecutions, the Anabaptists were often scattered to wider geographies, taking their message of regenerated life in Jesus with them.[16] No matter what the method, the Anabaptists' witness was confirmed by their lives; court documents testify that many new converts were attracted to the faith because of Anabaptist ethics.[17] Anabaptists were so well-known for their moral living that non-Anabaptists were sometimes brought up on charges as Anabaptist heretics simply for living ethically.[18]

---

9. Friesen, *Erasmus*, 44, 52, and 54.

10. See Thomas Finger on the diversity of eschatological thought among early Anabaptists in *Contemporary*, 512–39.

11. Meihuizen, "Missionary Zeal," 90, and Barrett, "Rethinking," 162.

12. Shank, "Anabaptists and Mission," 209.

13. Shank, "Anabaptists and Mission," 214.

14. Roth, "Anabaptist Missions," 94.

15. Kasdorf, "Anabaptist Approach," 57–58.

16. Kasdorf, "Anabaptist Approach," 55–58, and Roth, "Anabaptist Missions," 93–94.

17. Schäufele, "Missionary Vision," 80; Roth, "Anabaptist Missions," 95; Klaassen, "Quest," 20.

18. Bender, "Anabaptist Vision," 26.

Evangelization for the early Anabaptists was a risky endeavor; they risked their lives, property, reputation, vocations, and relationships with those they loved. Despite these risks, many Anabaptists passionately believed that witness was essential to an authentic faith. The effectiveness of the Anabaptist witness caused an uproar in the state-run Church and government: in preparation for one public debate, Anabaptists were promised safe passage only as long as they did not evangelize along the way.[19] Soldiers took to using tongue screws on the Anabaptists before their executions to keep them from evangelizing from the fire.[20] Some Anabaptist women were chained to their kitchen tables to prevent them from going out to witness (although this did not keep eager seekers from coming to them).[21] The government increased the penalties for evangelism to include the confiscation of property, imprisonment, expulsion, or even death.[22] These risks did not dampen the fervor of the early Anabaptists to bring others into their faith; at its height, the Anabaptist movement may have reached 15,000–20,000 followers throughout Central Europe and the Netherlands.[23]

"The Anabaptist movement of the first generation was deeply defined by its missionary character," describes Mennonite historian John Roth.[24] Despite their missionary fervor, however, they spent little energy on strategy. "At the most, they seem to have sought a common mind on certain key theological themes, made some ad hoc provisions for the economic support of itinerant preachers, and sought general understandings regarding a division of missionary labor in specific territories."[25] The 1527 missionary synod in Augsburg, Germany, during which the early Anabaptist leaders attempted to formulate a missionary strategy to "call people to repentance before the end

---

19. Augsburger, *Robe of God,* 65.

20. van der Zijpp, "Maeyken Wens."

21. Schäufele, "Missionary Vision," 80. Thomas Finger adds that although "fairly little is known about individual Anabaptist women, this grassroots movement likely owed its spread and sustenance at least as much to women as men" (*Contemporary,* 258).

22. Kasdorf, "Anabaptist Approach," 54.

23. Roth, "Anabaptist Missions," 88. Because much of Anabaptism was spread and practiced in secret, exact numbers are difficult to determine. Robert Bainton suggested that, if not for persecution, the Anabaptist missionary zeal may have led to Anabaptism becoming the dominant faith in Germany ("Anabaptist Contribution," 321).

24. Roth, "Anabaptist Missions," 92.

25. Roth, "Anabaptist Missions," 92.

time"[26] has been remembered, instead, as the "Martyr's Synod;" more than half of the participants were executed within the year.[27]

In response to a variety of Anabaptist radicalism, some streams of Anabaptists sought to differentiate themselves from others. After Jan van Leyden and his followers' disastrous attempt at establishing God's kingdom on earth through force in the city of Münster, Germany, ecclesiastical authorities accused Anabaptists of violence, polygamy, and practicing the common purse. Other Anabaptists sought to distance themselves from the atrocities of Münster, stressing that they were peaceful followers of Menno Simons, or "Menno's people."[28] This attempt to prove themselves good citizens—not troublemakers—along with the movement to establish viable congregations, dampened later Anabaptists' enthusiasm for taking risks in mission.[29]

Within another generation, the persecution began to take its toll. What threat of death or expulsion could not accomplish, offers of safety and a peaceful, fruitful life could. By the end of the sixteenth century, state governments in the Netherlands, the Ukraine, and parts of Switzerland had reached an uneasy peace with the Anabaptists: they could live and work without interference as long as they kept quiet and stopped evangelizing.[30] "This 'bloodless persecution' of the Mennonites lasted till late into the eighteenth century. The Mennonites were only tolerated . . . . They had to keep 'silent and quiet,'" describes Dutch historian Nanne van der Zijpp. "This restricted their old missionary zeal. They could not spread their wings anymore."[31] Instead of fervent radicals, the Anabaptists moved to protect themselves from vulnerability; they became the "Quiet in the Land."[32] As the eschatological fervor of the Reformation faded, mission no longer seemed worth the risk.

MENNONITES GROW RISK-AVERSE

Protection from persecution and the promise of land eventually drew Anabaptists to migrate to the British colony of Pennsylvania, in what would become the United States.[33] There, the initial immigrants were called

26. Barrett, "Rethinking," 164.

27. Roth, "Anabaptist Missions," 95.

28. Friesen, *Erasmus*, 65. This was the beginning of the name, "Mennonites."

29. Van der Zijpp, "From Anabaptist," 129.

30. Van der Zijpp, "From Anabaptist," 124–26.

31. Van der Zijpp, "From Anabaptist," 124.

32. Gallardo, "Ethics and Mission," 152.

33. Historians estimate the number of Mennonite immigrants at 3,000–5,000 during the first half of the eighteenth century (Schlabach, *Gospel,* 27).

"Mennonists," a title that was then extended to cover all Anabaptists, even those who were not Dutch followers of Menno Simons; the majority of the new "Mennonists" were from Switzerland and the Palatinate.[34] Settled in the New World, Mennonites established themselves as good, law-abiding citizens in rural communities. They were surrounded by other pietistic groups like the Dunkers, Quakers, and Schwenkfelders.[35] There, the Mennonites could blend in and participate in society; there was no need to evangelize when the community was filled with others of like mind.[36] Perhaps this gave them their first taste of the "Christendom" experienced by other reformation branches: a Christian society in which mission was unneeded.

Over the next decades, as Pennsylvania saw increasing immigration by English-speaking peoples, Mennonites withdrew into their communities, refusing to intermarry with those outside the fellowship, and emphasizing their religious (and cultural) distinctives: simplicity and nonconformity, nonresistance, church discipline, ethical behavior, and adult baptism.[37] After decades of establishing their safe, "pure" communities, why would they begin to risk mission? Instead, Mennonites faced a different kind of risk: the loss of identity. Eighteenth- and nineteenth-century Mennonites struggled with how to maintain their identity and faithfulness as a separated Church in response to questions of war (*To whom should they be loyal in the War of Independence? Is it permissible to hire soldiers or pay a war tax to avoid fighting in the War Between the States?*), nonconformity (*Was it appropriate to use technology of any kind? What kind of clothing or jewelry was it permissible to wear? Could Mennonites belong to guilds, lodges, or other societies?*), and modernization (*Should the Mennonites have their own printing press, colleges, and institutions? What would be the impact of education or industry on Mennonite communities? Should the Church take minutes or use the rule of order at meetings?*). Struggles with these questions often led to an inward-looking focus and numerous schisms.[38] Mennonites had learned the lesson of the persecution years well: lay low, protect the community, do not try

---

34. Dyck, *Introduction*, 214.

35. Donald Durnbaugh describes the origins of these groups and their relationship to one another in *Believers' Church*, 12, 76–77, 106–15, and 120–30.

36. Dyck, *Introduction*, 197. Some early Mennonites settlers did briefly join with Quakers in half-hearted attempts to evangelize the local Native Americans.

37. Dyck, *Introduction*, 198.

38. "When people take their convictions seriously and seek purity, they may be tempted to make high demands on others . . . . It may be that Mennonites have not yet fully solved the problem of how to be earnestly seeking purity and hold strongly to deep convictions, without splitting over differences between equally sincere believers" (Dyck, *Introduction*, 127).

anything new. Desire for the purity of the Church prevented the opening of Mennonite fellowship to the risk of pollution by outsiders.

Like the faith communities surrounding them, however, the Mennonites could not avoid the impact of American revivalism. The "Awakening" or "Quickening"[39] introduced an emphasis on a conversion experience, a new simplicity and evangelical mainstreaming of theology, and the introduction of Sunday Schools, gospel music, and teaching materials written in English by those outside of the Mennonite Church.[40] The revivals emphasized an adult commitment to faith in contrast to the European State Church method; this resonated with American Mennonites. At the same time, Mennonites were skeptical of the "enthusiasm" of the movement, the integration with other Church traditions, and the lack of ethical accountability.[41] Slowly, under the leadership of preachers like John Coffman, Mennonites began to pursue revival within their own communities.[42]

THE INSTITUTIONALIZATION OF RISK

As the nineteenth century drew to a close, "quickened" Mennonites were gripped by the call to mission and benevolence. Up until this time, "evangelism" in the US-American Mennonite Church had referred to sending ministers to visit members who had migrated to the American frontier, calling these lost sheep back to faithfulness and evangelizing their children.[43] Now, in observing the denominations around them, young Mennonites called for the formation of mission boards for both home and international mission.[44] This movement was slow within the Mennonite Church, often taking decades to establish. Some problems were logistical: traditionally, Mennonites called bivocational leaders and, except for deacon's funds (for the purpose of mutual aid), had no system in place to collect money to support mission efforts;[45] Mennonites were concerned that the formation of mission societies was too

---

39. Weaver, "Quickening," 6. He takes this vocabulary from Schlabach, *Gospel.*

40. Dyck, *Introduction,* 415–20.

41. Weaver, "Quickening," 6.

42. Dyck, *Introduction,* 417.

43. Schlabach, *Gospel,* 37; Ruth, *Maintaining,* 350 and 376.

44. This reflects a wider move in western society toward institutionalization (Schlabach, *Gospel,* 83).

45. Schlabach, *Gospel,* 38 and 73. Mennonites did not pay their pastors, so many desired that missionaries become self-supporting (198). The professional missionary movement was one of the contributing factors that led to paid ministry in the Mennonite Church (199).

much like membership in labor unions and lodges;[46] and factionalism within the Mennonite Church initially prevented widespread cooperation.[47] Other concerns were ideological: Should Mennonites send individuals to do mission work or was it more consistent with their values to migrate in groups?[48] What was the balance of evangelism and service?[49]

Even as Mennonites got involved in mission work in the twentieth century, much of that work was performed by individuals in international settings or at mission outposts in US cities.[50] Risk was embraced, but only by a handful of special individuals sent to distant locations and idolized by those who remained at home: these were truly heroes of the faith. The efforts in church planting resulted in dozens of new congregations, some of them in response to the migration of Mennonites to cities[51] and others as mission outposts to people who were very different from the traditional Mennonite center: people of color, immigrants, and poor mountain folks.[52] For decades, these new converts were kept separate from existing Mennonite communities in their own special churches; the Mennonite Church could not tolerate the risk of embracing the "Other" into their fellowship.[53] Existing congregations grew only subtly, through witness to neighbors "here and there"[54] and the occasional influx of young people responding to revival preaching.[55] One of the Mennonite Church's mission leaders acknowledged in 1951 that many congregations preferred mission work at a distance because "they feared that new Christians from non-Mennonite backgrounds might bring a 'different cultural and religious climate' into the Church."[56] Those who were interested

46. Schlabach, *Gospel,* 72 and 151.

47. Schlabach, *Gospel,* 88 and 92–93.

48. Schlabach, *Gospel,* 40–41.

49. With a nod to the frugality of traditional Mennonites, Schlabach wonders if the word/deed debate "mixed questions of how to be faithful with a seeming desire to have missions without much cost. How much did the critics really believe in verbal evangelism as the best way to communicate gospel, and how much did they like it because it was cheaper?" (*Gospel,* 142).

50. Schlabach, *Gospel,* 106.

51. Boshart, *Becoming Missional,* xv.

52. Ruth, *Maintaining,* 417 and 486. Schlabach describes how the segregation of home mission at first led to benevolence for local people of color but not integration (*Gospel,* 76). This integration took decades (77–78) and, even then, was not universal or consistent. See my account of the Norristown, PA mission, which was eventually split into two congregations because of segregation (Ralph, "God's Dream," 77–78).

53. Schlabach, *Gospel,* 76–78.

54. Schlabach, *Gospel,* 54–55.

55. Ruth, *Maintaining,* 416.

56. J. D. Graber, as quoted by Schlabach, *Gospel,* 238.

in committing to the faith were often submitted to months (and even years) of teaching and quizzing before they were deemed dedicated enough to join the Church; one mission leader summed up the guiding principle quite clearly: "We want to keep the Church pure."[57]

The Mennonite Church had often struggled with moral legalism. With the influence of the North American fundamentalist movement, some streams within the Mennonite Church began to struggle with theological legalism as well.[58] When Mennonite historian Harold Bender introduced his synthesis of the "Anabaptist Vision" in 1942, he sought to pull Mennonites back from the theological abyss of the conservatism and liberalism divide by focusing attention on what he considered "Anabaptist distinctives" related to discipleship.[59] In suggesting that Anabaptists had a "usable past"[60] that set them apart from other faith traditions, Bender painted a picture of Mennonites offering a unique perspective and witness to the world. In order to resist the impulse for Mennonites to become more like the Protestants around them, the Anabaptist Vision emphasized the value of Anabaptist uniqueness. This vision of uniqueness served as a "glue" that could hold the Church together during a time of great turmoil and change following World War II.[61]

Meanwhile, Mennonites who had applied for conscientious objector status during the war served in volunteer roles in urban settings in which there had previously been no Mennonite churches. Many of these Mennonites never returned to their rural communities, instead settling in and helping to plant churches in their new neighborhoods.[62] These church plants integrated both new believers and those who joined from other faith traditions, introducing a new diversity into the Mennonite Church. For the conscientious objectors who did return home, the exposure to another world outside of the Mennonite enclave was profoundly transforming, fostering a commitment to mission and justice while simultaneously lowering commitments to social nonconformity in the form of dress and lifestyle.[63] Church leaders were faced with the question: If Mennonites no longer looked different from the "world," what would set them apart?

57. Schlabach, *Gospel,* 178.

58. Kraus, "American Mennonites," 132.

59. Friesen, *Erasmus,* 125–26.

60. Bush, "Anabaptism Born Again."

61. Bush, "Anabaptism Born Again," 31–32.

62. Stutzman, *From Nonresistance to Justice,* 108.

63. Stutzman, *From Nonresistance to Justice,* 110.

The answer seemed to be the Mennonite Church's traditional peace witness. The World Wars shook the Church as members were faced with questions about nonresistance and social responsibility in the face of devastating suffering. Is it enough to simply opt out of participation in war and to help care for the victims of war, as the Mennonite Church had historically done, or were members of the historic peace churches called to a greater type of witness that extends beyond the "plan of salvation?"[64] A generation of Mennonite conscientious objectors, studying for graduate degrees or engaging in voluntary service in post-War Europe, tried to make sense of their experience in the face of the brokenness around them.[65] Some Mennonites began to believe that the way they should live their nonconformity was through service programs and counter-cultural witness rather than through plain clothing and a rejection of education and technology.[66] Mennonites began to see both the content and field of their "witness" growing beyond the "unsaved" to the broader Church and government.[67] Mennonite scholars and leaders engaged with the World Council of Churches and the National Association of Evangelicals, advocating for a Christian peace witness,[68] particularly in the atmosphere of the Cold War.[69] New waves of activism broke out in response to the calls for advocacy issued by the Civil Rights Movement and Vietnam War protests.[70] Mennonites began to reclaim the peace witness as central to the gospel and not just something of secondary importance.[71] Some Mennonites undertook the risks of draft dodging,[72] the refusal to pay war taxes,[73] and nonviolent resistance.[74] These new directions in witness associated risk more with political action and less with evangelizing neighbors.

64. Hostetler, "Nonresistance."

65. Hostetler, "Nonresistance," 55.

66. Bush, "Anabaptism Born Again," 30.

67. Political advocacy was new for Mennonites, whose two-kingdom theology had not allowed the Church to seek influence over the State. Mennonite theologian and ethicist John Howard Yoder challenged this theology by arguing that "Christ was Lord over all the powers" and therefore "the state must ultimately be accountable to God for its conduct" (Stutzman, *From Nonresistance to Justice*, 142).

68. Bush, "Anabaptism Born Again," 32–37.

69. Stutzman, *From Nonresistance to Justice*, 132.

70. Stutzman, *From Nonresistance to Justice*, 142.

71. Shenk, *By Faith*, 58 and 65.

72. Some saw draft resistance and antimilitarism as the "defining elements in the American Mennonite identity" (Toews, *Mennonites*, 328).

73. Schmidt, "Tax Refusal."

74. Stutzman, *From Nonresistance to Justice*, 126–27.

Even as Mennonites were discovering an activist perspective on mission, the institutional mission of the Church was paying off. By the time that participation in international mission had slowed down at the end of the 1970s,[75] Mennonites had spread their brand of faith to all continents and, in some cases, the new associations of churches in other countries were larger than the conferences of congregations that had birthed them.[76] Today, the worldwide community of Mennonites in Mennonite World Conference (MWC) includes around 1.5 million people in about 10,000 congregations.[77] About 81 percent of baptized believers in MWC are in Africa, Asia, or Latin America.[78] Mennonite churches are thriving in Ethiopia, India, and Indonesia.[79] In the decade leading up to the turn of the millennium, more than half of Mennonite mission initiatives worldwide were launched by the Church in the Global South.[80]

RISK COMES HOME

For decades, Mennonites developed their missional practice and theology in response to what they encountered in their global partners,[81] including the Church Growth Movement, evangelical ecumenism (specifically the concepts of *missio Dei*, contextualization, "incarnational" mission, and "kingdom of God" language), and liberation theology (particularly its emphasis on social justice and identification with the poor).[82] It was only in the 1970s that Mennonites began to specifically wrestle with what a distinctive Anabaptist missiology might include.[83] Mennonite missiologist Wilbert Shenk has wondered if this movement toward a Mennonite missiology resulted less from a recognition of tension between mainstream missiology and Anabaptist theology than from a need to bolster Mennonite identity in response to the "two and three generations of Mennonites in some churches

---

75. Kraus, "Shifting Mennonite," 44.

76. Shenk, *By Faith*, 63.

77. Mennonite World Conference, "World Directory." These churches around the world include European congregations and conferences that pre-date the US denominations as well as Anabaptist groups that emerged out of mission programs from other US and global agencies.

78. Mennonite World Conference, "About MWC." This shift has happened across most denominations, as described in Jenkins, *Next Christendom*.

79. Nathan Hege, *Beyond Our Prayers*; Asheervadham et al., *Churches Engage*.

80. Shenk, *By Faith*, 84–85.

81. Shenk, "Developing," 46.

82. Kraus, "Theological Analysis," 19.

83. Shenk, "Developing," 49.

in Asia, Africa, and Latin America [that] look and feel like evangelicals."[84] Although Mennonite missiology has continued to evolve in the decades since, theologies of mission from Mennonite perspectives have not been drastically different from mainstream missiology;[85] perhaps it is fair to say that the differences are merely a matter of accent.

As Mennonites continued to expand their understandings of mission in the latter part of the twentieth century, they encountered other local mission movements: house and cell churches,[86] intentional community,[87] and, later, Purpose-Driven Church,[88] new monasticism, and emerging church.[89] In 1985, the Mennonite Church began Vision 95, a ten-year campaign for church renewal and mission, with the goals of doubling witness, church membership, and international mission workers, as well as of planting 500 congregations.[90] This decade of mission continued to focus on an attractional form of evangelism, with an emphasis on church growth and little analysis of culture and context.[91] As a result, instead of the desired doubling in size, after ten years the Mennonite Church had only grown by under 7 percent, financial offerings had dropped, and the number of international missionaries had fallen by nearly 30 percent.[92] Of the 200 congregations planted, only a fraction remain open and connected with the denomination today.[93]

In the late 1990s, in reflection on Vision 95 and during conversations about a merger between the two largest Mennonite denominations in the US (the "Old" Mennonite Church and the General Conference Mennonite Church), various Mennonite mission agencies met to imagine what a future joint agency might look like.[94] Several Mennonite missiologists

84. Shenk, "Developing," 47–48.

85. See, for instance, the regular references to Lesslie Newbigin and David Bosch throughout Mennonite missiology. Many of the Mennonite Church's most prominent missiologists worked ecumenically, including Wilbert Shenk and Paul Hiebert.

86. Barrett, *Building the House Church*; Birkey, *House Church*.

87. Fretz, "Newly Emerging Communes."

88. Pelkey-Landes, "Purpose-Driven Mennonites."

89. Sine, "Joining."

90. Mennonite Church, "Proceedings," 10–11 and 22.

91. James Krabill, MMN, interview (February 13, 2017).

92. Mennonite Church, "Vision 95," 32–35.

93. Noel Santiago, Leadership Minister for Mosaic Conference, interview (February 13, 2017). Dave Greiser, one of the founding pastors of West Philadelphia Mennonite Fellowship, a congregation planted during Vision 95, suggests that the denomination gave up too soon; perhaps the reason that few congregations survived was that the Church was not yet experienced enough in church planting and needed more time to learn (interview, September 1, 2017).

94. Krabill, interview.

were participants in the Gospel and Our Culture Network, out of which the ground-breaking book *Missional Church: A Vision for the Sending of the Church in North America* was published in 1998.[95] Seeing the need for engaging in mission in a less attractional and more missional way, the mission agencies suggested that their purpose would be to empower "every congregation and all parts of the church [to engage] in God's mission across the street and around the world."[96] Denominational leadership eventually took this mission on as a central organizing factor.[97]

By the time that the old denominations merged in 2002 to become MC USA, the new denomination had dedicated itself to "developing and nurturing missional congregations of many cultures" but soon found that "our vision and call to engage in God's purposes in the world is not adequately supported by our present relationships, behaviors and organizations."[98] In the years since the merger, Mennonite mission agencies, denominational leadership, and seminaries have been working to foster a missional culture within congregations,[99] with varying degrees of success; it appears that the engagement with various mission movements in the past few decades may have been embraced more by congregational and denominational leaders than by ordinary congregation members.[100]

In his 2006 survey of Mennonite Church USA members, sociologist Conrad Kanagy found that membership in the denomination has continued to decline; he suggests that this drop results from a combination of changing demographics (including lower fertility rates) and a lack of enthusiasm for evangelism and outreach.[101] In the past, he claims, our congregations maintained their membership because of large family sizes. Now, however, "as fertility rates have declined, it is apparent that we were never doing a very good job of reaching the world right around us for Christ, despite effective global mission efforts. Many of those who remain in our congregations are descendants of those who were in the pews

---

95. Barrett, "Defining Missional Church," 179. These missiologists included Wilbert Shenk, Lois Barrett, and Linford Stutzman.

96. Mennonite Church USA, "Church Structure."

97. Krabill, interview.

98. Boshart, *Becoming Missional*, 112.

99. For one example of partnership among mission agency, denomination, and seminary, see Green and Krabill, *Fully Engaged*.

100. Boshart, *Becoming Missional*, 126.

101. Kanagy, *Road Signs*, 71. This survey is now more than a decade old and significant changes have taken place within the denomination since then, including a significant loss of congregational and conference membership; no new data is available, however. See Guyton, "One Small Step."

several generations ago; and there are fewer of them today than in the past."[102] The majority of Mennonites reported having no close friends who were unchurched;[103] only half of those surveyed considered peacemaking and nonviolence to be important priorities while only a third considered evangelism to be important.[104] The more educated and wealthy Mennonites are, the less likely we are to sacrificially invest in evangelism or church planting.[105] Only two percent of the denomination's new members are new Christians,[106] which implies that, although the Mennonite Church is attracting converts from other denominations, we have not made much of an impact on the unchurched in our communities.[107] Within today's Mennonite Church, there seem to be three separate segments, describes former Mennonite Mission Network senior mission advocate, James Krabill: a group of more progressive, urban, educated white folks who are greatly concerned with issues of peace and justice and often less concerned with traditional mission or evangelism;[108] a more moderate, working-class group of rural white folks who are rapidly aging and somewhat resistant to change, yet remain committed to traditional expressions of mission; and a group comprised of the global majority, particularly immigrants on the margins of the institutional Church,[109] who are significantly more interested and involved in holistic mission and evangelism.[110] The moderate center is shrinking while the other two groups are growing—what does this mean for the future of the Mennonite Church, for mission and justice work, and for common vision?[111]

102. Kanagy, *Road Signs*, 71.

103. Kanagy, *Road Signs*, 80.

104. Kanagy, *Road Signs*, 82–83.

105. Kanagy, *Road Signs*, 85.

106. Kanagy, *Road Signs*, 180.

107. Former mission worker Alan Kreider describes his tendency to try to "convert" other believers instead of nonbelievers in "Tongue Screws."

108. While I advocate for a holistic understanding of mission that includes justice, the divide between advocates of "justice" and "mission" is still experienced in many US-American Mennonite settings.

109. Krabill estimates that this group comprises a quarter to a third of the current number of congregations in MC USA (interview).

110. See also Kanagy, *Road Signs*, 86.

111. Krabill, interview. A growing edge for MC USA is in the area of immigration. Although the percentage of first-generation immigrants has greatly increased, congregations, conferences, and the denomination struggle to incorporate the new ways of being in, understanding, and engaging the world that immigrants offer. For more on the impact of migration on the Church, the difficulties of multi-ethnic community and witness, and proposals for a vision of radical hospitality, see Wild-Wood, "Common

The disconnect is clear: white, US-American Mennonites, particularly those who grew up in the Church, have not caught the vision or found the motivation for taking risks in mission; yet this reality is very different when we look at those on the margins of the institutional Church.[112] Could this be because they are less worried about encountering the "Other" since, in the Mennonite Church context, they often *are* the "Other?" Perhaps hearing and responding to the voices of those on the margins of our Church could bring about a renewing of our minds.[113]

After years of teaching about why we *should* care about mission, many people in the pews "are told that they aren't living out their missional calling because they are lazy or not committed enough," suggests Mennonite educator Michele Hershberger.[114] Yet Mennonites should find no space in our theology or practice to coerce or manipulate others into missional behavior; this certainly does not lead to whole-hearted risk-taking for the sake of love. If risk-taking in mission could be developed simply by ideological motivation, Mennonite congregations would have grown exponentially in recent decades.[115] The problem, however, is much deeper, according to Hershberger: "We have a subconscious fear of others; we are afraid they will change us."[116] Transformation is the ultimate risk; human vulnerability can be defined as the "susceptibility to being changed."[117] This fear of loss may be what prevents Mennonites from wholeheartedly participating in risk-taking mission for the sake of love.

GOD-STORIES IN MENNONITE THOUGHT

Throughout these experiences of mission, Mennonites were developing their understandings of the world through the stories that they told about God. These narratives revolved around and were dominated by the Gospel stories

---

Witness."

112. This is reflected both in the US and globally.

113. Rom 12:2.

114. Hershberger, "Reading the Bible," 187–88.

115. Noel Santiago suggests that, when it comes to mission, the Mennonite Church has traditionally been motivated by ideology rather than compassion: "We seem to have a desire to do mission because we want to be faithful—it's about us" (interview). Likewise, (Ana)baptist theologian James McClendon argues Christians are "obliged by the content of Christian faith itself to [fulfill the Great Commission]. It is their own salvation, and not in the first place their neighbors', that is at stake in the task" (*Doctrine*, 424).

116. Hershberger, "Reading the Bible," 187–88. Hershberger suggests that this fear is well-founded. She argues that, although we need to be wise in responding to syncretism, a "missional lens" allows us to engage with those who are different.

117. Culp, *Vulnerability and Glory*, 2.

of Jesus. I will, therefore, begin this survey with Anabaptist stories about Jesus and continue with stories about the Spirit and the Father. This order will form a pattern for this book as I analyze existing stories in the Mennonite tradition and construct new narratives for risk-taking in later chapters.

Stories About Jesus

Early Anabaptists believed that Jesus, not Scripture, was the Word of God; therefore, Jesus was the best representation of God's desire for humans.[118] This insistence on Jesus as the Word did not mean a rejection of Scripture, but instead a deep respect and love for it, especially the Gospels, as our source for learning what Jesus did and taught. With a particular emphasis on the Sermon on the Mount,[119] the early Anabaptists insisted that Jesus meant for his followers to actually do what he taught: loving enemies, caring for the poor, living simply and sharing with those in need, refusing to engage in violence, avoiding oaths, washing feet, and enforcing church discipline. This stress on discipleship meant taking the teachings of Jesus seriously, and often, literally: belief is nothing, they taught, if that conviction is not accompanied by regenerated behavior.[120] Jesus was an example to follow and the authority for faith and life.[121]

Jesus had authority, not just as a virtuous person, but because he was God in flesh. The importance of the incarnation for the Anabaptists was that God became human, a new Adam,[122] to bring about the regeneration of humanity that God had always intended. The incarnation of Jesus means that humans can be changed, here, in this life, on earth. Jesus was unique, and the only way that humans could be saved.[123] God could have simply sent God's Spirit to save the world, Pilgrim Marpeck admitted, but instead, "he sent a Son who came to men as a lowly carpenter from Nazareth. . . . Jesus could have ordered the man born blind to be healed; instead he used such lowly means as mud and spittle. . . . God uses lowly means to

---

118. This is most clearly articulated in the writings of Hans Denck (Klaassen, *Anabaptism*, 20).

119. Neufeld, *What We Believe*, 42. See Driver, *Kingdom Citizens*, and Kraybill, *Upside Down Kingdom*.

120. Klaassen, *Anabaptism*, 21.

121. Roth, *Practices*, 54.

122. Menno Simons was so concerned that we understand Jesus to be the second Adam that he strayed into a non-orthodox belief in the celestial flesh of Jesus: If Jesus were born of sinful flesh, how could he be a sinless Adam to save humanity? See Kuiper, "Pre-Eminence," 120 and George, *Theology*, 280–85.

123. Roth, *Practices*, 55. See also Finger, *Contemporary*, 374.

communicate to us."[124] Because Jesus came in material form, we can know that his incarnation, life, death, and resurrection are more than myth;[125] they are a true story of God's participation in history.[126] Through Jesus, humans can be reconciled with God.[127]

The story of reconciliation, often called "atonement" in Western theology, has been described in various ways throughout Church history:[128] first, as God's victory over the devil, in the traditional, or "Christus Victor," theory;[129] later, as a gift which changes the hearts of humans to accept God's love, in what is known as the moral influence or "subjective" theory;[130] finally, and most significantly, as a restoration of God's honor or a fulfillment of God's law, called substitutionary, satisfaction, or "objective" atonement.[131]

Early Anabaptists varied widely in their perspectives on the atonement. While most of them embraced some combination of the three common atonement theories (describing the cross and resurrection as a battle with the devil, Jesus as the second Adam, and the human response to the love of God evidenced by the cross), most rejected a forensic justification theory of atonement. Instead, they emphasized that through the life, death, and resurrection of Jesus and the presence of the Spirit, the image of God within was reawakened, allowing humans to make a decision to follow God and participate in God's life.[132] Like the Eastern Church, Anabaptists called this "divinization," which was manifested as a visible new life transformed into God's image and in community with God.[133] This new life included a voluntary commitment to the Church through adult baptism, participation in the faith community through accountability and mutual aid, a radical love of the enemy that resulted in nonresistance, and a commitment to congregational discipline that did not involve coercion or violence.[134]

124. Klassen, "Anabaptist Hermeneutics," 83.

125. While Ascension Day has traditionally been honored as holy in Mennonite practice, the ascension does not frequently appear in Mennonite literature. For more on Ascension Day celebrations, see Nussbaum, "Ascension Day."

126. Roth, *Practices*, 56.

127. Augsburger, *Robe of God*.

128. Mary Grey suggests that these three categories are inadequate differentiations in atonement theories as there are elements of each in all (*Redeeming the Dream*, 115).

129. This theory, the most common among the Church fathers, was reintroduced by Gustaf Aulén in *Christus Victor*.

130. Abelard, *Commentary*.

131. Anselm, *Why God Became Man*.

132. Hiebert, "Atonement," 129–31.

133. Hiebert, "Atonement," 128.

134. Bender, *Anabaptist Vision*.

It was not until the mid-twentieth century that leaders in the American Mennonite Church began to investigate and challenge the changes in theology and practice that emerged from the American revivals, including an unquestioning acceptance of satisfaction atonement theories.[135] As a result of historians like Harold Bender[136] and allied with the social movements of the 1950s, 1960s, and 1970s, Mennonites once again engaged with the particularity of their traditional nonresistant theology, exploring new ways of expressing this theology in both word and practice.[137] Beginning in the 1960s, Mennonite theologians including Gordon Kauffman, John Howard Yoder, Norman Kraus, and Thomas Finger articulated Christologies and theories of atonement that sought to reclaim the Anabaptist distinctive of nonresistance and suffering love.[138] These theologies often rejected the underlying claims of substitutionary atonement, while not rejecting those claims altogether; instead they integrated aspects of substitutionary atonement with elements of the moral influence and the classic Christus Victor theories.

In the most recent *Confession of Faith*,[139] Jesus is named not only as prophet, priest, and king, but also as teacher. No atonement theory is named, but the confession describes how in "his suffering, he loved his enemies and did not resist them with violence, thus giving us an example to follow. In the shedding of his blood on the cross, Jesus offered up his life to the Father, bore the sins of all, and reconciled us to God."[140] Kanagy's survey gives evidence that most lay Mennonites have not been influenced by scholarly debates on atonement: 85 percent said that "Jesus had to die to complete God's plan of salvation." These numbers may change in the near future since fewer pastors agreed with that statement (only 64 percent); an increasing number of pastors responded, instead, that "Jesus willingly died to show the power of nonviolent love" (24 percent).[141]

This difference in pastoral theology reflects the shift in the late twentieth and beginning of the twenty-first centuries from "nonresistant" to "nonviolent" atonement theories. Anabaptist theologians like Robin Collins[142]

---

135. Dyck, *Introduction*, 420.

136. Bender, *Anabaptist Vision*.

137. Stutzman, *From Nonresistance to Justice*.

138. Koontz, "Liberation," 171–92.

139. Mennonite Church USA, *Confession of Faith*.

140. Mennonite Church USA, *Confession of Faith*, 13–14.

141. Kanagy, *Road Signs*, 95–96.

142. Robin Collins calls his an "incarnational" or "participatory" theory ("Girard and Atonement").

and Christopher Marshall[143] responded to René Girard's work on scapegoats and mimesis while others, like Ted Grimsrud, engaged with the American penal (retributive) system of justice.[144] One of the most influential nonviolent atonement theories in both academic circles[145] and popular Mennonite culture[146] is the narrative Christus Victor theory developed by Mennonite theologian J. Denny Weaver. As theologians and pastors in the Mennonite Church continue to strive for language to express a shifting theology based less on the "ethical perfection and absolutism of nonresistance" and more on "the ambiguities of peace and justice,"[147] Weaver's nonviolent theology and others like it will increase in importance.[148]

Mennonite stories about Jesus do not end with his death, however; Anabaptists live "on the resurrection side of the cross," according to Harold Bender.[149] The *Confession of Faith* declares that "God then raised [Jesus] from the dead, thereby conquering death and disarming the powers of sin and evil."[150] In 2006, 94 percent of Mennonites in MC USA believed that Jesus physically rose from the dead.[151] "The doctrine of new life in the power of regeneration and of the Holy Spirit, with its confident hope of growth in holiness, lived by walking in the resurrection, is the true source of the powerful dynamic for holy living and discipleship in the Anabaptist movement," Bender suggested.[152] Mennonites believe that the resurrection brings about new life, not only in the individual believer, but in the world: "New creation is possible, thanks to the resurrection," described Bender. "New creation is powerfully promoted by the Holy Spirit of God and the church of the risen

143. See Christopher Marshall's "Atonement," where he describes a mimetic theory of atonement without referencing Girard's work (91).

144. Grimsrud, *Instead of Atonement*.

145. See the November 2007 symposium at the Mennonite and Friends Forum on Weaver's nonviolent atonement (published in *CGR*, Spring 2009), his inclusion and dominance as a conversation partner in Sanders, *Atonement and Violence*, and the anthology *The Work of Jesus Christ in Anabaptist Perspective: Essays in Honor of J. Denny Weaver* (edited by Alain Epp Weaver and Gerald J. Mast), in addition to the numerous other engagements cited in my footnotes.

146. For example, see Heinzekehr, "On Women," and Joanna Shenk's interview with Drew Hart, "Becoming an Anablacktivist."

147. Stutzman, *From Nonresistance to Justice*, 48.

148. Robin Collins asks why traditional atonement theories have remained unquestioned for so long and whether these theories are the only alternatives ("Defense," 186).

149. Bender, "Walking in the Resurrection," 96.

150. Mennonite Church USA, *Confession of Faith*, 14.

151. Kanagy, *Road Signs*, 97.

152. Bender, "Walking in the Resurrection," 96–97.

Christ. But there is much more to come in a future moment, when God once more will intervene visibly in human history."[153]

The belief in God's future intervention and the second coming of Jesus was particularly strong during the Reformation. The early Anabaptists lived in expectation, believing that the coming judgment would be a time of vindication for the faithful and condemnation for their persecutors.[154] While some of the more radical preachers dabbled in predictions, Anabaptists, for the most part, were not interested in timetables[155] but were more concerned with being found obedient when Christ returned, a pure and unblemished Church.[156] This hope in the resurrection of the body and promise of vindication helped persecuted Christians to persevere in the midst of great suffering.[157] Just as no servant was greater than his or her master, so too would true believers suffer with Jesus; just as Jesus was vindicated in the resurrection, so too would his faithful followers triumph in the Day of the Lord.[158]

Anabaptist apocalyptic expectation began to wane as years passed and persecution diminished. Although eschatological urgency faded, belief in the second coming of Christ remained an important tenet in Mennonite confessions of faith.[159] The Mennonite Church was steadily influenced on issues of eschatology by the US-American Fundamentalist movement in the beginning of the twentieth century, with some coming into contact with premillennialism through their studies at Moody Bible Institute; the theology's popularity rose and faded in the US-American Mennonite Church most noticeably between the World Wars[160] (although many Mennonite leaders remained staunchly amillennial).[161] At times, the Mennonite Church reawakened to eschatological urgency, often in response to spiritual awakening and cultural anxieties.[162] When Mennonites did embrace a more urgent apocalypticism, it was often accompanied by a renewed emphasis on the experience of the Spirit and renewing of the Church, manifested in calls for holiness and purity.[163]

153. Neufeld, *What We Believe*, 49.

154. Finger, *Contemporary*, 526–27 and 534.

155. Finger, *Contemporary*, 518.

156. Finger, *Contemporary*, 517.

157. Finger, *Contemporary*, 520.

158. Estep, *Anabaptist Story*, 264.

159. Loewen, "Mission of Theology," 104.

160. Wenger et al., "Apocalypticism."

161. Schlabach, *Gospel*, 115.

162. Kraus, "American Mennonites," 147–48.

163. It is possible that this emphasis, in tandem with the Fundamentalist anxiety

In the latter part of the twentieth century, some Mennonites began expressing their eschatology in the language of the "reign of God," with less concern about the timing and order of end-time happenings and more enthusiasm about the nature of the "now and not yet" Kingdom. In the *Confession of Faith*, the final article states that we

> place our hope in the reign of God and in its fulfillment in the day when Christ our ascended Lord will come again in glory to judge the living and the dead. He will gather his church, already living under the reign of God according to the pattern of God's future. We believe in God's final victory . . . and in the appearance of a new heaven and a new earth.[164]

While a diversity of perspectives on eschatology remain within the Mennonite Church,[165] this movement away from mystical triumphalism and towards physical continuity and participatory consummation[166] reveals the influence of modern ecological theologies, experiential/standpoint theologies, and process theology.

Stories about the Spirit

Mennonite theologian James Reimer describes the early Anabaptists as the "charismatics of the sixteenth century."[167] Their emphasis on the "inner word" of the Spirit meant that "the doctrine of the Holy Spirit was the key to the Anabaptist faith."[168] Conflict arose within the church, however, because of the Anabaptists' desire to be true to the teachings of Jesus ("outer word"). Reimer contends that, eventually, "the 'outer word' people won the day, but all early Anabaptists were convinced that the inner regeneration (baptism of the Holy Spirit, if you like) was essential for discipleship."[169]

---

over worldliness and faithfulness, led to the renewed enforcement of "plain" clothing and the "restrictions" around the turn of the twentieth century (Wenger et al., "Apocalypticism").

164. Mennonite Church USA, *Confession of Faith*, 85.

165. See Finger, *Contemporary*, and Augsburger, *Robe of God*, for just two examples. In 2006, about 83 percent of Mennonites believed that Jesus would come again (Kanagy, *Road Signs*, 97).

166. Finger, *Contemporary*, 556–57.

167. Reimer, *Mennonites*, 428 and 264. "The Pentecostal movement [was in the 20th] century the closest parallel to what Anabaptism was in the sixteenth" (Yoder, "Marginalia," 78). See also Murray, "Spirit, Discipleship, Community," 198–201. James Dunn claims that the neglect of the Spirit in the Protestant Church for so long after the Reformation was due to their suspicion of the Anabaptists (*Baptism*, 225).

168. Reimer, *Mennonites*, 428.

169. Reimer, *Mennonites*, 428.

Mennonite theologian John Rempel describes the shift in Mennonite spirituality between the Reformation and the twentieth century as a pattern of renewal and institutionalization:

> The singlemindedness of Anabaptist spirituality . . . was corroded even in the first generation by apocalypticism and legalism. In subsequent generations a cycle set in: renewal would come and then be codified (and thereby eroded) through a preoccupation with prescribed behavior and outward nonconformity. . . . By the late nineteenth and early twentieth centuries the spirit of rationalism . . . further shifted the focus of the spiritual life from the divine initiator to the human actor.[170]

In the 1950s and 60s, the Mennonite Church, like many North American denominations, encountered and was shaped by the Charismatic movement.[171] This happened in part through inter-denominational interactions with other local individuals and churches[172] and in part through the influence of returning missionaries, shaped by their experiences of Pentecostalism in South America and revival in East Africa.[173] Although slow to accept and embrace the movement, by the mid-1970s the Mennonite Church had taken time to evaluate the Charismatic renewal and encourage cautious participation.[174] In response to the Charismatic experience, the Mennonite Church saw a wave of books and studies released on the topic of the Spirit.[175] In 2006 Kanagy found that 61 percent of US Mennonites believed in the gifts of the Spirit for today and 44 percent had experienced these gifts during their lifetime.[176] Pentecostal historian Vinson Synan suggests that, "of all the church families that have

---

170. Rempel, "Spirituality," 595. Just before this book went to press, Mennonite Church Eastern Canada announced that it had terminated Rempel's ministerial credentials after substantiating recent accusations of sexual misconduct in the 1970s and 1980s. More work still needs to be done to "reconcile the tension that human beings [like Rempel] have the capacity to cause much harm and pain even while they have also done much good for the church" (MCEC press release, quoted in Anabaptist World, "Theologian").

171. Synan, *Century*, 192–98.

172. Koch, in "My Personal Pentecost," 17.

173. See MacMaster and Jacobs, *Gentle Wind,* and Rempel, "Spirituality," 595.

174. See *Anabaptist Wiki*, "Holy Spirit."

175. See Koch and Koch, *My Personal Pentecost*; Bauman, *Presence and Power*; Kraus, *Community*; Augsburger, *Quench Not*.

176. Kanagy, *Road Signs*, 98–99. More pastors than lay people (66 percent vs. 44 percent) claim to have experienced the gifts of the Spirit.

been touched by the renewing power of the Holy Spirit in this century, none have been more deeply affected than the Mennonites."[177]

Meanwhile, elsewhere in the Mennonite Church, a growing interest in liturgical practices and spirituality was emerging.[178] These spiritualities were more concerned with the inner ecstatic experience than the outer, manifesting in spiritual practices like contemplation, silence, spiritual direction, and mindfulness.[179] In addition to being linked at times to issues of justice and activism,[180] these streams of spirituality were embraced and propagated by leaders and thinkers within the Church. If the Charismatic movement overwhelmingly (but not entirely) affected the layperson and the bi-vocational pastor,[181] the spirituality movement was embraced by the educated and those in the academic world.[182] This may help to explain why many of the works published in recent years related to Mennonite theology and practice express more of a contemplative than Charismatic spirituality.[183]

Stories about the Father

Throughout Mennonite history, the doctrines of God, God the Father, and the Trinity have been intertwined.[184] In the *Confession of Faith*, for instance, while there are individual articles on Jesus and the Spirit, there is no separate article on the Father, only an article on "God," which incorporates references to the Trinity.[185] Earlier confessions stress "God's unity, attributes, trinity, and fatherhood. . . . [God] is the creator of the world and of all things. In his preservation and providence God is seen as the sustainer, governor, supporter and ruler of the universe."[186] This view of God seems to be changing, however; Kanagy found that only around half of twenty-first century Mennonites

177. Synan, *Century*, 192.

178. Rempel, "Spirituality," 595.

179. See Mennonite Church USA, "Mennonite Spiritual Directors," and Smucker, "Spiritual Direction."

180. See Boers, *On Earth*.

181. Koch, in "My Personal Pentecost," 22.

182. "By contrast, the materials I am reviewing have a European, nostalgic, white, college-educated flavor. . . . [They] are unintentionally elitist and limited in their ability to address the post-denominational religious world and the dominant North American culture that is its medium" (Rempel, "Spirituality," 596).

183. See, for instance, the description of "Spiritual Life" at AMBS.

184. Catherine Mowry LaCugna shows that, prior to Nicaea, understandings of "God" and "Father" were synonymous (*God for Us,* 54). Likewise, much of the New Testament uses the terms interchangeably (116).

185. Mennonite Church USA, *Confession*, 10–12.

186. Loewen, "Mission of Theology," 99.

believe that God has ultimate control over daily life, while another 44 percent believe that God provides guidance instead.[187]

The early Anabaptists' primary concern with the doctrine of the Trinity was that, through this doctrine, the divinity of Jesus was understood: if Jesus is the very essence of God, then we know the character of God by looking at the Son; in other words, the unity of the Father and the Son prevented them from "ruling" separate worlds (i.e. the Church and the State).[188] Additionally, the theology of the Trinity underscored the Anabaptist practice of mutual aid and (for some Anabaptists) the common purse.[189] Anabaptist emphasis on the essential equality and mutuality of the Trinity reflected their desire for society.[190] Beyond this, the Anabaptists (and, until recently, most Mennonites) have spent very little energy on issues of origin, priority, or the *filioque* debate.[191] While Anabaptists/ Mennonites have remained orthodox on issues related to the relationship of the Father and Son, the nature of God, and the Father's role of sending in mission (including an embrace of *missio Dei*), they have not spent much time considering, evaluating, or rethinking those doctrines. Traditional ways of talking about God remain in common practice.[192]

THE IMPACT OF GOD-STORIES ON MISSION

Mennonite missiology clearly reflects many themes prominent in wider missiological thought as well as themes that are less commonly engaged; the theme of risk-taking, for instance, is rarely explored, fleshed out, or grounded in theology.[193] The Mennonite accent (the emphasis on following Jesus

187. Kanagy, *Road Signs*, 95.

188. Finger, *Contemporary*, 431.

189. Finger, *Contemporary*, 431.

190. Finger wonders, "Might an Anabaptist trinitarian theology then display commonalities with feminist criticisms of divine and social hierarchy?" (447).

191. Finger, *Contemporary*, 444–45. A concern with the efficacy of the ancient creeds (starting with immanent vs. economic Trinity) has re-arisen in Mennonite circles in debates about the nature of Christ and atonement (Finger, "Christus Victor"; Reimer, *Mennonites*; Weaver, "Christus Victor," and "Narrative Theology").

192. 73 percent of those Kanagy surveyed disliked references to God as Mother or using the female pronoun for God (Kanagy, *Road Signs*, 95).

193. The exception to this is Lois Barrett, who describes missional communities as those who take risks as contrast communities. Her emphasis is on the battle between the powers and, therefore, the resistance missional communities experience by "the world" when they choose God's values and priorities over their culture's. Like other Mennonite theologians, she continues to emphasize risk-taking for the sake of a mission (cause). Additionally, her chapter describes what missional congregations do without exploring how they are formed ("Taking Risks," 74–82).

in community) can be heard in the prominence of the Messianic nature of the life of Jesus, the call to make disciples who follow Jesus in life and thus willingly submit to the reign of God, the suffering nature of discipleship and mission, the understanding of the Church as a set-apart community witnessing to reconciliation, and the inclusion of peace (*shalom*) as an essential characteristic of the gospel. While many of these emphases may issue needed challenges to some mainstream missiological conversation, they carry their own significant weaknesses in their ability to form congregations into the image of a God who takes risks for the sake of love.

The christocentrism of Anabaptist thought is obvious in Mennonite missiology. Mennonites emphasize that Jesus is central to faith and mission,[194] particularly as the source of reconciliation and *shalom*.[195] Traditionally, the focus of many of the Mennonite stories of Jesus has been discipleship and holy living: the life of Jesus provides a model for holy living; the death and resurrection of Jesus make possible holy living; anticipating the return of Jesus encourages holy living. In the context of these stories about Jesus, Mennonite missiologists describe mission as an invitation to costly discipleship that submits to the reign of God,[196] rooted in accountability to the faith community.[197] For those who choose the path of discipleship, they argue, mission is an act of obedience,[198] one that will involve "vicarious, sacrificial suffering."[199] They wrestle with the balance of witness through word and deed,[200] particularly stressing the importance of ethics in Anabaptist mission.[201] Although this focus is important, it may not be a helpful narrative for

194. Krabill, *Is it Insensitive*, 51; Shenk, *By Faith*, 21, and *Changing Frontiers*, 11–13; Becker, "What is an Anabaptist," 134–37).

195. Augsburger, *Robe of God*; Krabill, "God's Shalom Project," 60; Shenk, *God's Call*, 39–40.

196. Shenk and Stutzman, *Creating Communities*, 26–27; Roth, *Practices*, 25; Shenk, *God's Call*, 78–79; Shenk, *Changing Frontiers*, 9–11.

197. Shenk and Stutzman, *Creating Communities*, 103–4; Stuart Murray, *Church After Christendom*, 26–31; Kreider and Kreider, *Worship and Mission*, 253–55.

198. Shenk, "Developing," 57; Jacobs, *Pilgrimage in Mission*, 160; Shenk and Stutzman, *Creating Communities*, 27–28.

199. Shenk, "Developing," 56. See also Shenk, *God's Call*, 73; Shenk, "Essential Themes," 83; Roth, *Practices*, 167. The *Confession of Faith* refers to the traditional Anabaptist concept of the baptism of suffering and blood (46–49). This is often described in Mennonite literature as "nonresistance" or "suffering love" (Stutzman, *From Nonresistance to Justice*, 132 and 185).

200. Shenk, "Essential Themes," 75–81; Shenk, *Changing Frontiers*, 28; Sider and Unruh, "Keeping Good News," 47–56.

201. Kraus, *Intrusive Gospel*, 53; Blough, "Messianic Mission," 178–98; Roth, *Practices*, 81–82.

Anabaptist congregations who desire to take risks in mission. The Anabaptist emphasis on Jesus as "fully God," that is, divinely equal to God and therefore representative of God, tends toward portraying his perfection as a model for his followers, while ignoring the vulnerability and struggles he encountered as "fully human." The stories of his self-sacrificing willingness to suffer as a witness to God's "kingdom" do not illustrate the breadth of risk we might encounter or provide a healthy understanding of how to respond to suffering and failure as we take risks for the sake of love. Mission as an act of obedience discounts mission motivated by love. A partially realized eschatology and an apocalypticism that emphasizes purity may exclude rather than welcome as congregations engage in missional risk-taking.

Mennonite stories of the Spirit are more limited than those of Jesus and many are linked to the life and work of Jesus, with the "outer word" and "inner word" collapsing into one another as we talk about the "Spirit of Jesus." Mennonite missiologists reflect this reality when they describe how the Spirit, who continues the mission of Jesus,[202] is already present in the world,[203] and gives direction and power to the Church in mission.[204] They encourage engagement with culture in the light of the teachings of Jesus, both as a challenge to culture and for the purposes of contextualization.[205] The two parallel streams of Charismatic and contemplative understandings of the Spirit have created a dichotomy in the Church, setting those with differing spiritualities at odds with one another and causing many in academic circles to dismiss the experiential nature of the Spirit. Our stories of the Spirit as the "Spirit of Jesus" tame the third person of the Trinity, making the Spirit predictable in light of the gospel narratives: the Spirit provides insight without challenging the status quo. By highlighting the Spirit's role in sanctification (the Spirit's purpose is to help us follow Jesus), we miss the relational function of the Spirit, actively and creatively drawing us into relationship with God, others, ourselves, and the whole of creation, which is essential to taking risks in mission.

---

202. Shenk, *Changing Frontiers*, 13; Kuitse, "Holy Spirit," 112; Kidane, "Holy Spirit Empowerment," 91.

203. Krabill, *Is it Insensitive*, 141 and 145. John Howard Yoder challenged the assertion that the Spirit is at work in the world, saying that the Spirit's work is in the Church (*Theology of Mission*, 137–38).

204. Shenk, *God's Call*, 46, 74, and 175; Shenk, *Church in Mission*, 35; Shenk and Stutzman, *Creating Communities*, 24–25, 33–34, and 112; Yoder, *Theology of Mission*, 89; Kreider and Kreider, *Worship and Mission*, 29.

205. Shenk, *God's Call*, 189–201 and 156–57; Krabill, *Is it Insensitive*, 98–100; Shenk and Stutzman, *Creating Communities*, 119.

The Anabaptist focus on following Jesus in community also creates a void in which God the Father serves as either only a reflection of Jesus, the original Creator, the final judge, or even shorthand for the Trinity—in all, irrelevant for today. Although many Anabaptist/Mennonite missiologists ground their arguments in the story of the missionary God[206] as told throughout Scripture,[207] because Mennonites have not spent much time considering the doctrine of the Trinity for the Anabaptist context, our simple embrace or rejection of traditional understandings of the Trinity have prevented us from considering what impact the Community of God has on shaping a community of risk-takers in mission. Mennonite missiologists have a well-developed missional ecclesiology. They describe how, as a free Church traditionally calling for voluntary commitment to the way of Jesus, Mennonite mission should never be coercive or manipulative;[208] the work of mission belongs to the entire congregation[209] and includes the witness of worship,[210] church planting,[211] alternative lifestyle,[212] and interfaith dialogue;[213] and, although the Church partners with God in mission,[214] the focus of mission is the world.[215] Mennonite missiologists point to the Church as an instrument of reconciliation[216] and a sign of the kingdom that is coming and yet already here.[217] These understandings of the Church in mission are the result of an Anabaptist ecclesiology, however, not a trinitarian theology. While the

206. Shenk, *Changing Frontiers*, 106; Berry, "Mission of God," 167; Kreider and Kreider, *Worship and Mission*, 23–27.

207. Krabill, *Is it Insensitive*, 25. Kreider and Kreider, *Worship and Mission*, 48–53; Shenk, *God's Call*, 21–40; Jacobs, *Pilgrimage in Mission*, 102–62.

208. Krabill, *Does Your Church Smell*, 14, and *Is it Insensitive*, 117; Roth, "Anabaptist Missions," 99; Kraus, *Intrusive Gospel*, 49; Lois Barrett, "Anabaptist Vision," 307.

209. Shenk, *God's Call*, 163–70; John Driver, *Images*; Escobar, "Present and Future Realities," 40. John Howard Yoder goes so far as to argue that groups of believers should migrate together, thereby forming a new congregation wherever they go ("As You Go," 399–421).

210. See Kreider and Kreider, *Worship and Mission*; Kreider et al., *Culture of Peace*, 22.

211. Shenk and Stutzman, *Creating Communities*; Murray, *Church Planting*; Boshart, *Becoming Missional*.

212. Driver, *Images*, 44; Kraus, *Intrusive Gospel*, 58 and 76; Biesecker-Mast, "Recovering," 206.

213. Shenk, "Gospel and Religions" 171–86, and the many works by David Shenk including *Christian, Muslim, Friend* and *Global Gods*.

214. Driver, *Images*; Shenk, *Church in Mission*; Krabill, *Is it Insensitive*, 59–72.

215. Murray, *Church Planting*, 39–40; Kasdorf, "Towards," 4; Shenk, *Changing Frontiers*, 17.

216. Kreider and Kreider, *Worship and Mission*, 52; Stutzman, *With Jesus*, 87–99; Kreider et al., *Culture of Peace*.

217. Shenk, *Church in Mission*, 27–29. Kreider and Kreider, *Worship and Mission*, 49; Augsburger, *Robe of God*, 91.

existing stories of the Father and Trinity may not necessarily be harmful to the spiritual lives of Anabaptists today, they form a truncated understanding of the gospel by limiting our experience of God and failing to identify ways in which the Father relates to a Church in mission.

CONCLUSION

In this chapter, I have considered the Mennonite practice of mission from early Anabaptism through today's MC USA, showing how, over time, the early Anabaptist inclination to take risks in evangelism diminished in response to the threat of persecution, offers of security, and the building of an insular, homogenous community. This brief survey of Mennonites in mission suggests that many modern-day Mennonites do not share the early Anabaptists' inclination to risk-taking. While the Mennonite Church contains individuals who are willing to take these kinds of risks—individuals who are often on the front lines of international or domestic mission—many congregations have not fostered communities of risk-taking by engaging in vulnerable relationship in their very own neighborhoods. Mennonites often celebrate the stories of risk-takers involved in peacemaking around the world[218] while struggling to participate in everyday risk-taking that results in the vulnerability of being changed by our encounters with the "Other" across town or next door.

In response to this understanding of mission, I have also considered the stories that Mennonites have traditionally told about God in theology and missiology, suggesting that the Mennonite accent of following Jesus in community can be a gift to the broader Church, but can also be a stumbling block to Mennonite congregations who desire to engage in mission. Not only have many of the stories highlighted in this chapter been ineffectual in promoting risk-taking in mission, but I will argue in chapter 5 that some of them might actually have undermined the efforts of leaders to promote missional engagement by emphasizing suffering, duty, separatism, and a resistance to change.

In the next chapter, I will argue that, if the Mennonite Church wants to experience transformation as risk-takers in mission, we must develop new stories that do not undermine our efforts. In order to change our existing theological and missiological stories, we must take the risk of being changed by dialogue with voices from outside or on the margins of our tradition. Changing our stories may allow us to experience transformation as we open ourselves to people who are not seeking to preserve the status quo or defend the establishment; exploring new stories might empower the Church to be formed into the image of a God who takes risks for the sake of love.

218. For example, see Houser, "MJ Sharp."

2

A Methodology for Change

INTRODUCTION

A POPULAR ADAGE HAS described the foolishness of repeatedly doing the same thing and expecting different results. In the Church, however, we continually attempt to create fresh theology or new practices while drawing on the same theological sources and voices. As I illustrated in chapter 1, the stories we have traditionally told in Mennonite congregations have not fostered a culture of risk-taking in mission; instead, the stories we have been telling may have undermined our mission efforts. If the stories that we tell in our churches—our theology—are inadequate to shape us into people who take the risk of vulnerable relationship for the sake of love, the time has come for new stories. In order to imagine new stories instead of simply recycling old ones, the Church cannot rely on the same methods and voices that have maintained the established stories throughout our history. Creative risk-taking in mission calls for creative risk-taking in theology. Creative risk-taking in theology calls for a creative, risk-taking methodology.

In the development of theology, the Church establishes criteria to decide what stories are valid, who is allowed to articulate new stories, how those stories are evaluated as truth claims, and whether those stories will come alongside existing stories or replace them. The process of discernment includes foundational values, practices, and relationships that determine, ultimately, which stories are heard and what theology is articulated. In the construction of new Anabaptist theologies, we first establish the guidelines for how we will know whether these new stories are harmonious with the Mennonite Church's underlying values and practices. In other words, if change is called for, to what degree can we change while ⟩⟩ remaining Anabaptist?

To set the foundation for the rest of this book, in this chapter I will articulate a correlational method of liberation, designed to utilize a broad range of sources and voices in order to bring about transformation in the Church. I will first consider the transformational nature of narrative and the importance of acknowledging and respecting perspective in theological storytelling, arguing that a change in standpoint is needed if we are to tell new stories that will shape us in new ways. Then I will explore and define what it means for theology to be "Anabaptist" by establishing the context of Anabaptist hermeneutics. Based on these Anabaptist values and narrative principles, I will articulate a correlational method of liberation, which will guide my selection of dialogue partners and the ways in which I validate truth claims. This method will engage with the social and behavioral sciences while dialoguing with feminist and liberationist theologians.

(RE)STORYING LIFE AND THEOLOGY

The work of re-visioning, re-imagining, and "calling forth new worlds"[1] out of established traditions and patterns is not new;[2] the practice of narrative therapy is built upon the premise that people understand their lives through the telling of stories and that these stories determine how an individual creates meaning and relates to others.[3] An individual's stories are not randomly constructed, however; the way that he[4] tells his stories and the meaning he attaches to those stories are culturally determined. The dominant culture in which an individual lives teaches him to ascribe meaning to some parts of his story, which he then remembers or tells, and to reject other parts of his story as meaningless and to be forgotten. Those single story-events form a longer

---

1. Johns, "Grieving," 145.

2. For a list of germinal works about narrative in a number of disciplines, see Bochner, *Coming to Narrative*, 12.

3. Narrative therapy was introduced to North American practice by Michael White and David Epston with the publication of *Narrative Means to Therapeutic Ends*. Critics have accused practitioners of getting caught up in oppressive patterns by clinging to narrative therapy's own "hard" normative story without being open to input or context (Amundson, "Why Narrative Therapy"). Critics also raise concerns that narrative therapy may be so motivated to empower the marginalized that they miss the therapeutic purpose of therapy (Minuchin, "Where Is the Family?").

4. In my use of gender-neutral language, I alternate between the use of female and male pronouns, sometimes specifically using one or the other if it helps to clarify the sentence or intentionally challenges gender roles.

story that becomes the narrative *of* a person's life. Eventually, as he tells and retells that story, the narrative *becomes* his life.[5]

The language we use and the stories we tell have been shaped by the dominant narrative of the culture around us. The power of this dominant narrative is that it is subconscious and, until something challenges it, the only reality that an individual knows, a narrative that is internalized to the point that she believes its message about her reality or identity is true. The individual often cannot imagine other possibilities; therefore, those who control the narrative shape her perceptions of reality simply because of repetition.[6] When this dominant cultural story is oppressive, individuals and communities must rediscover alternative stories: "A key to [narrative] therapy is that in any life there are always more events that don't get 'storied' than there are ones that do," write therapists Jill Freedman and Gene Combs. "This means that when life narratives carry hurtful meanings or seem to offer only unpleasant choices, they can be changed by highlighting different, previously un-storied events or by taking new meaning from already-storied events, thereby constructing new narratives." So, they conclude, "narrative therapy is about the retelling and reliving of stories."[7] One of the goals of this book is to challenge some of the dominant theological narratives in the Church so that we might become aware of new possibilities and imagine new ways of living.[8]

Narrative therapy was not the only twentieth-century application of narrative to life; a new understanding of narrative in theology was developed out of the Yale School as Stephen Crites explored the storied nature of life[9] and Hans Frei argued that biblical interpretation had been reduced to apologetics and analysis instead of opening space for Christians to enter into the story of God.[10] This postliberal theology was further developed by theologians and ethicists such as Stanley Hauerwas[11] and George Lindbeck;[12] the narrative lens has become so commonplace in the decades since that it can be seen in the writings of mainstream theologians as well

5. Freedman and Combs, *Narrative Therapy*, 32.

6. Freedman and Combs, *Narrative Therapy*, 39.

7. Freedman and Combs, *Narrative Therapy*, 32–33.

8. In my master's thesis, I argued that the stories we tell as congregations shape the way we see the world and, by changing those stories, we can change our sense of identity and purpose (*God's Dream on Earth*).

9. Crites, "Narrative Quality."

10. Frei, *Eclipse*.

11. See *Community of Character* and *Why Narrative?* among his other works.

12. See *Nature of Doctrine* and "Story-Shaped Church."

as liberation and feminist theologians.[13] Narrative theological method has been used in the work of Anabaptist theologians like James McClendon[14] and J. Denny Weaver;[15] narrative theology and a narrative style will be foundational to this book as well.

Until the twentieth century, much of Mennonite theology was "lived theology,"[16] written only in confessional form or in response to contextual challenges; many Mennonites distrusted intellectual speculation as a hindrance to practical discipleship.[17] Mennonite *systematic* theology has only been developed in the last few decades of the twentieth century and is still much in dispute.[18] Weaver argues that in the formulation of a systematic Mennonite theology, narrative theology is a useful tool because it allows for a normative story (that is, the story of Jesus) that shapes the behavior and ethics of the Church. "When Jesus is identified by a narrative, to accept Jesus is to put oneself into that narrative and to be shaped or guided by it," argues Weaver. "Accepting Jesus as defined by story does not reduce the gospel and Christian commitment to ethics, but it does make clear that ethics is intrinsic to the gospel and an inherent dimension of what it means to accept Jesus as the Lord."[19]

Mennonite philosopher and theologian Chris Huebner suggests that narrative theology can only benefit the Mennonite Church if it results in discipleship, meaning that the response to the text matters as much as the story of the text. The emphasis on ethics and discipleship that theologians like Weaver say characterizes Anabaptist tradition may cause tension with the values of narrative theology, Huebner maintains, since narrative theology emphasizes letting the text speak for its own sake. For a religious tradition that has historically valued its particularity, this could result in an inability to respect other stories because it is so "concerned with protecting its own story that it results

13. For mainstream theologians, see Wright, "Narrative Theology" or "Israel's Scriptures." For liberation or feminist theologians, see the authors cited later in this chapter.

14. McClendon encourages the use of "picture thinking" (*Doctrine*, 75–89).

15. Weaver, "Narrative Theology."

16. Weaver, *Keeping Salvation Ethical*, 225.

17. Walter Klaassen argues that the initial Anabaptist leaders were highly trained clerics and writers; their skepticism, he suggests, was not about learning itself, but about the tendency of religious academics to over-think and make abstract what should be clear and practical readings of Scripture (*Anabaptism*, 40–51).

18. Cramer, "Mennonite Systematic Theology." See also Swartley, *Explorations*. McClendon argues that one reason Anabaptists have produced so little theology over the centuries is that they were unaware that they had anything valuable to offer (*Ethics*, 26). Walter Klaassen challenges the prevailing assumption that Mennonites have not been involved in the construction of systematic theology ("Keeping Salvation Ethical," 244).

19. Weaver, "Narrative Theology," 175.

in the oppressive exclusion of others."[20] Mennonites may be risk-averse when it comes to theology; we are afraid of being changed.

By protecting our own story, Mennonites may create a normative story that is inflexible. The possible rigidity of this normative story is a cause for concern to Mennonite rhetorician Gerald Biesecker-Mast. Although enthusiastic about Weaver's articulation of the normative story and its implications for discipleship, Biesecker-Mast nevertheless describes Weaver's story as a "hard narrative," sometimes too shaped by traditional ways of knowing to see outside of itself. Biesecker-Mast suggests this narrative gets caught in a cycle of interpretation, reflecting that "the Mennonite reading of Jesus as a pacifist is justified by the Mennonite reading of Jesus as a pacifist."[21] This should not result in a rejection of the normative story, he claims, but instead, an acknowledgment "that this story comes to those whom it structures through layers of cultural and historical sediment, and that our reading of it originates in our contemporary circumstances and formative traditions."[22] He recommends, instead, a "soft narrative," which accepts "ethical and political responsibility for our particular presentation of this normative story in the contemporary context."[23]

The ethical responsibility for our own narratives begins by naming the lens through which the narrative has been shaped. Who constructed the normative story by which we judge our ethics and how might our normative stories be oppressive or exclusionary of others? In 1983, feminist philosopher Nancy Hartsock published an essay in which she claimed that each individual's cultural context shapes his or her perspective on life and knowledge.[24] This became known as "standpoint theory;" proponents suggest that a person's standpoint, shaped by the people and environment surrounding a person as she develops, not only determines *what* she comes to know but also becomes the filter through which she judges and validates knowledge, both her own knowledge and the assertions of others.[25] Because all knowledge is filtered, no one can see the world objectively; the idea of a normative, objective reason is in itself a construction.[26]

20. Huebner, "Mennonites."

21. Biesecker-Mast, "Reply," 331.

22. Biesecker-Mast, "Reply," 331.

23. Biesecker-Mast, "Reply," 332.

24. Hartsock, "Feminist Standpoint."

25. Thomas, "Womanist Theology," 494. See also Koontz, "Trajectory," 206.

26. Kwok Pui Lan suggests that the historical critical method of studying the Bible, hailed by its practitioners as "scientific, objective and value-neutral," was born out of a movement to set Christianity apart from the mythical, superstitious religions encountered during Europe's colonial expansion (*Introducing*, 44–45).

Because no standpoint is value-neutral, argue standpoint theorists, some standpoints have more value in theological interpretation than others since the filters through which some people see the world are less distorted than others.[27] Individuals who are systematically given power because of race, socioeconomic status, education, gender, or physical/military strength may not see the full picture of their reality, since maintaining the status quo will keep them in a position of privilege and power while relegating others to the margins.[28] Those on the margins, however, are positioned to more accurately see reality since they are not concerned with maintaining the status quo; they have an epistemological advantage that leads to a more just society.[29] Since not all standpoints are created equal, suggests womanist theologian Kelly Brown Douglas, filters on biblical interpretation that lead to oppression and hatred, maintaining power and privilege for a select few, should be discarded while those that lead to liberation and love for those on the margins should be embraced.[30]

As a basic building block of life,[31] story is powerful. This narrative power must be carefully wielded, however, when the dominant narrative is oppressive or exclusionary. In the context of biblical interpretation, it is important for theologians to evaluate what voices have been germinal in the formation of the normative narrative and to consider what other stories have been unheard or suppressed in the process. Once we become aware that our narratives are unhelpful or, even worse, hurtful, theologians can take responsibility for finding ways to re-story our narrative toward liberation and life.

For Anabaptists, this also means acknowledging the ways in which we are no longer on the margins ourselves. As a faith tradition that began as a persecuted, minority group and, over the last century, has become more influential to those in the center of Church and society,[32] we have struggled to release our "marginalized" identity.[33] Yet, as our history shows, those on the

27. White feminist theologian Rebecca Chopp has critiqued standpoint theory, suggesting that a better model is social constructionism, which still maintains that knowledge is shaped by power and context, but also takes into consideration race and class among other factors, refusing to generalize about women's experiences and thus allowing for more diversity ("Eve's Knowing").

28. Hartsock, "Feminist Standpoint," 288.

29. Douglas, "Marginalized People," 43.

30. Douglas, "Marginalized People," 42.

31. White and Epston, *Narrative Means*, 9–10.

32. See Ross and Stoner, "What Anabaptists Bring," 260–61; Kreider, "West Europe," 211; and Shenk, "Developing," 50.

33. See Gingerich Stoner, "Our Victim Mentality."

margins of the institutional Church challenge the status quo and bring about needed change: the minority voice of the early Anabaptists brought about changes including adult baptism, separation of Church and State, and a charge to live like Jesus. While it is true that Anabaptists were once a persecuted minority, now, in many ways, we have become a new center that itself needs challenging.[34] As long as we self-identify as the marginalized ones, we will not receive the gift of transformation offered by the voices and experiences of those who are actually marginalized. If we continue to claim the margin, our stories—and the practices shaped by them—will not change.[35]

"I believe we poor folks, we black folks, the disinherited, the Pentecostals, the charismatics, the radical Christians—we are today's Anabaptists," claims Black Mennonite pastor Hubert Brown. "Most present-day Mennonites do not fit these categories, and have drifted away from what it means to be Anabaptist, from what it means to be part of a movement, part of a prophetic, dynamic oppressed minority that listens to God and not society."[36] Therefore, Brown suggests, God's gift to the Mennonite Church is "non-white"; as a tradition that has borrowed heavily from other streams in the past, today's white Mennonite Church will only experience revitalization if we now learn from the voices on the margins. Only then, he argues, will we recover the true "Anabaptist Vision."[37]

(RE)COVERING THE ANABAPTIST VISION

Over the last century, one of the most significant debates within the US-American Mennonite/Anabaptist stream has been the definition of Anabaptism: What are the bare essentials of Anabaptism, beyond inherited Mennonite culture and family relationships,[38] and is it possible to agree upon a core principle as the lens through which Scripture is interpreted and congregational decisions are made?[39] Is Anabaptism really a unified movement?[40] This debate has become even more important over the last few decades as people who did not grow up in the tradition have been

34. Goossen, "Mennonite Privilege."

35. For a longer discussion of Anabaptism and the margins, see Ralph Servant, "Gentrification."

36. Brown, *Black and Mennonite*, 94.

37. Brown, *Black and Mennonite*, 94–96.

38. See, for instance, Stuart Murray's *Naked Anabaptist* and Mark Thiessen-Nation's response, "Naked Anabaptist."

39. See Swartley, *Essays.*

40. Enns, "Challenge of Diversity."

attracted to Anabaptism, exploring whether there is space for them within the Mennonite/Anabaptist family.[41]

The struggle began in the turmoil between the World Wars, when members of the US-American Mennonite Church began to research Anabaptist origins. Up to that point, most Mennonites had been suspicious of academic involvement,[42] but a new generation of scholars sought to defend the tradition in a society that was suspicious of the Mennonites' German roots and pacifist positions. Harold Bender first published *The Mennonite Quarterly Review* in 1927[43] and, with other Mennonite scholars like Guy Hershberger, J.C. Wenger, and Robert Friedman, began working to rehabilitate the image of Anabaptism within the wider Church.[44] With his speech on "The Anabaptist Vision," Bender constructed a narrative of Mennonite roots that described Anabaptism as a radical wing of Protestantism committed to discipleship, community, and nonviolence.[45]

Bender encouraged the Mennonite Church to find a "third way" between the twentieth century's fundamentalism and liberalism.[46] To do this, he focused on *historic* connections among Anabaptists instead of doctrinal ones in order to build faith and identity.[47] This meant doing some careful work to exclude sixteenth-century radicals who did not fit his vision of Anabaptism. "By creating the category 'evangelical Anabaptism,' as defined in *The Anabaptist Vision*, he was able to eliminate all undesirable elements, a sort of posthumous excommunication," describes historian James Coggins.[48] Bender's positioning of Anabaptism as the birthplace of the democratic notion of separation of Church and State transformed the Mennonites almost overnight from "traitors (as a result of their refusal of military service in the Second World War) to the founders of essential Americanism."[49]

As Anabaptist studies continued to expand into the 1950s and 1960s, a wave of "New Mennonite" scholars, building on Bender's legacy, developed slightly different theories of Anabaptist origins and primary values.

41. See Boyd, "Can Traditional Anabaptists Change"; Grimsrud, "Part of the Conversation?"; and Schirmer, *Reaching Beyond.*

42. Harder, "Naming Myself," 196.

43. Dyck, *Introduction,* 33.

44. Dyck, *Introduction,* 34.

45. Bender, "Anabaptist Vision." Biesecker-Mast describes how Bender's vision overshadowed the alternative described by his contemporary, C. Henry Smith ("Persistence of Anabaptism," 29).

46. Dyck, *Introduction,* 34.

47. Biesecker-Mast, "Persistence of Anabaptism," 25.

48. Coggins, "Toward a Definition," 187.

49. Coggins, "Toward a Definition," 188.

These scholars found that the emphasis in the early Anabaptist movement was less a difference from the State Church on matters of ecclesiology and more a profound difference of soteriology; it was the matter of free will and discipleship that set the early Anabaptists apart from the Protestant Church. Early Anabaptists saw faith as a commitment to following Jesus. "Harold Bender had been right in stressing the importance of discipleship for Anabaptism," maintains Coggins. "He was wrong in limiting discipleship to sanctification as a corollary to justification by faith. Discipleship constituted a replacement for justification by faith."[50] This radical discipleship resonated with a generation of US-American Mennonites swept up in the activism of the Civil Rights Movement. At the same time, the Charismatic movement made it more acceptable to embrace the increasing evidence of early Anabaptism's spiritualism, including an emphasis on the Holy Spirit in biblical interpretation.[51]

The weaknesses of Bender's vision became even more apparent in the 1970s, when scholars began to look at the social, political, and economic factors surrounding the rise of Anabaptism.[52] Making connections between Anabaptist groups and the Peasants' War, acknowledging the geographic and ideological polygenesis of the movement, and articulating the differences in both theology and practice among the groups, these scholars challenged the idea that there was a single Anabaptist vision.[53] "There seemed to be only an endless variety of separatist groups and individuals, making the writing of Anabaptist history, not to speak of a common or normative theology, almost impossible," observes historian C. J. Dyck.[54] Within the chaos of that historical moment, there seemed to be only one characteristic that all of these groups held in common: the practice of rebaptizing.[55] "For the most part," suggests Biesicker-Mast, "Mennonite historians found nothing offensive or even surprising about the claim that Anabaptism had a variety of origins or that it was not unified about doctrine, or that theology had limited value in defining Anabaptism;" this was probably because twentieth-century Mennonites "were nearly as difficult to define as were sixteenth-century Anabaptists."[56]

50. Coggins, "Toward a Definition," 191.

51. Coggins, "Toward a Definition," 192 and 194.

52. Dyck, Introduction, 35. This perspective emerged in Mennonite circles with the publication of Stayer et al., "From Monogenesis to Polygenesis."

53. Coggins, "Toward a Definition," 198.

54. Dyck, Introduction, 35.

55. Coggins, "Toward a Definition," 198.

56. Biesecker-Mast, "Persistence of Anabaptism," 31.

In more recent years, scholars have once again begun to look for common origins and relationality among the groups.[57] The debate remains about whether Anabaptism should be defined in relationship to the broader Church or in relationship to its own uniqueness, which Biesicker-Mast calls its "hard-won difference from Christendom."[58] Despite its weaknesses, Bender's vision of Anabaptist identity and theology continues to influence the Anabaptist community. It provided a "usable past" for twentieth-century American Mennonites, according to church planter Stuart Murray, "with which to orient themselves and from which to draw resources for contemporary church life."[59] The Anabaptist/Mennonite identity is strong for those who grew up in the Mennonite community.[60]

It is possible, however, that the twentieth-century quest for the Anabaptist vision was not so much a dis-covery or a re-covery but simply a cover-ing—an intellectual or cultural establishment seeking ways to protect and elevate Mennonite/Anabaptist identity over and against that of the "Other."[61] This raises some important questions about the nature of Anabaptist identity and theology. Should Anabaptist theology be evaluated against its roots or its present expression?[62] Should Anabaptist theology be determined by what it is or by what it could be? Have idealized visions of Anabaptist communities and practice,[63] such as that described in Bender's vision, paralyzed the Church,[64] preventing congregations from evaluating traditional theology and praxis in light of contemporary experience? For a theology to be Anabaptist, must it be uniquely Anabaptist? Does accepting the polygenesis of the Anabaptist vision(s) create room within Anabaptist theology for new stories about the nature and character of a risk-taking God, which develop into new practices within the Church?

57. See, for instance, Finger, *Contemporary.*

58. Biesecker-Mast, "Persistence of Anabaptism," 38.

59. Murray, *Biblical Interpretation,* 216.

60. This has resulted in increasingly diverse research on Anabaptist/Mennonite relationships with politics, gender, economics, literature, and other disciplines beyond theology (Koop, "Anabaptist and Mennonite Identity").

61. According to Lydia Neufeld Harder, this has been a defining characteristic of Anabaptist/Mennonite theology from the beginning ("Power and Authority," 9). This tendency can also be seen in Weaver, *Keeping Salvation Ethical.*

62. Hannah Heinzekehr wrestles with this in "On Neo-Anabaptism."

63. For one such idealized vision, see Frantz, "Theological Hermeneutics." In "Naming Myself," Harder describes her existential struggle after realizing that the real life of the Church was nothing like its idealized teaching (194).

64. Biesecker-Mast, "Persistence of Anabaptism," 28.

The ambiguity highlighted by these questions presents a space in which the "hermeneutical circle" can be broken. According to Mennonite feminist theologian Lydia Neufeld Harder, hermeneutical circles are formed when community practices and the biblical text interact over time to justify one another; this continues until an external influence interrupts the cycle.[65] Relevant Anabaptist theology, therefore, can only be developed when evaluated against both Anabaptist roots and present experience, maintains Harder, by both the current expression of the Church and a hope for transformation, and in conversation with voices from outside of and on the margins of the circle.[66]

If it is to transform congregations into risk-takers in mission, Anabaptist theology must be flexible, confessional, and open to new ideas. In *Slavery, Sabbath, War, and Women*, Mennonite theologian Willard Swartley suggests that congregations are most likely to hear God in Scripture when the context of the text (historical-cultural) is considered, when diversity within the canon is recognized and, ultimately, evaluated in light of Jesus, and when the over-arching moral principles of the Bible are prioritized over specific proof-texts.[67] Anabaptists emphasize that Scripture is self-interpreting, argues Murray, especially when the New Testament can help to interpret the Old. Most significantly, Anabaptist interpretation is highly christocentric, elevating the Gospels above the rest of the canon. Since Anabaptists interpret Scripture as a community, we depend on the inspiration of the Holy Spirit to make contemporary interpretations clear. The Holy Spirit also makes the Anabaptist "Hermeneutic of Obedience" possible, since theology is not meant to be only understood, but practiced.[68]

Harder defines the historical Mennonite hermeneutic as one of obedience and discipleship; it is only through obedience that one could truly understand Scripture to interpret it.[69] "Anabaptists stressed the reciprocal relationship between obedience and understanding, suggesting that although it was obedience that opened the mind to the revelatory Word of God, it was the Spirit that made the Word powerful and alive,

---

65. Harder, *Obedience*, 53 and 24. See Biesecker-Mast's previously mentioned suggestion that "the Mennonite reading of Jesus as a pacifist is justified by the Mennonite reading of Jesus as a pacifist" ("Reply," 331).

66. Harder, *Obedience*, 55–56.

67. Willard Swartley, *Slavery*, 23.

68. Murray, *Biblical Interpretation*, 211–15.

69. Harder, *Obedience*, 32. Ben Ollenburger reflects that this perspective could easily lead to a hermeneutical circle, as it did for Menno Simon ("Hermeneutics of Obedience," 51).

kindling the kind of obedient response that makes knowing possible."[70] By living the text, Anabaptists could complete the divine cycle in which the Word became flesh by allowing our flesh to become the Word.[71] A hermeneutic of obedience also requires a hermeneutic of trust; the two go hand in hand. Anabaptists believe that the biblical witness is true and can be trusted; therefore they shape their lives based on their reading of it.[72] "The theology of discipleship depends upon a notion of divine incarnation or embodiment in history that continues beyond the historical event of Jesus," describes Harder. "The present authority of God is mediated by the embodiment of God's activity in a human text, a human community and a human discernment process. . . . Therefore, a hermeneutic of obedience clearly describes the openness of a community to God's authority, as mediated through these human intermediaries."[73]

Despite this rich tradition, embracing a hermeneutic of obedience throughout Anabaptist history has resulted in the oppression of women and people of color, argues Harder. Not only have Mennonites been guilty of literal, oppressive readings of Scripture, but a hermeneutic of obedience has also allowed the misuse of authority within the Church:[74] "It can hide the fact that some interpreters within the community may be using biblical interpretation to seek their own interests. A hermeneutic of obedience can encourage an uncritical, naive acceptance of a human authority rather than promoting an openness to God."[75] The Church especially experienced this abuse of power throughout its history because the only part of the "community" allowed to participate in "communal hermeneutics" was male.[76] This resulted in a model of interpretation that moved the Church "away from dynamic change to a more static acceptance of the status quo."[77] Instead, Harder suggests a hermeneutical stance that "assumes that suspicion of our limited human perspectives must go together with obedience to the divine Word."[78]

70. Harder, *Obedience*, 35.

71. Frantz, "(Inter)Textuality," 139.

72. Harder, *Obedience*, 31 and 56.

73. Harder, *Obedience*, 37. Gayle Gerber Koontz suggests a "functional" understanding of Scripture that sees the text as *mediating* God's presence in the interpretive community ("Trajectory," 216).

74. Harder, "Postmodern Suspicion," 277.

75. Harder, *Obedience*, 39.

76. Harder, *Obedience*, 52 and "Naming Myself," 198.

77. Harder, *Obedience*, 39.

78. Harder, "Biblical Interpretation," 30.

Rather than dualities that could not be reconciled, Harder has found that both hermeneutics are important in developing new theologies that lead to liberation within the Anabaptist context. "This is because God's authority is powerful in its ability to reveal and save but vulnerable in its embodiment in humanity and in human structures," according to Harder,[79] and, therefore, neither a "suspicion that rejects these texts completely nor an easy obedience that fails to see the freedom of living a new life in Christ does justice to these texts in which the human and divine are so thoroughly intertwined."[80] The tension created in conversations between two hermeneutic communities with differing interpretations of Scripture is therefore necessary, she suggests, because they create accountability that allows us to recognize our human limitations and make "self-conscious choices between various claims to truth while, at the same time, opening up a space to listen again to God's disruptive Word."[81]

While Mennonites have been comfortably suspicious of other faith traditions for centuries, embracing a hermeneutic of suspicion alongside a hermeneutic of obedience means opening conversations that will illuminate the weaknesses, distortions, and sin in our own theology, Harder maintains. Being a minority tradition cannot be a claim to infallibility, but "in this context Mennonites can no longer hide from the admonition of other Christians."[82] This will require building relationships with the "Other" and with those who are on the margins of our communities.[83] "Love and intimacy with God are connected to love and intimacy with each other. Both are crucial for any knowledge which can be termed revelational," suggests Harder. "Intimacy always carries with it a certain vulnerability because it means opening ourselves to change, to salvation in its fullest meaning. This is both risky and exciting."[84]

For Pentecostal feminist theologian Cheryl Bridges Johns, the cycle of hermeneutical suspicion and obedience parallels the Spirit's creative process in birthing the cosmos. Followers of Jesus join with the Spirit in "groaning over the brokenness, brooding over the chaos, and calling forth new worlds."[85] Even when the hermeneutic of suspicion creates chaos out of the biblical text, the Spirit performs the same work in Scripture as she

---

79. Harder, *Obedience*, 148.

80. Harder, *Obedience*, 149.

81. Harder, "Naming Myself," 201 and *Obedience*, 148.

82. Harder, "Postmodern Suspicion," 274.

83. Harder, *Obedience*, 148. See also Koontz, "Trajectory," 217.

84. Harder, "Biblical Interpretation," 32.

85. Johns, "Grieving," 145.

does in creation, declares Johns: "The Spirit who enters into the broken-ness of human history and brings about its restoration is the same Spirit who enters into the textual landscape of the Bible in order to affect salva-tion history."[86] The Spirit joins with us in grieving over the pain portrayed in Scripture and times it has been used to bring harm; "The Spirit spreads her wings over the sinful times recorded in Scripture as well as over our own sinful times. Reading the Bible is to experience the hovering, waiting, gestating work of the Spirit."[87] Out of the brokenness, the Spirit brings new light, new life, and new imagination.

A hermeneutic of suspicion can become paralyzing for the Church because its members feel guilty or are afraid of being wrong, claims Harder. It must be accompanied by hope, by a "new freedom to speak and listen to each other in order to enrich and enlarge the convictions of truth that we all have."[88] This calls for a deep imagination, a re-visioning of theology, and a new narrative created in relationship with other voices and other com-munities.[89] As traditions are revisited and reconstructed, piece by piece, "repressed or neglected experiences and convictions of God's intervention are illuminated and interpreted in a new way, providing new models, im-ages and concepts. Familiar experiences and central convictions are reinter-preted in a different framework, creating new visions to direct our lives."[90] These new visions and models disrupt the status quo, moving the Church toward transformation and risk.

(RE)CONSIDERING CORRELATIONAL METHODOLOGY

Imagining new stories that may move the Church toward transformation and risk calls for a methodology that takes change and context seriously. One such methodology is the method of correlation. Practical theologians have long depended on correlational methodologies to shape their thought and praxis.[91] This methodology, later developed by David Tracy,[92] was origi-nally articulated by German systematic theologian Paul Tillich.[93] Tillich argues that no method for theological work is sufficient for all contexts

---

86. Johns, "Grieving," 150.

87. Johns, "Grieving," 152.

88. Harder, "Postmodern Suspicion," 278.

89. Harder, "Postmodern Suspicion," 278.

90. Harder, "Postmodern Suspicion," 279.

91. For instance, see Browning, *Fundamental* and Chopp, "Practical Theology."

92. See Tracy, *Blessed Rage* and "Foundations." Browning's work derives from a fu-sion of Tracy and Chopp (*Fundamental*, 47).

93. Tillich, *Systematic Theology.*

and that the method arises out of the theology itself. His system suggests systematic theology should be apologetic, that is, answering the questions implied by human existence.[94] Humans have asked the same existential questions throughout history, Tillich claims; even young children ask questions about their very being.[95] The message of the gospel, which is eternal,[96] is "the answer to the questions implied in [a theologian's] own and *in every human situation*."[97] A theologian's task is to focus on the *ultimate concern* and prevent *preliminary* (secondary) *concerns* from crossing the boundary into theology; only those *preliminary concerns* that point to the *ultimate concern* beyond them can be considered by the theologian. Therefore, the social sciences, politics, and art can only be addressed by a theologian when they point to the *ultimate concern*.[98] These other disciplines, then, can only participate in the formation of the question, not the answer.

Tillich names three sources for theology: the Bible (as both the chronicle of and a participant in revelation), Church history and tradition (specifically shaped by a theologian's denominational context), and the history of culture and religions (since the Christian message is the answer to the questions raised by other religions).[99] These sources for theology are received through the medium of experience. Experience itself cannot be a source for theology but is the mechanism through which the theologian participates in the sources.[100] The sources are evaluated against the norm, which is developed in the Church's encounter with the Christian message.[101] The Bible cannot be the norm, although the norm is shaped in encounter with the Bible,[102] but the Bible must be judged against the norm.[103] Tillich's correlational method, then, "makes an analysis of the human situation out of which the existential

94. Tillich, *Systematic Theology*, 60, 34, and 6.

95. Tillich, *Systematic Theology*, 62. In contrast, Mennonite theologian Gordon Kaufman argues that there are only particular and contextual experiences ("Religious Diversity," 5).

96. Tillich, *Systematic Theology*, 3.

97. Tillich, *Systematic Theology*, 8, emphasis mine.

98. Tillich, *Systematic Theology*, 12, italicized terms his.

99. Tillich, *Systematic Theology*, 35, 38, and 39. Kaufman suggests that this dialogue is mutual: other religions may also answer the questions that Christianity presents ("Religious Diversity," 5).

100. Tillich, *Systematic Theology*, 42, 46, and 40.

101. Tillich, *Systematic Theology*, 48. Tillich's norm is his ultimate concern, "New Being in Jesus as the Christ" (50).

102. Tillich, *Systematic Theology*, 50–51. Tillich further explores the relationships among these sources in *Biblical Religion*.

103. Tillich, *Systematic Theology*, 51.

questions arise, and it demonstrates that the symbols used in the Christian message are the answers to these questions."[104]

There are many ways that Tillich's framework may be helpful for a new theology of risk-taking in mission: he suggests that the message of the gospel must be contextualized for modern questions; he utilizes the social sciences in his attempts to understand the human condition; he places all his sources, even the Bible, under the scrutiny of his "norm." His method of correlation is also problematic, however: he claims that the human condition and existential questions are universal; he insists that experience cannot be a source of theology; he warns that theology loses sight of the *ultimate concern* if it provides sociological or political recommendations; he locates his epistemological foundation in a Euro-Enlightenment reason.[105] Tillich's universalizing of existential questions and his rejection of experience as a source for theology could be seen as a dismissal of women and those who have experienced oppression and marginalization. By rejecting the need for theology to participate in real sociological or political transformation, he continues to promote a status quo in which he maintains his own position as a powerful man who used and abused women and objectified people of color in order to stimulate his own intellectual and physical gratification.[106] This allows the experience and perspective of others to be consumed rather than transformationally and relationally embraced.[107]

Although David Tracy and Don Browning (among others) have revised Tillich's correlational method, their critiques have come from the perspective of white, Euro-American males and do not go far enough in building a methodology that challenges established ways of knowing and validating knowledge.[108] Earlier in this chapter, I explored how voices on the margins of the institutional Church can provide a necessary corrective to a theology or methodology that has been shaped within the dominant narrative. With these concerns about Tillich's method of correlation in mind, reconsidering this methodology through the lens of a liberationist critique will provide a

104. Tillich, *Systematic Theology*, 62. Mary Ann Stenger and Ronald Stone describe Tillich's method as flexible in responding to changing contexts, suggesting that this makes him particularly helpful in the construction of feminist theology (*Dialogues*, 87).

105. As does Browning (*Fundamental*, 34–54).

106. Tracy Fessenden documents Tillich's behavior and attitude toward women and African Americans in "'Woman' and the 'Primitive.'" Fessenden also suggests that Tillich's universalizing of the ultimate concern "opened the way for the study of religion as the study of something more and other than specific beliefs and practices" (71).

107. Fessenden, "'Woman' and the 'Primitive,'" 73.

108. I will highlight in the footnotes some of the ways in which their critiques resonate with or are challenged by liberationist critiques.

method that is more consistent with the spirit of constructing a new theological narrative for risk-taking.[109] In order to do this, I will identify themes in the methods articulated by liberationist, womanist,[110] white feminist,[111] Latina,[112] and Asian feminist theologians and compare those themes with Tillich's method of correlation.[113]

One of the primary tenets of liberation theologies is the particularity of experience. Korean women's experience is "not the universal, abstract, and standardized human experience as alluded to by some traditional European male theologians," argues Asian feminist theologian Chung Hyun Kyung.[114] As such, Korean women's experience is not just a medium through which theological sources are received, but a source in and of itself.[115] Womanist theologian Jacquelyn Grant also stresses the importance of avoiding universal assumptions. "When theology and Christology are contextualized," she contends, "the oppressed become actual participants in the process rather than mere recipients of theological and christological dogma which has claims of universality."[116] White feminist Elizabeth Say argues that liberation theology "makes a conscious effort to account for multiple realities which inform human existence rather than presupposing a 'generalized other,' assuming that all persons are, in essence, similar to oneself."[117] She critiques traditional approaches that say they address the human experience "while at the same time erasing the actual experiences of those who differed from

---

109. Stenger and Stone describe how Tillich's religious socialism predated liberation theology but note a growing interest in Tillich's theology among liberation theologians (*Dialogues*, 188–89).

110. Mercy Amba Oduyoye suggests African feminist theologians find it difficult to self-name because of the multiplicities of culture and language on the continent. She indicates that most African feminists would feel "at home" in North American womanism, which she calls the "wise precocious young woman, indeed girl, who wants to get involved and actually does have something to offer" (*Introducing*, 123).

111. I have used the term "white feminist" to honor the critique of womanist, *Mujerista*, and Asian feminist theologians who have rightly argued that "feminism" implies a universal woman's experience that does not take into consideration the differences of race or class (Grant, *White Women's Christ*, 200). See also Isasi-Díaz, *En La Lucha*, 3 and Kwok, *Postcolonial Imagination*, 7.

112. Latina theology includes *Mujerista* and *evangélicas* theologians.

113. For Mennonite engagement with liberation theologies, see Rutschman, "Anabaptism and Liberation" and Schipani, *Freedom and Discipleship*.

114. Chung, "'Han-Pu-Ri,'" 35–36.

115. Chung, "'Han-Pu-Ri,'" 35.

116. Grant, *White Women's Christ*, 1.

117. Elizabeth Say, "Many Voices."

the normative elite."[118] *Mujerista* theologian Ada María Isasi-Díaz takes it one step further, suggesting that if not even *Mujerista* theologians can speak for all Latinas, then the "conceptual frameworks and epistemological presuppositions of the world of theology . . . cannot hold the meaning of our daily lives and our concerns, knowledge, and understandings of the divine without distorting them."[119]

As such, all liberation theologies hold human experience to be a primary source. In contrast to Tillich, who is concerned that allowing experience as a source would introduce the influence of extra-Christian experiences or even, within the Christian experience, "add some new material to the other sources,"[120] liberation theologies delight in diversity of experience, *pursuing* new material or insights to theology. Isasi-Díaz describes the impact of using lived-experience on theology as providing an opportunity "to be self-defining, to give fresh answers, and, what is most important, to ask new questions."[121]

While Tillich also hopes for "fresh answers," he describes how the nature of the question on a fundamental level has remained the same, even if it has taken on a new form or vocabulary.[122] The underlying assumption of liberation theology, on the other hand, is that the questions asked will vary by context. Isasi-Díaz suggests that much traditional theology is about coming up with different answers for centuries-old questions: "This results in so-called 'new' answers, which are most often nothing but reinterpretations of old answers."[123] So while Tillich's approach uses the "symbols of the Christian message" to answer the world's existential questions, liberation theologies would suggest that the world's questions demand a rediscovery of new or reinterpreted symbols within the Christian message.[124] Theology's "answer" is not final; in fact, theology is more of a conversation.[125]

The rediscovery or reinterpretation of symbols within the Christian message happens in conversation with the social sciences. In contrast to Tillich's emphasis on the role of social sciences, which he sees as helping provide insight into the nature of human existence and therefore shaping only the question, liberation theologies depend on other disciplines to help

---

118. Say, "Many Voices."

119. Isasi-Díaz, *En La Lucha*, 64–65.

120. Tillich, *Systematic Theology*, 46.

121. Isasi-Díaz, *En La Lucha*, 73.

122. As in his discussion of existential questions.

123. Isasi-Díaz, *En La Lucha*, 74.

124. Kwok, *Introducing*, 38.

125. Say, "Many Voices."

shape the answer as well. Liberational methodology demands a practical outcome. As such, liberation theology relies on other disciplines not only to help understand the sources of human experience, but to develop strategies for change.[126] While Tillich argues that systematic theology should only be concerned with general concepts (it is the role of practical theology to identify ways in which these theories are lived out in local contexts),[127] liberation theologies argue that all theology should be practical.[128] "In the very telling and retelling of the stories and memories of the tradition, narrative performs," claims white feminist theologian Rebecca Chopp; that is, "it converts, informs, and changes us."[129] Therefore, liberation theology's pattern of "practice—reflection—practice"[130] does not stop the process at theological thought but instead requires action.

This practical outcome does not result in action that perpetuates the status quo, however, but instead calls for action that works for transformation. Douglas suggests that the Bible "can be used as a weapon of oppression or a source of liberation."[131] She describes the task of the theologian as denouncing "any attempts to use the Bible in ways that terrorize others," saying "inasmuch as any text or interpretation of a text diminishes the life and freedom of any people, then those texts and/or interpretations must be held under 'suspicion,' critically re-evaluated and perhaps lose authority."[132] Chung suggests that if a source does not lead to liberation, it is bad theology, even if it contributes to Church unity or comes from biblical or Church tradition.[133] Liberation is the norm against which sources and the resulting theologies are measured.

This liberation must not be only theoretical but real, local, and contextualized. Liberation theologies are not developed in the academy,[134]

126. Chopp, *Praxis of Suffering*, 136.

127. Tillich calls practical theology "technical theory" and does claim that systematics and practical theology are interdependent (*Systematic Theology*, 32–33).

128. See Chung, "'Han-Pu-Ri,'" for an example of how theology, arising from the experience of Korean women in conversation with behavioral and social sciences, resulted in action (35). In *Fundamental*, Browning suggests that fundamental practical theology is the over-arching umbrella of theology, under which are four submovements (42 and 47).

129. Chopp, *Praxis of Suffering*, 141.

130. Browning critiques Tillich's method as moving from theory to practice and advocates this practice—reflection—practice pattern (*Fundamental*, 43).

131. Douglas, "Marginalized People," 47.

132. Douglas, "Marginalized People," 47. See also Say, "Many Voices;" Chopp, *Praxis of Suffering*, 143, and Kwok, *Introducing*, ch. 3.

133. Chung, "'Han-Pu-Ri,'" 36.

134. Browning supports practical theological development in local contexts but

claims white feminist theologian and ethicist Sharon Welch, but in "actual communities in the concrete experience of women and men struggling to build a new world."[135] Theology cannot and should not represent a single voice but must speak for a community while letting the diversity within that community be heard.[136] The theologian cannot be an objective outsider but must work from within the community, explains Isasi-Díaz. "When she has no vested interest in the liberation of those involved because her liberation is not connected to the liberation of those in the group," she argues, "the dialogue becomes dishonest, the group being researched is objectified, and the theology itself becomes a tool of oppression."[137]

White feminist theologian Anne Carr suggests that there have been moves toward liberation throughout Church history, only to be "marginalized, suppressed, and ultimately forgotten in the dominant patriarchy."[138] The task of this wave of feminist scholarship, she argues, is to "reclaim the center," so that "feminist perspectives, if not feminist methods, are so incorporated into the whole of theology that theology itself is transformed."[139] If the theology of the Mennonite Church is going to be transformed so that the Church is shaped into a community of risk-takers in mission, these feminist perspectives will need to be privileged in theological dialogue.

(RE)COMMENDING A CORRELATIONAL METHODOLOGY OF LIBERATION

Keeping in mind the importance of voices from the margins, Lydia Neufeld Harder's three stances toward hermeneutics—obedience, suspicion, and imagination—draw together the three streams shaping my methodology. In order to develop an Anabaptist theology of risk-taking in mission, my methodology embraces the Anabaptist trust of the story of Scripture, with an emphasis on the Gospel narratives, believing that Scripture is both transformational and lived. At the same time, my methodology responds to a liberationist critique of Scripture and tradition, evaluating theology in light of its value to bring about freedom and wholeness. Finally, my methodology is constructive, delving into both tradition and experience to write new

---

also advocates making space for it in the academic setting, suggesting that those working in the academy should attempt "distancing maneuvers" (*Fundamental*, 50).

135. Welch, *Communities of Resistance*, 33.

136. Isasi-Díaz, *En La Lucha*, 69. See also Browning, *Fundamental*, 50.

137. Isasi-Díaz, *En La Lucha*, 71.

138. Carr, "New Vision," 25.

139. Carr, "New Vision," 25.

narratives that will help the Church to be formed into vulnerable risk-takers in the image of our risk-taking God.

What makes a theology of risk-taking specifically Anabaptist? How much transformation can our theology undergo while remaining within the Anabaptist family? We have already seen that the definition of "Anabaptism" is fluid. Based on both the historical and contemporary manifestations of Anabaptism, however, we can safely say that an Anabaptist theology is christocentric, formational, and practical. Earlier in this chapter, I evidenced how Mennonite theologians ground their work in the story of the historical Jesus; Anabaptism has stressed from the beginning that all interpretations of Scripture and all decisions about daily living must be made with the life and teachings of Jesus in mind. Even as the theology of risk-taking in this book seeks to bring a corrective to this overly narrow Anabaptist focus by building on a more robust trinitarian foundation, it cannot lose its Jesus-focus without losing its identity. Early Anabaptist leader Menno Simons included the same scripture at the beginning of all of his writings: "No one can lay any other foundation besides the one that is already laid, which is Jesus Christ" (1 Cor 3:11).[140] Jesus, for Anabaptists, is nonnegotiable.

As Harder evidenced and the "New Mennonites"[141] articulated, Anabaptists have always emphasized transformation, also known as "discipleship." Menno Simons called this regeneration "The New Birth."[142] Anabaptists believe that Jesus brings about a complete life-change and that this renewal is a sign of the Spirit at work. Yet with Harold Bender's Anabaptist Vision in 1942, the emphasis on *acting* like Jesus overcame the traditional desire to *become* like Jesus. Decades after that ground-breaking speech, Stephen Dintaman reflected that the "next generation of 'Anabaptist vision' theologians taught passionately about Christian behavior and greatly deepened and expanded the concept of discipleship, but gave only passing, nonpassionate attention to the work of Christ and the work of the Spirit in the inner transformation of the person."[143] The result of this approach was that several generations of church leaders learned how to behave like good Christians without learning that "discipleship is only meaningful and possible because it is an answer to who God is and what God is doing in the world."[144]

---

140. Harder suggests that this scripture has been a sort of Mennonite "motto" (*Obedience*, 29).

141. See my earlier discussion in ch. 2.

142. Simons, "Fundamental Doctrine," 167–76.

143. Dintaman, "Spiritual Poverty," 205.

144. Dintaman, "Spiritual Poverty," 205.

Traditional language of obedience and discipleship does not adequately articulate the relational nature of this transformation. It is not simply a new "doing," but a new way of "being." Contemporary Mennonites are apt to quote early Anabaptist leader Hans Denck as saying, "No one can wholly know Christ, unless he is willing to follow him in his life" but rarely remember to add the second half of the quote: "And no one can follow after him except insofar as one previously knows him."[145] For this reason, I prefer the term "formation" instead of "discipleship." Those who know and follow Jesus are formed into his image as risk-takers for the sake of love.

The need to remember "being" as essential to discipleship does not negate the importance of "doing," however. An Anabaptist theology, therefore, is also practical. As we have seen, until the twentieth century, Anabaptism was resistant to systematic theology, believing that theology is lived, not written. If theology does not impact how we live, Anabaptists believe, it is useless. Menno Simons described the practical bent of theology in *The New Life*, saying that true evangelical faith

> cannot lay dormant; but manifests itself in all righteousness and works of love; it . . . clothes the naked; feeds the hungry; . . . shelters the miserable; aids and consoles all the oppressed; returns good for evil; . . . prays for those that persecute it; teaches, admonishes and reproves with the Word of the Lord; . . . heals that which is diseased and saves that which is sound.[146]

This living of the Scripture comes out of the relational formation of the Spirit and takes the life and teachings of Jesus seriously. If formation transforms humans into the image of a loving God, then those transformed humans naturally perform the action of loving, whether that means caring for the poor and marginalized, refusing to return violence with violence, or taking risks so that others can also participate in God's Community of life.

I have argued that feminist and liberationist perspectives will be transformative for theological reflection, particularly if the goal of that reflection is actual change: privileging experience, particularly the experience of those on the margins; not only giving new answers but asking new questions; using other disciplines to form those questions and to articulate a possible way forward; emphasizing conversation over monologue; evaluating sources against the norm of liberation; "doing" theology in community, as a member

---

145. For the original quote, see Denck, "Whether God," 108. The truncated quote is used in as diverse sources as Neufeld, *What We Believe Together*, 90; Green, "Cultivating a Spirituality," 161; Rutschman, "Anabaptism and Liberation," 58; Roth, *Practices*, 42; and by three separate authors in Swartley, *Essays* (6, 27, and 30).

146. Simons, "Reason Why," 246.

of that community. The Anabaptist foci of christocentricity, formation, and practice are both in harmony with and in tension with these liberative theological methods. As Harder demonstrated, however, this tension can be a benefit to both streams as it breaks down hermeneutical circles, challenges assumptions, and balances suspicion with trust.

A CORRELATIONAL METHOD OF LIBERATION IN ACTION

This book presents an Anabaptist theology of risk-taking in mission that is built on a correlational methodology. I use the behavioral and social sciences to help understand the current reality of my context by exploring the history of Mennonite mission (chapter 1), by constructing best practices of risk-taking from the fields of anthropology, psychology, disability studies, business, child development, and philosophy (chapter 3), and by evaluating the literature on risk and existing theological stories against those practices (chapter 4). The shape of this book reflects a praxis—reflection—praxis structure: beginning with my current context of practice (the missional context of the Mennonite Church in which I minister) in the introduction and chapter 1, reflecting on that practice in relationship with a new methodology and existing literature and theology on risk-taking in chapters 2 through 5, and then returning to practice with the development of a new theology of risk-taking for Anabaptist contexts in chapters 6 through 8.

Additionally, my method of correlation is distinctly liberationist. Throughout this book, I engage Anabaptist theologians who are not in the mainstream of Anabaptist thought as well as theologians from other spiritual streams, privileging the voices of women and people of the global majority. This engagement happens most significantly in this chapter and in chapters 5 through 8, in which I critique the Mennonite Church's existing stories and develop alternative narratives. I choose my sources based on their usefulness[147] and their potential for bringing about real transformation in the Church, transformation that leads to liberation for the poor and marginalized, liberation for those at the center of power and privilege, and therefore, liberation for the whole Church. I have worked out my theology within my context and

---

147. While this method is pragmatic, it is not pragmatist. Feminist thought has been influenced by pragmatism, as can be seen in the collapse of the material and spiritual in the work of Rita Nakashima Brock (*Journeys by Heart*) and Sharon Welch (*Feminist Ethic*). My method does not collapse apparent dichotomies as pragmatism does (Stuhr, *Pragmatism*, 194); rather, I hold them in tension. Instead, my methodology reflects Letty Russell's emphasis on the "usability" of theology (*Human Liberation*, 72–103) and what Darby Ray refers to as theology's "lived-out consequences" (*Deceiving the Devil*, 110).

community, creating space for that community to provide feedback and thus to determine whether they see themselves in the theology that is developed.[148]

A liberationist methodology requires an awareness of the standpoint through which I and others engage in our theological work. While it is impossible to identify the lens of every individual with whom I dialogue within this book, the internal consistency of my argument and methodology requires that I at least identify the standpoint of my major dialogue partners. This may include ethnicity, gender, geography, or theological identity.[149] Many liberation theologians have articulated their own "naming" preferences (i.e. womanist, *Mujerista*). Unfortunately, many theologians who are part of the more dominant theological traditions have not; because they are the "norm" against which divergent theologies are measured, they often retain only the title of "theologian," with perhaps a modifier of denomination or discipline. How do you identify the standpoint of someone who has not acknowledged their own lens of experiential bias?[150]

A correlational methodology that is distinctly liberationist also emphasizes the importance of language. Although whenever possible I use gender-neutral and culturally-sensitive language in this book, I leave quotes from other sources as they are. By allowing each person to speak for themselves (as well as their time and culture), we can see their patterns of language and ideas. For God, I prefer the use of ungendered language whenever possible ("God's self"), although I use the masculine when referring to the life of Jesus. In my chapter on Jesus and the Spirit, I use the female pronoun for the Spirit when a pronoun is unavoidable so that the stories of the Spirit's interactions with Jesus have the most possible clarity.

Although I have made every effort to identify gender, racial, and class inequities in the writing of this book, there may be ways in which I have not acknowledged my privilege. My story (shared in the introduction) clarifies how I am situated at both the center (as a middle-class white person with educational and positional credentials) and the margins (as a woman and an "outsider" of my community); I can identify with Asian feminist theologian Kwok Pui Lan's analysis of being both the recipient of oppression

148. Isasi-Díaz, *En La Lucha*, 72. I began this research in response to questions raised in my ministry (see the introduction for more). In the years that I developed my original dissertation, I repeatedly explored the implications of it through teaching and preaching, conversations and coaching, and by observing and asking questions; therefore, the continual pattern of practice—reflection—practice was a reality throughout my doctoral work.

149. I will do this the first time each conversation partner is mentioned in a chapter.

150. This finds ironic expression in J. Denny Weaver, who identifies this problem in the work of others without acknowledging his own position of privilege (*Anabaptist Theology*, 123).

and part of systems that oppress.[151] White feminist theologian Rosemary Radford Ruether suggests that advocates of liberation will always be limited by their social context, regardless of their desire to speak inclusively for all oppressed groups. Just as the Hebrew prophets spoke out against the oppression of their people by the wealthy classes or by conquering empires but ignored the oppression of women and slaves within their own social systems, so today's prophets may also be "aware of who is hurting them and the groups of people with whom they feel primary bonds. They may be insensitive or oblivious to other oppressed people who are the underside of social systems from which they themselves benefit."[152] My story identifies the groups with whom I may feel bonded and for whom I may be most vocal in my advocacy, the voices whom I may be most inclined to privilege. My story also identifies ways in which I may be indifferent to other voices, unaware of or resistant to their perspectives.

I have experienced what it feels like to be an outsider, to be excluded or oppressed. I have also participated in and taken advantage of systems in which I collude with the oppression of others. Therefore, although my voice could bring critique of those systems that marginalized me and those with similar life experiences, I must also listen to voices that critique me and my participation in systems of marginalization. This is the lens through which I read and develop theology; I cannot avoid it. I do hope that, by listening to voices of those who have been marginalized, I can become more aware of the ways that my lens distorts reality. Only then can I share in developing theology that brings liberation to *all* people, so that all may participate in the life of God, taking risks in mission for the sake of love.

CONCLUSION

So far in this book, I have provided an overview of Mennonite mission in practice and considered the stories that Mennonites have traditionally told about God in theology and missiology. I have suggested that images of a risk-taking God are absent in these conversations; additionally, the unique Mennonite emphasis on following Jesus may undermine congregational leaders in their attempts to promote risk-taking in mission. I have also argued that if the Mennonite Church wants to experience transformation as risk-takers in mission, we must develop new stories that do not undermine our efforts.

In response, I have suggested utilizing a correlational method of liberation, in which new narratives are constructed in conversation with the

151. Kwok, *Introducing*, 41.

152. Ruether, "Feminist Interpretation," 119.

social and behavioral sciences and voices of liberation from the margins of the institutional Church. In the next two chapters, I will apply this method by engaging with the behavioral and social sciences and with a wider theological literature on risk. As very little research has been done on risk in the Church, I will develop the practical implications of congregational risk-taking in mission by exploring literature on risk across other disciplines. These implications will provide a set of best practices in light of which the existing literature on risk in theology and Mennonite missional literature and practice can be critiqued.

3

The Practice of Risk-Taking

INTRODUCTION

ALTHOUGH TODAY'S MENNONITE CHURCH was born out of the fiery evangelism and bold risk-taking of the Radical Reformation, the historical overview in chapter 1 illustrates how it has become increasingly risk-averse in local, congregational mission. As a result, rather than promoting vulnerable risk-taking in mission, I have identified how some of the stories that Mennonites tell about God in our theology, ecclesiology, and missional literature may have undermined the efforts of pastors and leaders as they have encouraged congregations to make changes and take risks essential to mission. These unhelpful narratives revolve around following Jesus in life: first, following Jesus results in suffering and is an act of duty or obedience that motivates mission; second, following Jesus calls for the separation of a pure Church and, therefore, clinging to the uniqueness of a "Mennonite identity;" and third, following Jesus depends on the predictability of the "Spirit of Jesus" and Jesus as the divine model. These stories about God may shape our congregations into communities who resist taking risks in mission because of the risk of being changed.

In order to revise some of these stories, in chapter 2 I developed a correlational methodology of liberation, bringing voices from the margins of the institutional Church into conversation with Anabaptist hermeneutics and values. In engaging a correlational methodology of liberation, I have chosen to explore the behavioral and social sciences as an avenue to building a theology for change. As we will see in chapter 4, little has been written about risk-taking in the Church, particularly risk-taking in mission; most of the thinking about risk in the Church has been in the field of theology. To learn about the practical implications of risk-taking, therefore, we need to turn to other disciplines. By investigating how risk is understood in the worlds of anthropology, disability studies, psychology, business, child development, and philosophy, we can draw parallels with behaviors and relationships in the Church and begin to formulate corporate understandings of the nature of risk as well as a set of best practices related to risk and mission. These understandings and best practices will then be used to critique literature on risk and mission and identify areas in which different narratives might better help the Church to be formed into a community of risk-takers.

This exploration of the behavioral and social sciences identifies five understandings of risk that lead to best practices. Foundational to all these understandings is the reality of risk-taking as relational vulnerability; the other four principles—the need for risk-taking to be practiced out of a safe and loving community; risk-taking as an expression of creativity; the inevitability of failure in risk-taking; and loving justice as the ethical grounding for risk-taking—are rooted in vulnerable relationship. These five foci for risk-taking arose out of the spiral of research in theology, methodology, and practice. Each was identified in response to questions raised by and in conversation with my theological dialogue partners and with practical concerns identified in my historical and experiential research. With these five elements in mind, local congregations can evaluate their practices of formation, community, and outreach as they re-shape their corporate life around risk-taking in mission.

THE NATURE OF RISK: VULNERABILITY

According to disability theologians and shame researchers, the essential nature of life is vulnerability; living as a human being in relationship with others requires taking risks. To be a creature is to be contingent, suggests disability theologian Thomas Reynolds, formed in relation to and dependent on others for existence.[1] This interdependence can be a good thing, but it can also result in struggle and suffering. Humans are created in God's image to seek life, to avoid pain, and to pursue wholeness.[2] The desire for life is a reflection of "a God of Life who desires that human beings choose being over nonbeing, life over death, and who becomes incarnate so that humanity might have life in abundance," argues white feminist Elizabeth Gandolfo. "It is not only legitimate but good that we are structured in such a way as to seek such abundance for ourselves and avoid that which threatens it."[3]

1. Reynolds, *Vulnerable Communion*, 163.
2. Reynolds, *Vulnerable Communion*, 184.
3. Gandolfo, *Power and Vulnerability*, 121.

Interdependence also causes humans to seek abundance for those we love or those with whom we feel a connection. In this way, a mother cares for her children or for the children of other mothers in whom she sees a reflection of her own children.[4] Humans search for ways to flourish in a vulnerable world. This includes the basic needs of food and shelter, but more specifically, it means "being welcomed into relational space, a home where one's unique value is revealed and affirmed."[5] This unique value and worth is our dignity as human beings. Dignity, according to psychologist Donna Hicks, "is an internal state of peace that comes with the recognition and acceptance of the value and vulnerability of all living things."[6]

Vulnerability is a necessary and important characteristic of human life and yet humans resist our vulnerability, striving instead to protect ourselves from the suffering and weakness it could cause. Vulnerability, then, is at the heart of sin and suffering, Gandolfo argues. In our efforts to protect ourselves from vulnerability, humans violate the vulnerability of others, leading to injustice, violence, and oppression.[7] This cycle of anxiety and vulnerability causes further harm to vulnerable others as well as to those who violate them.[8] In attempting to protect ourselves from the vulnerability of living within an unpredictable and potentially devastating world, humans hoard resources, creating privileged classes, genders, and races. "Privilege, then, can be interpreted as an unjust, unequal, and ultimately violent means of (mis)managing human vulnerability."[9] While understanding systemic issues of oppression and injustice are important, Gandolfo argues, theology and anthropology need to dig deeper if they are to address systemic sin and violation: "A robust understanding of the dynamic of vulnerability and violation offers not only an alternative to sin as the root problem of the human condition. It also calls for an alternative understanding of what human beings need in order to experience wholeness, flourishing, and life in abundance."[10]

Fear of vulnerability results in broken relationships, according to shame researcher Brené Brown. When humans are faced with our own vulnerability, we often experience shame: the feeling that we are inadequate

---

4. Gandolfo, *Power and Vulnerability*, 121.

5. Reynolds, *Vulnerable Communion*, 104.

6. Hicks, *Dignity*, 3. Hicks points out how much easier it is to recognize and affirm the value of children (4).

7. Gandolfo, *Power and Vulnerability*, 104–5.

8. Gandolfo, *Power and Vulnerability*, 168.

9. Gandolfo, *Power and Vulnerability*, 138.

10. Gandolfo, *Power and Vulnerability*, 171.

and unworthy of love.[11] Shame is not based on what we have done, but on a sense of who we are.[12] "We are physiologically, emotionally, cognitively, and spiritually hardwired for connection, love, and belonging," describes Brown.[13] Shame, at its core, is the fear of disconnection.[14] In our shame, humans hide from, attack, or try to appease one another.[15] Vulnerable people, instead of embracing their vulnerability, lash out and hurt others; the chance of disconnection is too great to risk exposing vulnerability. Rejection and the sense that we are not "good enough" leads us to fear being wounded again, suggests Reynolds. We deny our need for others and "try to prove that we are okay, hiding behind masks of self-sufficiency. The irony, however, is that this is an illusion, for this belies the fact that we need to be recognized by others as of value."[16]

When humans try to avoid their vulnerability, however, they also fail to experience the joys of connection and belonging. "When we spend our lives (knowingly or unknowingly) pushing away vulnerability, we can't hold space open for the uncertainty, risk, and emotional exposure of joy," maintains Brown.[17] When someone numbs themselves to the negative emotions and experiences of vulnerability, she also numbs herself to the positive emotions and experiences of vulnerability.[18] This is why vulnerability can be defined as the "susceptibility to being changed" that is basic to human life, argues theologian Kristine Culp.[19] "Vulnerability encompasses not only the capacity to suffer harm and to be damaged, but also capacities implied by contrast: to be kept safe and whole, to have integrity and dignity, and to be healed and lifted."[20] Vulnerability brings with it the capacity for devastation or transformation. Cutting oneself off from the pain of vulnerability necessarily cuts one

---

11. Brown, *Daring Greatly*, 69.

12. Brown, *Gifts of Imperfection*, 39. Brown's concerns about shame and vulnerability are developed in a US-American context and not within cultures in the world that are built on an honor-shame value system. While research among those cultures might yet produce similar results, until that research has been done, universalizing the human experience according to Western experience could be considered another form of colonialism.

13. Brown, *Daring Greatly*, 68.

14. Brown, *Daring Greatly*, 68.

15. Brown, *Daring Greatly*, 77–78.

16. Reynolds, *Vulnerable Communion*, 109.

17. Brown, *Daring Greatly*, 122.

18. Brown, *Daring Greatly*, 122.

19. Culp, *Vulnerability and Glory*, 2.

20. Culp, *Vulnerability and Glory*, 3.

off from the joy.[21] Vulnerability risks disconnection and wounding but also promises connection and healing: "Staying vulnerable is a risk we have to take if we want to experience connection."[22]

The key to living wholeheartedly is developing resilience in the face of vulnerability, argues Brown. The opposite of shame is empathy:[23] the willingness to show up, to see others and to be seen by others. This kind of seeing cannot happen from a distance but must be built in close relationships of trust and mutuality. "The bottom line is that we need each other," claims Brown. "And not just the civilized, proper, convenient kind of need. Not one of us gets through this life without expressing desperate, messy, and uncivilized need. The kind we are reminded of when we come face-to-face with someone who is in a deep struggle."[24] While Brown's work focuses on the vulnerability of emotional need, for congregations engaged in mission, these desperate, messy struggles could also include tangible experiences like poverty, systemic racism, illness, or domestic violence.

Opening ourselves up to others is a vulnerable experience, whether that vulnerability involves emotional exposure or acknowledging physical needs: we risk rejection, misunderstanding, inadequacy, and shame. Being present to someone else's vulnerability and pain can be just as difficult;[25] the human default is to self-protect in the face of someone else's suffering or shame, according to Brown. Humans look for someone to blame, hide behind judgment, or go into "fix-it" mode.[26] Being truly present to another person, building connection "when they feel seen, heard, and valued: when they can give and receive without judgment; and when they derive sustenance and strength from the relationship"[27] is the gift of empathy. "The willingness to show up changes us. It makes us a little braver each time."[28] While vulnerability can lead to empathy, vulnerability could also be wielded as a weapon, a crutch, or a coping mechanism when used to anticipate or deflect criticism, manipulate the emotions of others, or avoid difficult conversations. This kind of negative vulnerability may not be true vulnerable

---

21. Culp, *Vulnerability and Glory*, 16.

22. Brown, *Gifts of Imperfection*, 53.

23. Brown, *Daring Greatly*, 74.

24. Brown, *Rising Strong*, 182.

25. Brown, *I Thought*, 56.

26. Brown, *Gifts of Imperfection*, 16.

27. Brown, *Gifts of Imperfection*, 19.

28. Brown, *Daring Greatly*, 42.

presence, however, but another mask humans use to avoid real connection or to hide from moments of shame or unworthiness.[29]

In the complexity of our world, connection takes more than courage, argues blogger Rachel Cohen-Rottenberg. While Brown's emphasis on worthiness and shame resilience is important, "It's a question of people being battered by the bigotry and violence and distortions that surround them in their lives," writes Cohen-Rottenberg. "While I agree that developing one's inner resources is crucial, it is only half the story." Many individuals who do take the risk of vulnerability are harmed repeatedly by systemic issues beyond one-on-one interaction. What is someone to do when her society rejects her vulnerable self? "The world we live in must be a place of connection. The world must create loving connections that create a sense of worth in the first place. . . . It takes more than one side to make connection."[30] Being present to and empathetic in response to another's suffering and pain also means working together to fight systemic injustices that hoard resources for resilience and violate the vulnerability of marginalized people. The human condition of vulnerability calls for both empathy and resistance.

For congregations who desire to take risks in mission, accepting the vulnerability of life is an essential first step. While many people may consider the risks involved in losses of property or finances, failed programs or community development initiatives, or even the loss of membership or viability, perhaps the most difficult risk of mission is the act of showing up and being seen. In mission, congregations are called to a radical closeness beyond programs and charity: continually giving of themselves, investing in relationships, and enduring both the pain and joy of connection, while risking rejection, disappointment, embarrassment, or broken relationships. Relationships are not a quick fix, but a long-term investment in other human beings, as messy and unpredictable as those relationships can be. Congregational risk-taking in mission requires the vulnerability of connection: in the community as well as inside the church's walls. In order to take those risks, members of the congregation must have a safe home base of loving relationships from which they can draw the courage to keep venturing out and showing up.

29. Brown does argue that vulnerability requires boundaries and trust and is not indiscriminately dumping private thoughts on a public audience (*Daring Greatly*, 45) but does not adequately discuss how to respond to weaponized vulnerability. See also her interchange with Adam Grant about whether there is such a thing as "too much authenticity" (Grant, "Unless You're Oprah," and Brown, "My Response").

30. Cohen-Rottenberg, "Connection Takes More." See also "Shame and Disconnection." Heather Hackman makes some connections in "Addressing Shame."

THE COURAGE FOR RISK: COMMUNITY

Attachment theory,[31] which looks at how a baby's relationship with her caregiver affects her development and emotional competency, provides one picture into why these secure and loving relationships matter. As the theory shows, a baby does not feel confident to explore or experiment within her environment unless she knows that she has a safe haven of loving relationships to surround and protect her. When it comes to venturing out and risk-taking in mission, the church is no different.

Attachment theory is based on two universal needs: that of a baby to be protected and cared for and that of a caregiver to use energy and resources to care for the baby.[32] Babies can be attached in healthy and unhealthy ways with their caregivers. In healthy attachments, the caregiver becomes both a "secure base" from which a child can explore her environment and "haven of safety" to which a child can return when she feels threatened or in danger.[33] The baby is also shaped by her relationship with her caregiver to behave in ways that are socially and culturally acceptable: "Cultures define to a large extent what children should explore and in what skills they should become competent," explain developmental psychologists Klaus Grossmann, Karin Grossmann, and Anika Keppler. "Attachment theory posits that caring by committed parents who understand the child's needs, and who respond appropriately to the child's emotional expressions of needs and desires will have children who comply with their goals as individuals and members of the culture."[34] A healthy attachment to a secure base gives the baby confidence to explore and experience the world. In Western cultures, this encourages independence and experimentation; in Eastern cultures, this encourages interdependency and mutual exploration.[35] Secure attachment will not just protect the developing child, but also expose her to her environment, helping her to learn, adapt, and understand her social world.[36]

The developmental outcomes that particular cultural groups value create significant differences in how they provide care, say psychologists and anthropologists Vivian Carlson and Robin Harwood. "Among caregivers who emphasize obedience, respect, and fulfillment of familial roles, child behaviors

31. While attachment theory is cited by advocates of attachment parenting, the two are not the same thing (Kulkarni, "Attachment").

32. Grossmann et al., "Universal," 76. Recent research into the cultural context of attachment is an important corrective to traditional attachment theory.

33. Grossmann et al., "Universal," 80.

34. Grossmann et al., "Universal," 91.

35. Rothbaum and Morelli, "Attachment and Culture," 112–13.

36. Weisner, "Socialization of Trust," 265.

are carefully monitored and directed;" caregivers who are encouraging more traditional behaviors "tend to follow the child's lead more responsively and gently shape the child's motivations to match traditional values." On the other hand, caregivers who "strongly value the development of individual agency allow and encourage autonomous activity on the part of the child and reward creativity and the violation of norms."[37]

One of the roles of caregiving relationships is to correct behavior that is not considered acceptable to the child's social network: in response to a child's actions, the caregiver will reinforce desired behavior and punish or discourage undesired behavior. This repeated interaction of "reinforced meaning" can either build trust and relationship between the child and caregiver when they have the same goal, or it can break down trust when their goals are conflicting.[38] There is no such thing as a dysfunctional system:[39] members of a family unit or church community are shaped by their surroundings to behave in socially acceptable ways, even ways that appear to others as unnecessary or undesirable. Similarly, attachment theory describes how a baby who is attached to his caregiver in healthy ways is more likely to grow competent in the behaviors desired by his family and their culture. Unhealthy attachments may result in behaviors that conflict with social expectations.[40]

Another role for the child's network of caregivers is to nurture such a trusting and safe relationship with the child that she feels secure in venturing out, exploring her environment, and trying new things. Child development researchers Fred Rothbaum and Gilda Morelli see this as a "balance between contact with the attachment figure and re-engaging the wider social world."[41] The child's attachment must be secure enough that, when she feels threatened, she focuses her attention on, and increases her contact with, her caregiver but "when children feel secure they broaden their social involvements to include other partners and activities (i.e.,

---

37. Carlson and Harwood, "Precursors," 285.

38. Carlson and Harwood, "Precursors," 283.

39. Jeff Lawrence, as quoted in Heifetz et al., *Practice*, 17.

40. Carlson and Harwood, "Precursors," 283. Critics of attachment theory suggest that it puts too much emphasis on the "nurture" side of the "nature/nurture" debate, does not adequately take into consideration the breadth of attachment figures beyond the mother, and does not account for the role of external environment on the development of a child. See Harris, *Nurture Assumption* and Field, "Attachment and Separation." Some of these concerns have been addressed by the expansion of attachment research into other cultural contexts.

41. Rothbaum and Morelli, "Attachment and Culture," 112.

exploration)."[42] By considering the role of caregivers in risk-taking and exploration in this manner, it "reconceptualizes exploration as a social, not solitary, process and it downplays other western connotations of exploration."[43] The child is not left to explore the world on her own, but does so in loving relationship with her caregiver.

When the Church creates a nurturing community, it can become a haven of safety and a secure base that makes risk-taking possible.[44] Attachment theory describes a baby's need for someone "strong and wiser"[45] to protect and nurture him. Research shows, however, that adult attachment relationships can be mutual,[46] and this is the kind of relationship appropriate for the Church: not one of dependency or that strips a person of his agency, but relationships of mutuality and trust. The Church forms a caregiving "secure base" for Jesus-followers as they are nurtured into the image of God; or, in the words of attachment theory, shaped into the cultural expectations of their social network.

Asian American feminist theologian Rita Nakashima Brock and white feminist Rebecca Parker note, however, that "socially organized religion is seen as hypocritical or oppressive because people often adapt their behavior in groups to conform to group ideals and expectations."[47] In this way, the culture of the community matters. What are the desired behaviors cultivated within the faith community? Which behaviors are rewarded, and which are discouraged? Are members who challenge church tradition conditioned to comply or to explore? Is the community a haven of safety where members can return after they feel threatened or experience failure? Does the love of the community foster courage? Is this a place where risk-taking can happen? The fruit of the congregational system will reveal the culture into which its members are being cultivated.

Congregations who desire to take risks in mission will foster an intimacy with God and others that gives their members courage. They develop intimacy with one another as they focus on loving one another well. They foster creativity and novelty. They encourage and challenge one another

---

42. Rothbaum and Morelli, "Attachment and Culture," 112.

43. Rothbaum and Morelli, "Attachment and Culture," 113.

44. In a 2006 study, Richard Beck found that college students who were secure in their attachment to God were more willing to engage in theological exploration and extend generosity to other Christians with differing perspectives ("God as a Secure Base," 126–7). Beck found that students with secure attachment "wandered" but maintained a clear sense of their theological home (130).

45. Grossmann et al., "Universal," 70.

46. Boccia, "Human Interpersonal Relationships," 23.

47. Brock and Parker, *Proverbs of Ashes*, 82.

toward spiritual growth and union with God. As congregations engage in risk-taking together, they remain present to one another after the risk, regardless of the outcome, graciously helping to bear the consequences of the risk. This fosters courage for members to take more risks, knowing that they will not be abandoned because of their mistakes or failure.[48] The congregation provides a haven of safety to which risk-takers can return, where they can learn from their experiences and remember how deeply they are loved by God and by one another, regardless of the outcome.

Risk-taking in mission should not be a solo sport; risk-taking without the support and accountability of a church community can be dangerous, both to the risk-taker and to others.[49] Communal risk-taking not only prevents lone rangers, but provides an environment in which the ethics of risk can be evaluated. Taking risks as a community is not simply a hindrance to bad risk, however; it can also be a stimulant for good risk. Within the community of the Church, creativity can flourish as members work together to foster an environment of learning, exploration, and safety.

THE ENERGY FOR RISK: CREATIVITY

"Imagination, full-bodied and courageous, is exactly what today's world with its complex character and challenges requires of Christian persons and communities," suggests theologian Darby Ray. "For Christians, creativity is not an option but a mandate."[50] This kind of imaginative creativity is often considered an elusive concept, an experience that comes suddenly to a certain type of person—usually artistic and antisocial—in a moment of genius and a flurry of activity. Yet research on creativity has shown quite the opposite: the best creativity is the result of skill cultivation, ongoing practice, diverse community interaction, and hard work.

Research has shown that the work of formation is essential to building capacity for creativity: those who are most creative in their fields have spent many years developing their knowledge and experience.[51] Creativity

48. See Beck's findings on how students with an insecure attachment to God are less tolerant of those with differing Christian beliefs and more afraid of God's abandonment if they should make a mistake ("God as Secure Base," 130).

49. One example of this within the Mennonite Church is theologian John Howard Yoder. Yoder spent decades experimenting with a new theology of sexuality that resulted in the abuse and harassment of dozens of women. During that time, Yoder refused to be accountable to his local congregation or theological community (Ruth Krall, "Mennonite Church" and Mennonite Church USA, "John Howard Yoder Digest"). Yoder's story underscores the importance of cultivating entire communities of risk-taking.

50. Ray, *Incarnation*, 142.

51. Sawyer, *Explaining Creativity*, 94–95.

seems to be the result of the interaction between a general creative energy and experiences that have built knowledge and skill within the domain.[52] It is not sudden but is built over time, with new pieces of information added to accumulated knowledge, rearranged, and constructed into a new idea.[53] The experience of the "A-ha!" moment is often simply the final piece coming into place. "We only think we see dramatic leaps of insight because we didn't observe the many small, incremental steps that preceded it," explains psychologist Keith Sawyer. "Instead of the light bulb, a better metaphor for an insight would be the tip of an iceberg, or the final brick in a wall."[54] Psychologist Mark Runco describes the "A-ha!" moment as a dramatic shift in the way someone is structuring their thoughts. "A person's thinking actually changes, and changes quickly, which is why insights may appear to be sudden."[55]

Often, these final leaps of insight are the result of ongoing processing in times of silence and disengagement. The brain continues to work, even when it appears to be resting: rearranging, making connections, and constructing new combinations of ideas.[56] These times "away" are incubation periods[57] where ideas grow. Mindfulness (being fully present in the moment) as a practice can help us to be aware of old patterns and intentionally develop new ones.[58] Creativity is the result of balance: action and reflection, knowledge and inspiration, movement and stillness.[59]

Social psychologist Vlad Glaveanu argues that "new" ideas are not in conflict with what has been done in the past but are in essential relationship with it. He suggests that the relationship between the two is more complex, since change is "neither random nor disconnected from the past, [but is] a creative continuation of what exists in ways that constantly bridge the gap between performance and potential, between the here-and-now and the not-yet-here."[60] Novelty[61] and conservatism, therefore, work together in

---

52. Sawyer, *Explaining Creativity*, 60.

53. Sawyer, *Explaining Creativity*, 93. Mark Runco suggests that we should take our time in problem-solving because the more original ideas often come later in the process (*Creativity*, 11).

54. Sawyer, *Explaining Creativity*, 139.

55. Runco, *Creativity*, 13 and 21.

56. Sawyer, *Explaining Creativity*, 97 and Runco, *Creativity*, 19.

57. Sawyer, *Explaining Creativity*, 88.

58. Runco, *Creativity*, 34.

59. Kim, *Holy Spirit*, 41.

60. Glaveanu, "Unpacking," 14–15.

61. "Novelty refers to the quality of not being previously experienced or encountered, while surprise refers to the result of encountering something suddenly or unexpectedly;" Barto et al., "Novelty or Surprise?," 1.

creativity as part of the development process. Creativity does not invent something from nothing but, rather, rearranges past constructs in expressions that have not yet been seen.

The new combination of ideas often happens as a result of exposure to a diversity of experiences and thought, suggests Glaveanu.[62] When new ideas encounter an existing depth of knowledge, people are able to conceptualize their field in new ways;[63] even experts need other perspectives to help them overcome their own assumptions.[64] Creativity happens neither inside of a person or outside of her, but in the space where she encounters the world.[65] When diverse experiences and domains engage, ideas will emerge that are formed from the encounter, describes Korean Canadian feminist theologian Grace Ji-Sun Kim. "It is in this particular third space that creativity can arise so that new ways of articulating faith, beliefs, and theology can emerge and be born."[66]

This third space allows the partnership between convergent and divergent thinking. In traditional research on creativity, convergent thinking has been defined as thinking of the one right answer to a question while divergent thinking was defined as thinking about a variety of possible answers. Researchers are starting to realize, however, that both types of thinking are needed for problem-solving:[67] divergent thinking can create a broad range of ideas, but convergent thinking allows someone to develop the good ideas more fully. In the same way, some people are gifted in "problem-finding" while struggling with "problem-solving;"[68] yet without clearly identifying the problem or question that needs to be addressed, opportunities for creativity are significantly limited.[69] This need for diverse thinking and experience shows that creativity and risk-taking are best practiced in community.[70] Creativity in community is also a much-neglected avenue for social change, argues Glaveanu. He calls for more attention to be paid to the important work of societal creativity, which is

---

62. Glaveanu suggests that creative expression is context-specific ("Unpacking," 18).

63. "Cross-fertilization and distant combinations are often the source of surprising creative insights" (Sawyer, *Explaining Creativity*, 125).

64. Runco, *Creativity*, 26.

65. Glaveanu, "Unpacking," 21.

66. Kim, *Holy Spirit*, 99.

67. Runco, *Creativity*, 10. He adds that it is important to recognize that not all creativity involves problem-solving and not all problem-solving is creative, yet the two fields overlap enough to make the connections helpful (16).

68. Runco, *Creativity*, 16.

69. Sawyer, *Explaining Creativity*, 91.

70. Sawyer, *Explaining Creativity*, 141.

"simultaneously individual and collective acts of creativity that respond to pressing social problems of general interest in ways that have important developmental consequences for larger communities."[71]

In addition to diversity, community can also provide the safety, security, and structure that some people need to exhibit creativity or to encounter circumstances that challenge their expectations.[72] In addition to security, research shows the importance of confidence: those who believe they can be creative are more likely to be creative.[73] This shows how important both encouragement and formation are in the life of the Church.

As we approach risk-taking in mission, our question is not only "What shall we do?" but "In what do we need to be formed?" We are not just formed spiritually, however; we are also formed in our locality: our congregations, neighborhoods, and cities.[74] This takes time, which means a long-term commitment of individuals together in community in a certain place; "church-hoppers" are not settled in one congregation long enough to become experts of their domain. As members of a congregation make a commitment together to their place, they can begin to develop a deep love for the people, geography, history, cultures, gifts, and challenges of that place.[75] Congregations experience creativity as they learn more about their community and the people who live in it. These relationships lead them to take risks as they engage with those they have come to love in their own backyard. Most of all, the congregation values the ideas and insight of those who are already in their community, seeing expertise not just in trained pastors and church planters, but in their neighbors as well.[76]

Surprisingly enough, those who, stereotypically, are perceived to be the most risk-averse (often, older or long-term members of a congregation) may also be the most valuable participants in risk-taking because of their knowledge and experience in the congregation and neighborhood. For these members, encouragement is key for them to believe that they have a contribution to make and that they are valued. Congregations need both people who think outside the box (divergent thinking) and people who can make the box bigger (convergent thinking). As these members are formed in relationship with God, they will experience the Spirit's energy to participate in mission as they

71. Glaveanu, "Developing Society," 192.

72. Gocłowska et al., "Whether Social Schema Violations."

73. Sawyer, *Explaining Creativity*, 81–82.

74. In *New Parish*, Paul Sparks et al. describe long-term commitment to local community.

75. Sparks et al., *New Parish*, 93–114.

76. Sparks et al., *New Parish*, 125–27.

are, not as who others want them to be. "Acceptance indicates the ability to see past cultural, moral, ideological, and other differences to the worth of the other person" that is more than just tolerance, suggests Mennonite theologian Norman Kraus. "Affirmation indicates respect for other persons in their own cultural context. Jesus saw in the vacillating Simon a rock; in the quiet Nathaniel 'an Israelite in whom there is no guile;' and in the weeping prostitute a woman with a deep capacity for love. He affirmed them for what in their best moments they most wanted to be."[77]

We are formed in our own culture, which is necessary but also limiting. We need to be exposed to people who are different from us, to experience discomfort and disequilibrium. This means diversity within our congregations (diversity of ethnicity, socioeconomics, gender, generation, education, level of able-ness, etc.) but also partnership with our communities, with other congregations, and with local ministries.[78] This cross-fertilization is the breeding ground for creativity, creating "third spaces" for hybridization and the possibilities of chaos.[79]

Not all congregational life can be focused on missional behavior and taking risks, however. Congregations are also formed in times of togetherness, fun, and rest. In these times of disengagement, ideas incubate, develop, rearrange, and come together. Enjoying the community of the Church and finding new and creative ways to love one another are important aspects of risk-taking as we are formed into a creative community in mission together. *balance*

Formation is transformative, but it takes time. Congregations often desire quick results and have walked away from creative mission because it seems not to "work." Commitment to one another and to the world means following through and persevering instead of looking for a quick fix. Risk-taking may not be just a one-time occurrence, but a series of risks that work together toward an ultimate goal. Risk involves the possibility of failure, yet failure is simply a step along the continuum of the creative process. Taking risks from the secure base of the congregational community allows congregations to endure failures and keep going; the depth of the love they have experienced in God and one another will not allow them to stop trying.

---

77. Kraus, *Community*, 176. Missiologist Emma Wild-Wood suggests that many efforts towards multiculturalism revolve around mere tolerance; congregations that embrace "interculturalism" instead move beyond tolerating difference to an exploration of real mutuality that results in sacred community ("Mission," 53 and 62). For more on re-storying congregational identity toward interculturalism, see Ralph, *God's Dream*.

78. See Cleveland, *Disunity in Christ*.

79. Kim, *Holy Spirit*, 99.

THE CONSEQUENCE OF RISK: FAILURE

"Vulnerability is not knowing victory or defeat," suggests Brené Brown, "it's understanding the necessity of both; it's engaging. It's being all in."[80] Creativity cannot exist without the possibility of failure,[81] argues Brown, yet many people are afraid to "put anything out in the world that could be imperfect."[82] This results in "life-paralysis," she suggests—opportunities missed and dreams not followed "because of our deep fear of failing, making mistakes, and disappointing others. It's terrifying to risk when you're a perfectionist; your self-worth is on the line."[83] When a person or congregation starts from the image of perfection, however, "there is nowhere to go but down," argues Brown; goals are unattainable and failure is guaranteed. Often this failure results in shame, a sense that we have not lived up to who we should be,[84] and a fear of disconnection from the relationships around us.[85]

Failure is impossible to avoid when taking risks, however; the very nature of creativity and experimentation means that innovators should not expect to be right the first time, describes business and leadership researcher Amy Edmondson.[86] Although many leaders see failure as bad, this view of failure is often misguided. Failure can be negative, she argues, but it can also be a source of learning and a pivotal step toward success. While some failure is the result of incompetence or the intentional breaking of rules, most failure comes from the inevitable uncertainty and interconnection of life; some failure even results from intentional and thoughtful experimentation. Failure is essential for organizations who are on the frontier, encountering new situations that have not been experienced before. There is no guidebook for these situations and an organization's goal should be to fail quickly and efficiently in order to learn how to succeed.[87]

Failure is difficult enough on the business level; it can be particularly painful in a congregational setting in which failure involves more than just a failed product launch or miscommunication around marketing. Failure

---

80. Brown, *Daring Greatly*, 2.

81. Brown, *Daring Greatly*, 15.

82. Brown, *Gifts of Imperfection*, 56.

83. Brown, *Gifts of Imperfection*, 56–57. With our emphasis on purity in the Church, Mennonites could be seen as perfectionists, although not in the technical (theological) sense—a charge which Harold Bender vehemently refutes in "Perfectionism."

84. Brown, *I Thought*, 196. Perhaps the Church's recent emphasis on developing "missional churches" is an unattainable goal?

85. Brown, *Daring Greatly*, 68.

86. Edmondson, *Teaming*, 55.

87. Edmondson, "Strategies," 50–51.

as a result of risk-taking in mission can often result in emotional and relational brokenness and pain: rejection, embarrassment, or a devastating loss of resources or reputation. For a Church shaped by a drive for purity and perfection, failure could be debilitating. "If we're going to put ourselves out there and love with our whole hearts, we're going to experience heartbreak," admits Brown. "If we're going to try new, innovative things, we're going to fail. If we're going to risk caring and engaging, we're going to experience disappointment."[88] When we do not acknowledge the pain of failure, however, we are more likely to act out of that pain and hurt others. Failure often leads to a feeling of powerlessness "because we didn't achieve our purpose and/or effect the change we wanted to see," argues Brown.[89] This can be dangerous because it leads to fear and desperation, which can lead to acts of violence.[90] In order to protect ourselves, we blame others as a mode of "discharging" our own pain and discomfort.[91] "It's a way to puff up and protect myself when I'm afraid of being wrong, making someone angry, or getting blamed," describes Brown.[92] Our tendency as humans is to minimize or deny our own mistakes or failures while quickly blaming others for theirs.[93]

Organizations who are quick to assign fault or blame for failures are less likely to cultivate a culture of risk-taking and learning, however. In contrast, in safe social environments, "people believe that if they make a mistake, others will not penalize or think less of them for it. They also believe that others will not resent or humiliate them when they ask for help or information," suggests Edmondson.[94] This psychological safety makes it possible for people to speak up when they notice or make a mistake; the earlier the mistake or failure is identified, the more quickly it can be addressed so that bigger, more dangerous, mistakes are avoided.[95] Individuals with positive attitudes toward mistakes are not enough; teams or other work or social groups need to share common values around failure and psychological safety in order to effectively take risks and innovate.[96] These values

88. Brown, *Rising Strong*, xx.

89. Brown, *Rising Strong*, 200.

90. Brown, *Rising Strong*, 200.

91. Brown, *Daring Greatly*, 195.

92. Brown, *Daring Greatly*, 202.

93. Edmondson, *Teaming*, 155.

94. Edmondson, *Teaming*, 118–19.

95. Edmondson, *Teaming*, 63 and 153–54 and "Strategies," 52.

96. Edmondson, *Teaming*, 123.

are best fostered through coaching and learning cultivation; a mission statement and "organizational culture" are insufficient.[97]

Once an environment is established in which it is safe to acknowledge
and respond to failure, conflict will most likely arise. Honestly speaking up can
lead to disagreement as members of a team strive to make sense out of their
experiences, apply differing values, or feel the tension of high uncertainty or
high stakes.[98] Teams with diversity across identity groups like gender, occupation, or race,[99] and with a variety of skills are more likely to experience success in innovation because of the wealth of experiences and perspectives they
bring. This will add to conflict, but the dissent can be productive, expanding
the group's awareness of the multiple alternatives that exist: "Learning about
the perspectives, ideas, and experiences of others when facing uncertainty
and high-stakes decisions is critical to making appropriate choices and finding solutions to novel problems."[100] Conflict, like failure, when handled well,
can be a positive outcome of risk-taking.

Brown has found that, in faith communities in particular, a search
for comfort, certainty, and absolutes keeps people from wrestling with
mystery and embracing their vulnerability.[101] In order to develop a safe
atmosphere for speaking up, conflict, and acknowledging failure, however,
communities must normalize discomfort.[102] "The simple and honest process of letting people know that discomfort is normal, it's going to happen,
why it happens, and why it's important, reduces anxiety, fear, and shame,"
she claims. "Periods of discomfort become an expectation and a norm."[103]
Creating a safe space for honest feedback is important, Brown argues, because it provides accountability, especially for organizations who are more
inclined to protect their own reputation or those in power than the dignity
of society's most vulnerable.[104]

Accountability is very different from blame, suggests Brown, because,
while blame is often used to protect our own fear and shame, accountability
is "often motivated by the desire to repair and renew—it is holding someone
responsible for his actions and the consequences of his actions."[105] Account-

97. Cannon and Edmondson, "Confronting Failure," 175.

98. Edmondson, *Teaming*, 64 and 68.

99. Edmondson, *Teaming*, 193.

100. Edmondson, *Teaming*, 169.

101. Brown, *Daring Greatly*, 177.

102. Brown, *Daring Greatly*, 198.

103. Brown, *Daring Greatly*, 199.

104. Brown, *Daring Greatly*, 196.

105. Brown, *I Thought*, 212.

ability is the counterbalance to psychological safety, describes Edmondson. Organizations can only foster healthy environments for learning and taking risks if they maintain high levels of both accountability and psychological safety.[106] If people are not challenged with high standards, they find it easy to stop learning or trying new things;[107] people who work in environments with both high accountability and high psychological safety, however, are more inclined toward collaboration, learning, and achievement.[108]

Congregations engaging in missional risk-taking will need to embrace failure as an essential part of both innovation and engagement. The vulnerability of human existence means that we open ourselves to both harm and failure when we risk relationships; exploring new territory and experimenting with new forms of community involvement will inevitably result in failure. This failure can be an important learning opportunity for congregations that remain open and non-defensive. In order to learn from failure, however, congregations need to foster safe environments where mistakes are not condemned, judgment is withheld, and failures are openly discussed. At the same time, clear expectations for discipleship and an articulation of the difference between failures to avoid[109] and failures to accept allow for a balance of accountability and psychological safety.

Failure is often extremely painful, especially when it involves something as valuable as the Church. Minimizing the pain of failure will not help congregations to take risks in mission; instead congregations should develop language and a culture in which failure can be grieved,[110] processed, and redeemed. Fear of failure and the judgment of others can paralyze a congregation if they expect that any risk taken in mission must achieve societally acceptable results if it is to be deemed successful.[111] A new definition of success or new expectations may allow congregations to escape the trap of perfectionism. This calls for courage, argues Brown; but if we are courageous enough often enough, we will fail. Committing to vulnerability is actually a commitment to fail. Failure is not just a risk; it is a certainty: "Daring is

---

106. Edmondson, *Teaming*, 129.

107. Edmondson, *Teaming*, 130.

108. Edmondson, *Teaming*, 131.

109. A failure in a congregation's child protection policy because guidelines were not followed, for instance, would not be acceptable.

110. Brown, *Rising Strong*, xxvii. Stephen Burrell suggests that church leaders who experience failure go through the stages of grief and therefore need to engage in an intentional grieving process in order to face future opportunities with courage ("Study"). Although Burrell reaches some interesting conclusions, his project reflects the weakness of his foundational assumption that only men are called as pastors (5).

111. See the parable of the talents, Matt 25:14–30.

saying, 'I know I will eventually fail and I'm still all in.'"[112] In the end, reflects Brown, "the result of daring greatly isn't a victory march as much as it is a quiet sense of freedom mixed with a little battle fatigue."[113]

THE ETHIC OF RISK: LOVE

Considering the vulnerability of human existence, the uncertainty involved in creative experimentation and exploration, and the frequency of failure as a consequence of risk, how does a congregation take risks ethically, in a way that does more good than harm? How does a congregation make decisions about risks when those risks involve people in the community, especially members of poor or oppressed groups? Churches have not always had a good track record when it comes to involvement in mission, community development, or poverty alleviation, say Steve Corbett and Brian Fikkert in *When Helping Hurts.* "Our concern is not just that [the] methods [used by North American churches] are wasting human, spiritual, financial, and organizational resources but that these methods are actually exacerbating the very problems they are trying to solve."[114]

In addition to knowing the best methods for community involvement, congregations also need to have an ethical framework for making risky decisions. In our complex world, making moral decisions is not as easy as picking a solution from a "good" column and avoiding any actions in the "bad" column, argues Darby Ray. Ethical decision-making "usually involves the careful sifting through of multiple possibilities, none of which may be ideal. . . . It ultimately requires that we step out in a mode of risk, wagering that we have done the best we could to make a humane and defensible choice."[115] One problem with making these kinds of moral decisions, however, suggests philosopher Sven Ove Hansson, is that we are rarely able to predict the outcome of our actions.[116] Consequences are affected by the actions and decisions of others, many of which we cannot anticipate, which give rise to compound effects.[117] Not only can we not predict the behavior of others, but we also cannot predict our own future behavior, including our ability and willingness to follow through on decisions we make today.[118] Yet despite these uncertainties, the ethics of our decision-making

112. Brown, *Rising Strong,* 5.
113. Brown, *Daring Greatly,* 43.
114. Corbett and Fikkert, *When Helping Hurts,* 27.
115. Ray, *Incarnation,* 142–43.
116. Hansson, *Ethics of Risk,* 1.
117. Hansson, *Ethics of Risk,* 16.
118. Hansson, *Ethics of Risk,* 19.

matter, since we cannot take risks in a vacuum. Human beings and our world are vulnerably interrelated: our risks affect others[119] and, often, the underprivileged in our societies end up with a greater exposure to the negative consequences of risks taken by others.[120]

Humans have a moral right not to be exposed to negative impacts—or even the risk of a negative impacts—to their health or property, Hansson argues.[121] Yet if society operated under only that principle, we could no longer live in community, as all of our actions affect others. There must be times, he suggests, when exceptions to this rule apply, times when we can ethically take risks that may or may not negatively affect others.[122] Exposing someone to a risk is acceptable if that exposure is outweighed by the benefit of the risk.[123] But what if the risk benefits some people and not others, or benefits all people, but not equally?[124] What if those affected by the risk have not participated in the decision-making?

Hansson suggests that risks must be considered within the context of justice and influence.[125] While it would be impossible to perfectly distribute both the consequences and advantages of risk to all, the impossibility of the perfect should not prevent us from striving toward more just outcomes.[126] He concludes,

> [exposing someone to a risk] is acceptable if (i) this exposure is part of a persistently justice-seeking social practice of risk-taking that works to her advantage and which she defacto accepts by making use of its advantages, and (ii) she has as much influence over her risk-exposure as every similarly risk-exposed person can have without loss of the social benefits that justify the risk-exposure.[127]

For congregations, this influence would mean involving as many of its members in the decision-making process as possible for risks that would affect the whole while also drawing members of the community into decision-making that involves those in the congregation's neighborhood or

---

119. Hansson, *Ethics of Risk*, 121.

120. Hansson, *Ethics of Risk*, 105.

121. Hansson, *Ethics of Risk*, 99, and "Ethical Criteria."

122. Hansson, *Ethics of Risk*, 99–100.

123. Hansson, *Ethics of Risk*, 102. For an in-depth discussion of paternalism and free choice, see Hansson, "Extended Antipaternalism."

124. Hansson, "Social Decisions."

125. Hansson, *Ethics of Risk*, 104.

126. Hansson, *Ethics of Risk*, 105.

127. Hansson, *Ethics of Risk*, 108.

town.[128] Justice insists that those involved in taking the risk carry as much of the negative consequence of the risk as possible. It would be unjust to take risks in which the risk-taker receives all or most of the benefits while others bear the consequences.

Researchers Nafsika Athanassoulis and Allison Ross argue that evaluating the ethics of a risk based on the possible benefits and consequences of the risk is insufficient, however. Since the consequences of a risk are outside of an agent's control, they suggest that the "reasonableness" of the risk is considered instead: *Would a virtuous person with knowledge of the risk's context decide to take it?* Thus, the ethics of the risk are dependent not on the risk itself, but on the character of the risk-taker. "Risk-taking will be best categorized as virtuous or vicious and only derivatively as right or wrong," they contend. "Good risks will be those that exemplify responsiveness to morally significant features of the context of risk-taking and . . . practical wisdom."[129] The difficulty with evaluating the ethics of a risk by the intent of the risk-taker, however, is that reasonableness may differ according to power dynamics, cultural expectations, and dominant narratives.[130] Just because someone's intent is good or virtuous does not mean that the risk is ethical, especially when the consequences of the risk might be carried by others. There must be mechanisms in place by which not only the benefits or consequences of the risk can be evaluated but by which the risk-taker's virtues or intent can be held accountable.

White feminist theologian and ethicist Sharon Welch argues for an ethic of risk that creates communities of solidarity working together to fight injustice. Welch draws on the writings of womanist authors and liberation theologians to develop an ethic that challenges what she calls the "ethic of control," masquerading as a societal sense of responsibility.[131] Welch suggests that the Euro-American middle-class believes responsible action in society means that they are responsible to make sure that everything turns out right. This entails a level of control over the outcome

128. Hansson argues that "consent" does not constitute influence over the decision, as consent usually happens later in the process and is often wrapped up in a package in which the benefits are only available if risks are accepted. People might consent to that package because the advantages cannot be obtained any other way, while still desiring a package in which there is less risk of negative consequences (*Ethics of Risk*, 119–20). See also Corbett and Fikkert, *When Helping Hurts*, 122.

129. Athanassoulis and Ross, "Virtue Ethical Account," 218.

130. For instance, Athanassoulis and Ross base their understanding of reasonableness on Aristotelean notions of "practical wisdom" ("Virtue Ethical Account," 219). This Greek way of evaluating ethics may not be adequate for evaluating virtue in today's complex, multicultural context.

131. Welch, *Feminist Ethic*, 14.

that they often cannot wield. When they cannot guarantee the desired result, they are often paralyzed into doing nothing at all:[132] "If one cannot do everything to solve the problem of world hunger, for example, one does nothing and even argues against partial remedies as foolhardy and deluded."[133] Welch calls this "middle-class despair,"

> grounded in privilege. It is easier to give up on long-term social change when one is comfortable in the present. . . . When the good life is present or within reach, it is tempting to despair of its ever being in reach for others and resort merely to enjoying it for oneself and one's family.[134]

Middle-class despair results in a give-up mentality that those who live under oppression or poverty do not have the privilege of experiencing.

Welch objects to a theology that describes God as powerful and omnipotent. While theologians use the theology of omnipotence to differentiate between human power and God's power, Welch suggests that absolute power, even attributed to God alone, validates a hierarchical concept that absolute power can ever be good. Absolute power "assumes that the ability to act regardless of the response of others is a good rather than a sign of alienation from others."[135] This valorization of absolute power has led many Western Christians and churches to organize their justice and mercy work around an ethic of control rather than an ethic of love, argues Welch.[136] German feminist Katja Heidemanns reflects,

> what Welch describes so aptly as a Western ethic of control also seems to guide the churches' current approach to mission. . . . In this sense, what is needed today might be called a missiology of risk which, fragile as it is, is shaped by the ever-present Spirit's call to lives of empathy, love, responsibility and accountability, instead of a missiology of control which assumes that it is possible to guarantee the efficacy of one's action if one only tries hard enough, and which all too often ends up in a kind of cultured despair.[137]

If the Church is going to resist the ethic of control, Welch suggests that a change in language is needed. The phrase "kingdom of God" is not "an

---

132. See also Corbett and Fickert, *When Helping Hurts*, 15.

133. Welch, *Feminist Ethic*, 15.

134. Welch, *Feminist Ethic*, 41.

135. Welch, *Feminist Ethic*, 111.

136. Welch, *Feminist Ethic*, 113.

137. Heidemanns, "Missiology of Risk?," 109.

appropriate symbol for the process of celebrating life, enduring limits, and re-sisting injustice," she argues, because "the kingdom of God implies conquest, control, and final victory over the elements of nature as well as over the structures of injustice." Instead, she believes that the phrase "beloved community" is more fitting, as it "names the matrix within which life is celebrated, love is worshiped, and partial victories over injustice lay the groundwork for further acts of criticism and courageous defiance."[138]

In contrast to middle-class despair, Welch describes an ethic of risk modeled by womanist authors. This ethic of risk includes three characteristics: "a redefinition of responsible action, grounding in community, and strategic risk-taking."[139] Responsible action, in contrast to the ethic of control, does not guarantee the short-term success of the desired outcome, but fosters an environment in which further action may be possible. Risk-assessment in an ethic of risk is not based on immediate chances of success, therefore, but "the contribution such an action will make to the imagination and courage of the resisting community."[140] This work is sustained in the community by love for oneself, for those who are oppressed, and for those who are working for justice.[141] Work for justice is not just for activists, but for all members of the community: while acknowledging that setting the world to rights will take generations, each generation must play its part to work at what they can do to make things better now.[142] This investment of time and energy may be challenging in a North American culture of busy-ness; many people seem to be willing to give their time for an occasional service project or work trip, but most are unwilling to do the hard work of investing in the long-term relationships that would foster love for their community or the oppressed.[143]

Communities cannot work toward justice alone; they must be in relationship with other communities that are very different from them. This allows for an ongoing outside critique, because "we cannot be moral alone."[144] Communities should engage in a constant cycle of work and as-sessment to make sure that their work is just.[145] "We can see foundational flaws in systems of ethics only from the outside, from the perspective of

---

138. Welch, *Feminist Ethic*, 161.

139. Welch, *Feminist Ethic*, 46.

140. Welch, *Feminist Ethic*, 46–47.

141. Welch, *Feminist Ethic*, 80 and 168.

142. Welch, *Feminist Ethic*, 70–71. See also Ruether, *Sexism and God-Talk*, 254–55.

143. Corbett and Fikkert, *When Helping Hurts*, 210.

144. Welch, *Feminist Ethic*, 127.

145. Welch, *Feminist Ethic*, 168.

another system of defining and implementing that which is valued," Welch suggests. "In order to determine which interests or positions are more just, pluralism is required, not for its own sake, but for the sake of enlarging our moral vision."[146]

Welch's ethic of risk is built unapologetically on the foundation of love. This love includes love of self and love of others, a distinction that Welch and other feminist scholars suggest may have been falsely constructed. As social beings who are created to live in relationship with others, the "dichotomy between love of self and love of others is a dangerous one, created by alienation and sustained by structures of alienation. To choose one or the other option is destructive."[147] Talking about risk as "self-sacrifice," then, promotes a faulty assumption that giving up parts of one's life or well-being entails giving up the essence of who one is. Acting on behalf of others, however, on the basis of love and relationship is actually enlarging one's self and, when the act is sourced by love for other people, "choosing not to resist injustice would be the ultimate loss of self."[148] This connection between one's self and others may be difficult for a society steeped in patriarchal systems to understand, Welch contends. It could be that women's ways of knowing and loving "cannot be contained in patriarchal depictions of logic or in patriarchal descriptions of a love predicated on a clear distinction between the self and other."[149]

This definition of love as the source for action conflicts with many popular teachings in the Church, which claim that love is a choice and not a feeling. These dominant narratives about the nature of love are harmful to the psychological and emotional development of Christians, argues New Testament scholar Matthew Elliot. The love that Jesus describes in the Great Commandment is not one that is just an act of will, he suggests, but is the cultivating of "a passionate love of God and neighbor . . . that flows from realizing that their neighbor is made in the image of God, specifically loved by God, and offered forgiveness by God just like they are."[150] Love is, then, intricately connected to thinking and reasoning, because it is fostered out of our perceptions and the value that we ascribe to others. "True knowledge results in genuine love and right action flows out of genuine love. [1 John] does not see love as knowledge or as action; rather, the three—love,

---

146. Welch, *Feminist Ethic*, 126.

147. Welch, *Feminist Ethic*, 162–63.

148. Welch, *Feminist Ethic*, 165.

149. Welch, *Feminist Ethic*, 170.

150. Elliot, "Emotional Core," 108.

knowledge, action—are linked together in a unified and interdependent whole."[151] Love is not an act of will or a forced commitment but is the motivation for action and commitment: rather than seeing our emotions as something to be managed and controlled, "Jesus taught that our love for God and neighbor should control us."[152] Our love is fostered by the value we ascribe to others; when we believe that others are worthy of love, our love is manifested in action for and with them. In this way, love *could* be perceived as a choice—the choice to change how we view others and therefore to value them enough to love them. This love is not a duty (with a goal or endpoint) but genuinely empowers us to "go the extra mile."[153]

Welch describes how middle-class people can engage with this ethic of risk and love to move from cultured despair to a learned hope. An understanding of this pilgrimage from cultured despair to learned hope could be helpful for congregations who have struggled to make the missional turn; releasing an ethic of responsibility and embracing an ethic of responsible action could be empowering. This hope then turns into action, in partnership with those who are oppressed and those who are working toward the alleviation of injustice.[154] The surplus of love that results from these partnerships is a manifestation of the divine.[155]

An ethic for risk-taking in mission, then, will be based on loving relationships. Risks are taken in community: within the church community, within the neighborhood community, and in community with other faith groups. In this way, risk-taking is accountable both to those whom it will affect and to diverse faith communities who can evaluate the morality of the risk through a different lens. Risk taken because of an ethic of love will bear its own consequences while sharing the benefits of the risk with others. Risks will be chosen in response to loving relationships and, by risking for others, result in the further personal and social development of the risk-takers. Although risk carries with it the possibility of failure, an

---

151. Elliot, "Emotional Core," 109.

152. Elliot, "Emotional Core," 112.

153. Elliot, "Emotional Core," 113. "[L]ove that's an act of the will, an obedience, or an obligation demands so little of us, because we typically invest only enough to accomplish our duty. . . . True love is about people you can touch" (Elliot, *Feel*, 167 and 169).

154. Welch, *Feminist Ethic*, 168.

155. Welch, *Feminist Ethic*, 178. In fact, Welch argues, God is not an "Other" outside of the human experience but is rather the love between humans living in right relationships. This does not work in an Anabaptist context, however. Anabaptists believe that everything we know or understand about God's love, we see in Jesus (Finger, *Contemporary*, 431). Therefore, any Anabaptist theology must be built on the foundation of who God is and how God has interacted with humans throughout history. A God-less theology cannot exist alongside a hermeneutic of trust (Harder, *Obedience*, 31 and 56).

ethic of love requires that congregations risk anyway; to be paralyzed by fear is not an option. An ethic of love leans toward justice and privileges risks that strive for liberation.

CONCLUSION

Risk-taking in mission is risk-taking for the sake of love. This risk arises out of personal relationships of vulnerability and mutuality, is fostered in communities of safety and diversity, is energized by creative experimentation, and learns from and redeems failure.

In this chapter, I have applied my correlational method through engagement with the behavioral and social sciences. As very little research has been done on risk in the Church, I have developed the practical implications of congregational risk-taking in mission by exploring literature on risk across other disciplines. In conversation with anthropology and psychology, I developed an understanding of vulnerability as the nature of risk. Vulnerable relationship is central to risk-taking in mission, not only in the risk of external relationships, but because, as attachment theory shows, the congregation's internal community provides the courage for risk. Within that risk-taking community, psychology has found that diversity results in creativity, which is an essential energy for risk. Business researchers have shown how the vulnerable relationships of community offer accountability and safety when risk results in failure. Knowing that failure is an unavoidable consequence of risk, philosophers have described how the community within and beyond the congregation can together evaluate risk against the ethical barometer of loving justice.

These understandings of risk provide a set of best practices against which the existing literature on risk in theology and Mennonite theological and missiological literature can be critiqued. In the following chapters, I will evaluate the literature and practice of the Church through these lenses, asking whether the stories we tell about God, ourselves, and mission reflect these understandings and how we might change our stories so that we are formed into a people who engage in missional risk-taking from an outpouring of authentic and vulnerable love.

4

The Theology of Risk-Taking

INTRODUCTION

As THIS BOOK WORKS toward an Anabaptist theology of risk-taking in mission, I have argued that some of the stories Mennonites tell about God in our theology, ecclesiology, and missional literature may have undermined the efforts of pastors and leaders to encourage congregations toward risk-taking in mission. After providing a historical overview of Mennonite mission in practice and considering the stories that Mennonites have traditionally told about God, I articulated a correlational method of liberation designed to facilitate change in the theological stories of the Mennonite Church. In chapter 3, I identified vulnerability as the nature of risk. When congregations engage in the risk of vulnerable relationship, they discover courage for risk in a secure and loving community, out of which flows the creative energy for risk even in the face of failure. In that community and beyond, vulnerable relationships provide space within which the ethics for risk can be evaluated against love and a desire for justice. These understandings provide a set of best practices against which the existing literature on risk in theology can be critiqued.

Literature on risk in the Church is limited.[1] Many missional authors use the term "risk" and describe missional engagement as "risky" without exploring what risk-taking looks like in the context of mission; in fact, risk often seems to be assumed rather than examined. In this chapter, I

---

1. Frost and Hirsch, *Faith of Leap*, 13. While Katja Heidemanns does entitle her article, "Missiology of Risk?," she focuses more on a feminist missiology and only mentions risk briefly, primarily in reference to Sharon Welch's ethic of risk. I have therefore engaged with her in response to Welch. Additionally, Lois Barrett briefly describes some risk-taking practices in "Taking Risks."

will consider existing literature on risk in theology and missiology, and, in keeping with my correlational method, identify areas of resonance and tension with the best practices from the behavioral and social sciences explored in chapter 3. This chapter focuses primarily on five authors: Alan Hirsch and Michael Frost encourage embracing a life of adventure in community while John Sanders[2] and Niels Henrik Gregersen[3] (and their precursor W. H. Vanstone[4]) engage with risk in the context of open theism.

These explorations of risk and theology highlight themes of relationality, sacrifice, love, creativity, vulnerability, and failure. Although these stories provide rich material for continued theological development, they are inadequate in and of themselves to support the efforts of congregations who desire to embrace risk-taking in mission. This chapter will reveal how those stories that present a picture of a risk-taking God do not take the final step in applying these insights to mission while those that discuss risk-taking in mission do not engage with a risk-taking God. These disparate pieces need to be engaged in conversation with one another and in dialogue with Anabaptist values and with voices on the margins to articulate a new theology of risk-taking for congregations in the Anabaptist tradition.

RISK-TAKING IN MISSION

In *The Faith of Leap*, Hirsch and Frost seek to address risk-taking in mission by engaging liminality, adventure, and *communitas* in the life of faith.[5] *The Faith of Leap* describes faithful discipleship as following in the Abrahamic tradition[6] and points to illustrations from Samuel, Elijah, Samson, David, Jesus, and Paul.[7] "All disciples of Jesus (not just a select few) are called to an ongoing, risky, actional, extravagant way of life—a life resonant with that distinctly wild—and yes, Christlike—faithfulness of their Lord and Master," Hirsch and Frost encourage.[8]

2. Sanders, *God Who Risks*.

3. Gregersen, "Faith." In March of 2002, Gregersen gave a paper at the Ninth European Conference on Science and Theology. This paper was published the following year under the title "Risk and Religion." In it, he expounds on the nature of risk and the history of risk-control. He references his chapter on "Faith" and the section on the trinitarian theology of risk in "Risk and Religion" is nearly identical to that earlier work. Therefore, I have chosen to engage with the 2002 chapter rather than the paper.

4. Vanstone, *Risk of Love*.

5. Frost and Hirsch, *Faith of Leap*, 13.

6. Frost and Hirsch, *Faith of Leap*, 16–17.

7. Frost and Hirsch, *Faith of Leap*, 62.

8. Frost and Hirsch, *Faith of Leap*, 17. They draw extensively on Joseph Campbell's work on the "hero's journey" (103–28).

The Faith of Leap suggests that disciples are positioned to take risks in mission when they are in spaces of liminality or disorientation—between spaces that are uncomfortable enough to require action.[9] Leaders work to bring their congregations to these spaces by utilizing crises, fostering urgency, standing up to opposition, and modeling desired behaviors.[10] Business and leadership researcher Amy Edmondson would add that leaders must also cultivate a safe environment for identifying and confronting failure, while fostering learning attitudes and accountability.[11]

The themes of liminality and community are intertwined throughout The Faith of Leap; Hirsch and Frost spend considerable time in a discussion of what they call "communitas," or the bonding that happens when individuals work together for some higher goal, enduring struggles and overcoming obstacles together.[12] Anyone who has experienced emotional closeness during and after a short-term mission trip or bonded with his or her comrades in the military can relate to their description of communitas, Hirsch and Frost suggest; getting out of one's comfort zone in the company of friends is transformative. This emphasis on risk-taking in community is essential to congregational risk and may be The Faith of Leap's most valuable contribution.

In their book, few of Hirsch's and Frost's examples are of women; within biblical examples, they completely ignore risk-takers like Rahab, Tamar, the Hebrew midwives, Ruth, Vashti and Esther, Mary, the woman who washed the feet of Jesus, the woman healed from bleeding, the Syrophoenician woman, and the women who cared for Jesus during and after his death.[13] Beyond biblical examples, Hirsch and Frost use numerous illustrations from fiction (Lord of the Rings, Chronicles of Narnia, Avatar, Defiance[14]) as well as real life illustrations from an African practice of boys' initiation, skydiving, sports, and the armed services.[15] When they finally do include examples of women, it is in the form of women in a "battle" against injustice, which seems to convey that even women can act adventurously or exhibit traits

---

9. Frost and Hirsch, Faith of Leap, 19.

10. Frost and Hirsch, Faith of Leap, 41–42.

11. Edmondson, Teaming, 118–19; Cannon and Edmondson, "Confronting Failure," 175.

12. Frost and Hirsch, Faith of Leap, 54.

13. Josh 2:1–21; Gen 38:6–26; Exod 1:15–21; Ruth 1:14–22 and 3:6–15; Esth 1:11–12 and 5:1–2; Luke 1:26–38; Luke 7:36–38; Luke 8:43–48; Matt 15:21–28; Luke 24:1–10.

14. Frost and Hirsch, Faith of Leap, 18–19; 37–38; 56 and 110; 60–61.

15. Frost and Hirsch, Faith of Leap, 55; 58–59; 41, 59, and 66; 67–68. They include musical and theater groups in the conversation about communitas as well (66).

traditionally attributed to men, at one point even suggesting that both men and women need to be holy warriors who are wild at heart.[16]

Significantly, Hirsch and Frost build their entire argument for risk-taking in mission around this idea of adventure. "It is not an overstatement to summarize Jesus's work on earth as that of starting an adventure," they suggest. "Thus we follow Jesus to the extent that we are part of the adventure he started."[17] On a foundational level, however, is it truly helpful to associate risk with adventure? Appealing to an innate sense of adventure not only "preaches to the choir" of people who are already inclined toward risk-taking, but also leads to expressions of risk that are exotic and distant. Our culture often dismisses the ordinary actions of everyday people as boring or meaningless, argues shame researcher Brené Brown:[18] "Heroics is often about putting our life on the line. Ordinary courage is about putting our vulnerability on the line."[19] Our pursuit of the extraordinary in mission could cause us to miss where God is moving in everyday life or ignore calls to take risks that are more personal and vulnerable.

Adventure can only go so far in describing or motivating risk-taking behavior; Hirsch and Frost are embarking on a pseudomasculine approach to risk that needs a feminist corrective.[20] Consider, instead of their illustrations from adventure movies, the armed forces, and sports, the decision of an expectant mother to forgo chemotherapy in order to protect the unborn child inside of her. The mother is unarguably taking a risk, yet who would call her experience an adventure? To then translate this illustration into mission, a congregation who invests their resources in neighborhood revitalization instead of internal maintenance may be choosing to risk their long-term survival. In both cases, the motivation of those who are risking is not an underlying attraction to adventure, but a deep and relational love.[21] Risk-taking in mission is motivated by a loving ethic, not a commitment to a cause.[22]

Risk-taking in mission, then, must be grounded in the loving nature of God. Hirsch and Frost seem to think that people can just decide to become risk-takers; for instance, they describe how the disciples "plucked up the

16. Frost and Hirsch, *Faith of Leap*, 90.
17. Frost and Hirsch, *Faith of Leap*, 31.
18. Brown, *Gifts of Imperfection*, 84.
19. Brown, *Gifts of Imperfection*, 13.
20. See LaCugna, "God in Communion," 91.
21. See Welch, *Feminist Ethic*, 162.
22. Welch, *Feminist Ethic*, 162–65.

internal courage to follow Jesus no matter where."[23] If leaders can tickle a congregation's adventurous imagination enough, they seem to say, the congregation will muster up their determination and overcome their risk aversion. "But we all know that we can't simply command ourselves to feel less fear, can we?" they ask. "What we can do is allow the fears themselves to be overwhelmed by bigger and better things—by a sense of adventure and the fullness of life that comes from relocating our fears and vulnerabilities within the larger story that is ultimately hopeful and not tragic."[24] While changing our stories is crucial to changing how we think and behave, the stories we tell instead must be the right stories,[25] and, thus, replacing stories of fear with stories of adventure may not be sufficient. Hirsch's and Frost's emphasis on the adventure of *communitas* misses the courage that comes from the secure base of connection to the congregational community and in relationship with God.[26] Only congregations who know they are loved and safe will have the courage to take risks in mission.

Hirsch's and Frost's focus on adventure creates a lack of theological grounding that is problematic. When we miss theology, we miss transformation; risk-taking becomes something we do instead of something we are, something limited to those who are already inclined toward it, rather than the creative posture of a transformative congregation, made in the image of a risk-taking God. W.H. Vanstone begins to fill in this theological gap.

THE RISK OF LOVE

Vanstone describes God's risk-taking in *The Risk of Love*. According to Vanstone, love by its very nature involves risk: the essence of love is complete self-giving, without a guarantee that the object of one's love will receive or respond to that love.[27] If the one loved is truly an "Other," then one cannot control the object of one's love. Vanstone calls this the "precariousness" of love: "But as specific achievement, love must often fail: and each step it takes is poignant for the possibility of failure."[28] Love which controls the other is not really love, because one who is controlled is not truly an "Other," and, therefore, one loves only oneself. God's love for the world is risky, Vanstone argues; for God's love to be authentic, God must not control humans or their response to God's love. God's love is vulnerable in

23. Frost and Hirsch, *Faith of Leap*, 37.

24. Frost and Hirsch, *Faith of Leap*, 87–88.

25. Freedman and Combs, *Narrative Therapy*, 32–33.

26. Grossmann et al., "Universal," 80.

27. Vanstone, *Risk of Love*, 45.

28. Vanstone, *Risk of Love*, 46 and 49.

that it can be rejected. For God to give everything that God is in love, God must allow God's self to be vulnerable to the impact of humans' responses. God gives humans the power to hurt God.[29]

While Sharon Welch would agree with Vanstone that authentic love cannot control the object of one's love, she argues that the act of love makes a clear distinction between self and other impossible to define. Our relational nature fosters a bond in which our self-emptying for the sake of the other is actually an act of self-fulfillment. By this assessment, the mother described earlier who forgoes cancer treatments for the sake of her unborn child may be sacrificing her health or long-term survival but is not sacrificing her "self;" she is, in fact, enlarging her "self" in her care for her child. The language of "sacrifice," Welch suggests, is rarely used by the one committing the act; rather, it tends to be observer-language.[30] In light of this critique, Vanstone's description of God as completely "other" does not take into consideration the relationality of self to others; humanity's impact on God may actually further develop the "self-ness" of both humans and God.

Vanstone describes how we can see the nature of God's love most clearly in the life and work of Jesus. Jesus showed the limitless, precariousness, and vulnerability of God's love in his death on the cross: he was willing to give everything, to be rejected, to experience the sorrow of that rejection. In Christ, we see the nature and activity of God. God gives up control over God's creation, working creatively in the world without coercion. God does not know the end of God's program, but works tirelessly to redeem evil and creatively respond to times when things do not "work out right."[31] In this way, God resists what Welch calls the "ethic of control" and trades responsibility for responsible action.[32]

Vanstone concludes that for love to be fully realized it must be recognized. The triumph or tragedy of love depends on humanity's response to it. Love requires two components: the ability to love and the response of the other to that love. The trinitarian God is able to both love and respond to love.[33] God's love for creation, therefore, comes not out of emptiness, but out of fullness. "Love has surrendered its triumphant self-sufficiency and created its own need," Vanstone argues. "This is the supreme illustration of love's self-giving or self-emptying—that it should surrender its

---

29. Vanstone, *Risk of Love,* 45 and 50–51.

30. Welch, *Feminist Ethic,* 165.

31. Vanstone, *Risk of Love,* 59 and 63–64.

32. Welch, *Feminist Ethic,* 46.

33. Vanstone, *Risk of Love,* 67–68.

fullness and create in itself the emptiness of need."[34] By emptying God's self of fullness and creating the need for response, God makes God's self vulnerable to humanity.

How, then, do humans respond to God's risk of love? Vanstone suggests that for many years, the Church has advocated a theology in which humans give God respect in response to God's supposed superiority and humans' inferiority. Because God created the world, God must be so much beyond the world, so much greater than the world. God, then, calmly rules over the universe in which everything goes according to plan and nothing is ever expended or jeopardized. But this description of God seems more about condescension, manipulation, or possessiveness than love, Vanstone claims.[35] A response of respect to superiority does not do Christian faith justice. "The argument that one who is great in power should therefore be respected is seen to involve a non sequitur; and, psychologically, the display of power has become an obstacle rather than an assistance to respect," Vanstone argues. "Power is seen as involving privilege rather than worth: why should the possession of privilege carry a further entitlement to respect?"[36] God's act in creation was not to show God's power, but God's love. By emptying God's self, God rejected God's power in exchange for a love relationship with the "Other" of humanity. Humans have the ability to recognize the love of God and thus, he claims, "we may say that the creativity of God is dependent, for the completion and triumph of its work, upon the emergence of a responsive creativity—the creativity of recognition. . . . We may say that the response of recognition celebrates the love of God."[37] Vanstone suggests that this recognition and celebration of God's love is the Church. When the Church recognizes the love of God and creatively responds, that creative response is an offering. This offering is the purpose of the Church.[38]

Vanstone does not, however, take his argument to its logical conclusion. Instead of suggesting that the Church embark on creative risk-taking in response to God's creative risk-taking on their behalf, Vanstone argues for maintaining the status quo. He suggests that the offering of the Church should be a sacrificial one; humans should worship in ways that force themselves to discipline and a form in which they are not comfortable—*How*

---

34. Vanstone, *Risk of Love*, 69. See my previous comparison with Welch on the connection between the self and the other as a critique of God's "emptying" God's self in order to need others.

35. Vanstone, *Risk of Love*, 61 and 73.

36. Vanstone, *Risk of Love*, 61–62. See also Welch's critique of God's power, *Feminist Ethic*, 111.

37. Vanstone, *Risk of Love*, 96.

38. Vanstone, *Risk of Love*, 97 and 106.

can an offering be anything but costly? he asks—and, since the forms of the Church have been developed over centuries, the Church should be slow in reforming them.[39] To respond to the creativity and love of God in a way that forces humans to limit their creativity and to be anything less than who they were created to be seems impossibly counter-intuitive. Vanstone's entire argument builds to this point in which he uses his creative thinking about God and the nature of love as an apologetic for the Church of England, of which he was a pastor.[40] Standpoint theory suggests that someone in such a central position in the institution might not have the best lens through which to evaluate the Church; such a person might be inclined to maintain what *is* at the expense of what *could be*.[41] Perhaps, in light of the womanist critique, the church's offering in response to God's risk-taking should be, instead, to fight the status quo and receive God's creative imagination for the Church's future.[42]

Vanstone claims that the contextual nature of visions means that we cannot know whether or not love is triumphing in the world.[43] While justice and wholeness can only be experienced in contextual practice, however, Scripture gives a clear vision for what God's final purpose is: to bring about a dream for the world in which everyone has enough, in which everyone is valued, is fulfilled, is healthy and loved, and in which everyone knows God intimately.[44] Thus, white feminist theologian Letty Russell would argue the opposite: rather than never knowing when love has triumphed, the contextual nature of freedom means that we can only know when liberation has been achieved when we experience it, for "the promises of liberation, like the promises of God, are not fully known except as they are experienced, and then they always have an 'overspill' of longing that points to the next fulfillment."[45] The Church's creative response (offering) to God's love is to join with God in God's work to bring everyone to the good news and *shalom* of Jesus. Vanstone's theology of risk falls short when it refuses to honor God's ability to respond to the world's brokenness with unlimited creativity and resourcefulness. Because of God's limitless love, God is working with humans toward a specific goal: to bring about God's Dream for the world.

39. Vanstone, *Risk of Love*, 107.

40. Vanstone was "ingenious in devising arguments in favor of 'Leave Well Alone'" (Webster, "Obituary").

41. Douglas, "Marginalized People," 43.

42. Douglas, "Marginalized People," 42.

43. Vanstone, *Risk of Love*, 89–90.

44. See Isa 65:17–25 and Rev 21:1–7 for example.

45. Russell, *Human Liberation*, 26.

A RISK-TAKING GOD

It is this very relational God that John Sanders attempts to describe in *The God Who Risks: A Theology of Divine Providence.* Sanders, a proponent of open theism, argues that open (or relational) theism provides the best answers to questions of prayer, evil, and free will. He describes God as one who chose to create the world with freedom; by creating the world in this way, God limits God's self to interacting with the world within those constraints.[46] God is resourceful, creative, and intelligent[47] and therefore can deduce what might come about as a result of human's free will.[48] God can even guess at which is the probable outcome but God cannot know for certain what will happen in the future unless God is predicting something that God is intending to do (and yet, even then, God can change God's mind).[49]

It is perhaps on this point that Sanders is most strongly critiqued.[50] Robert Picirilli argues that without divine foreknowledge, there is no room for open theism within the Arminian family. He suggests that God sees "necessities as necessities and contingencies as contingencies," knowing not only what will happen but what could happen.[51] Perhaps we might find a middle ground between the two: where God is aware of all possibilities without fully knowing which possibility will become a reality, and where God has the creativity and resourcefulness to work within any of the realities once they come to pass, using them all to move toward the final end of God's big project.

Because God is infinitely resourceful,[52] Sanders maintains, God will bring about God's desires in the end, but in the meantime, God responds creatively and authentically to what happens in the world and partners with humans in bringing about God's final project.[53] The open theism model is not meant to diminish God but to elevate God[54] through a greater

---

46. Sanders, *God Who Risks*, 15.

47. Sanders, *God Who Risks*, 159.

48. Sanders, *God Who Risks*, 206.

49. Sanders, *God Who Risks*, 76.

50. Critics suggest that Sanders creates straw men out of traditional views of theism, exaggerating traditional positions, or creating a larger distance between Calvinist and Arminian positions in order to argue that open theism can still fit within a free will paradigm (Caneday, "Putting God at Risk").

51. Picirilli, "Arminian Response," 473.

52. Sanders, *God Who Risks*, 116.

53. Sanders, *God Who Risks*, 65.

54. Sanders, *God Who Risks*, 184.

respect of the biblical portrayal of God.[55] We cannot know God outside of God's interactions with us.[56]

Sanders calls his model "relational theism" because he argues that this reality provides a relational foundation for God's interactions with humans: "The members of the Trinity mutually share and relate to one another. In this view personhood is the ultimate ontological category."[57] This emphasis on God's free and authentic interaction with humans, Sanders suggests, would not have been much of a stretch for the early Anabaptists, as their views, although still acknowledging foreknowledge, were radically free-will. Anabaptists have traditionally believed that God took a risk in granting humans free will, he argues, which means that God does not get everything God wants. Therefore, Anabaptists engage in a real relationship with God:

> Anabaptists emphasized . . . a transformation in which we are actually supposed to change our conduct and become like Jesus. Salvation is a process, a journey, in which we join the divine project by becoming collaborators with God, participating with God to bring about the kingdom. . . . They believed that God enters into genuine give-and-take relations with us.[58]

These "give and take relations" result in a reciprocal relationship between humans and God, one in which God takes all the risk (of being rejected) while humans rest secure in the knowledge that God's faithful character of love will remain unchanged.[59] Therefore, while God's character of love never changes, the way that God responds to the actions of humans in our world may. "If God gets involved in our lives and in history in genuine give-and-take relations," Sanders argues, "then the competence, resourcefulness and problem-solving abilities of God become significant. In relational theism God's creativity is highlighted."[60] In this view, God experiments, God "goes with the flow," God is responsive and redemptive. The image of God's creative Spirit that we see in Scripture is not, then, over and against the impassive or immutable character of God, but is, in fact, the very essence of who God is. Although Sanders does not make the connection between relational theism and mission, the intersection is unavoidable.[61]

---

55. Sanders, *God Who Risks*, 37.

56. Sanders, *God Who Risks*, 29.

57. Sanders, *God Who Risks*, 177.

58. Sanders, *God Who Risks*, 158.

59. Sanders, *God Who Risks*, 179–80. See also Hansson on who bears the consequences of risk (*Ethics of Risk*, 100–105).

60. Sanders, *God Who Risks*, 184.

61. Vaughn Baker touches on this in *Evangelism*, however his focus is largely on the

The theology that Sanders explores in his book thoroughly reflects many of the understandings of risk-taking articulated in chapter 3: God's vulnerability in taking risks in relationship with humanity, creativity as a result of formation, the risk-taker as the bearer of the consequences of the risk, God's resourcefulness in redemption. If our missional God's very essence is to become vulnerable and to take risks for the sake of love and relationship (most clearly seen in the incarnation of Jesus),[62] then we, made in the image of God and being restored to that image through Christ, also take risks and become vulnerable for the sake of restoring relationships with others, between others, and between others and God. Therefore we are not, as some critics argue,[63] making God in our own image, but acknowledging how we are made in God's image. In contrast to Vanstone's argument that there is no ultimate vision of how the world should be, Sanders declares that God's vision has been made known. "Though God's route into the future will contain many surprises for us and we cannot predict the precise way God will go, we are not left in the dark," Sanders explains. "We can be assured that Jesus is the trailblazer we are to follow. God will not lead us in a direction counter to our Lord since God is seeking to produce a Christ-like people."[64]

LIFE IS A RISK

Niels Henrik Gregersen draws from both Sanders and Vanstone in "Faith in a World of Risks." In this essay, Gregersen dialogues between a sociology of risk and a trinitarian theology of risk. We live in a world in which we have come to realize that there are dangers all around us, Gregersen argues. We have found that our attempts to control those dangers often result in the production of new risks, and therefore, that danger can never be fully removed.[65] Gregersen describes first-order risks (natural or social risks) and second-order risks (risks that we create in our attempt to remove or resist first-order risks).[66] In contrast to previous generations, today's society has developed a more complex understanding of risk-management,

---

impacts of traditional theism and open theism on evangelism, predestination, and the preaching/proclaiming of the gospel.

62. Sanders, *God Who Risks*, 187.

63. Caneday, "Putting God at Risk," 152.

64. Sanders, *God Who Risks*, 124. See also (Ana)baptist theologian James McClendon: "God is a pioneer, a trailblazer of destiny" (*Doctrine*, 285).

65. Gregersen, "Faith," 215.

66. For example, a first-order risk would be an illness that we treat with antibiotics. In the use of the antibiotic, however, we create a second-order risk because bacteria are growing resistant to antibiotics (Gregersen, "Faith," 217).

acknowledging that we create new risks any time we attempt to remove existing ones. We are then faced with the question of whether to address existing risks and take the chance of creating new dangers. Gregersen differentiates between "danger," which is a real and present threat, and "risk," which is the possibility of a threat in the future, saying that we often live as though future risks are present dangers.[67] Edmondson would agree with Gregersen's assessment, as she suggests that we are "hard-wired to overestimate rather than underestimate certain types of risk: it was better for survival to 'flee' from threats that weren't really there than to not flee when there was a real risk."[68] We attempt to prevent risks, contends Gregersen, because we see them as marring our movement toward a utopian society, a sign of disorder in a world that we desperately want to be ordered.[69]

In reframing this conversation theologically, Gregersen claims that religion can actually foster a risk-taking attitude.[70] Christianity is beginning to be reimagined in ways that claim "something important may be gained by risk-taking, and only by risk-taking."[71] Gregersen points to Jesus (his parable of the talents, his calling of the disciples, and stories from his life like calming the stormy sea), suggesting that the "recurrent idea in these biblical traditions is that only the one who is willing to risk a loss will prevail, and only the one who is willing to face uncertainty on the streets of life will find God. The gift of life demands a risk-taking attitude."[72] Risk-taking does not happen in a vacuum and all risks are made in context: they "exist for somebody in a given situation."[73] This contextual nature of risk-taking means that we risk for relationship, not ideology.

Gregersen describes the possibilities within both process theology and open theism for theologies of a risk-taking God. He further develops the work of Sanders and Vanstone by describing the two-fold risk of creation as humans receiving the gift of life and God giving the gift of love (God's self).[74] The world is created out of the trinitarian essence of love (the Father-creator, the Son-other, and the Spirit-ecstasy). This model within the Trinity shows us God's outward position toward the world.[75] God the

---

67. Gregersen, "Faith," 221–23.

68. Edmondson, *Teaming*, 54.

69. Gregersen, "Faith," 223.

70. Gregersen, "Faith," 224.

71. Gregersen, "Faith," 225.

72. Gregersen, "Faith," 225–26.

73. Gregersen, "Faith," 231.

74. Gregersen, "Faith," 229.

75. Gregersen, "Faith," 230.

Father took upon God's self the risk of creating *otherness* in both humans and in the natural world, giving up control and allowing both humans and the natural world to place others at risk as well.[76] This is the vulnerability of interrelatedness.[77] God, who created the risk in the first place, then bears the consequences of that risk in the cross. In the resurrection, God shows that God "does not only passively endure risks, but is also actively transforming those who lose in the game of risk-taking."[78] Failure is a given, but with endless creativity, God redeems failure.[79] As God waits for the fulfillment of creation, God the Spirit, sensitive to creation's sighs and laments, works tirelessly to overcome the risks of creation.[80]

CONCLUSION

While the writing on risk in the Church is limited, what has been written provides rich material for further development. Vanstone, Sanders, and Gregersen engage with a theology of a risk-taking God who loves deeply and creatively, but none take the next step to look at how humans are formed into the image of God as a risk-taker and none look at how a theology of God as a risk-taker impacts the Church's understanding of mission as risking vulnerable relationship. While Hirsch and Frost do engage with mission, they lack an adequate understanding of love as the motivation for risk and they stop short of a theology of God who forms humans in that love. None of these authors include more than a passing engagement with God's response to failure as a result of risk-taking, and, other than Hirsch's and Frost's work on *communitas*, none address the need for safe, loving relationships or communities (both human and divine) as the secure base from which risk-takers find courage to explore, experiment, and create. None address how creativity is cultivated or the ethics of risk-taking in real human interaction.

Anabaptists hoping to develop congregational communities of risk-takers in mission will need to consider the practices considered in chapter 3 and the theological insights explored in this chapter as we reevaluate the stories we tell in our churches; even these stories are not fully adequate to articulate a full theology of risk-taking in mission, however, especially in response to the particularities of Mennonite context and history. In the following chapter, therefore, I will analyze Mennonite practice and stories (theology)

76. Gregersen, "Faith," 232.

77. Reynolds, *Vulnerable Communion*, 163.

78. Gregersen, "Faith," 233.

79. See also Edmondson, "Strategies."

80. Gregersen, "Faith," 233.

of mission in light of the theological reflection on risk from this chapter and the understandings and best practices for risk that have been identified in chapter 3. Have the stories that Mennonites tell about God, mission, and the Church promoted formation in risk-taking practices and attitudes as we seek to become communities of risk-takers for the sake of love?

5

New Room to Breathe

INTRODUCTION

IF, AS I ARGUED in chapter 1, today's Mennonite Church has become increasingly risk-averse in local, congregational mission, and some of the stories that Mennonites tell about God may undermine the efforts of leaders as they have encouraged congregations to make changes and take risks essential to mission, then one of the tasks of today's leaders and theologians is to identify those unhelpful stories and to propose new stories that may shape congregations into communities of risk-takers. In chapters 3 and 4, I provided a critical foundation for evaluating growing edges for risk-taking in Mennonite theological and missiological literature by engaging with the behavioral and social sciences to develop best practices for risk-taking in mission and by exploring theological literature on risk. In this chapter, I will return to some of the themes I identified in chapter 1 from the history and literature of Mennonite mission that impact both the practice and narrative surrounding mission in contemporary life. These stories about God (and, as a result, the Church and mission) may weaken our efforts to be transformed into congregations who take risks in mission for the sake of love.

When we can honestly admit that what we have been doing in the past is no longer effective, we can begin to make changes that will move us in a new direction. Although change can be painful, it can also bring freedom. "Liberation is always experienced concretely," suggests white feminist Letty Russell, "as individuals and groups discover ways in which they have found new 'room to breathe' in society."[1] This new room to breathe will allow the Mennonite Church to see how our old narratives can be reinterpreted

1. Russell, *Human Liberation,* 51.

in ways that bring about new possibilities; what has been familiar can be re-storyed, "creating new visions to direct our lives."[2]

THE VULNERABLE CHRIST

While the stories that Mennonite missiologists tell about Jesus are important, they tend to focus more on the *idea* of Jesus than the *person* of Jesus.[3] Jesus is valued and loved because Jesus represents *shalom* and brings about reconciliation among people. Relationship *with* God through the radical presence of Jesus *with* us is mostly overlooked. Mennonite theologian Myron Augsburger gets close to this understanding with his emphasis on reconciliation with God: "Christology is the truth that reconciliation doesn't happen at a distance. This is true in experiences between individuals and even more so in our relation with God. God is not aloof. God took the initiative and came to us in Christ."[4] Even Augsberger, however, focuses mainly on reconciliation through the cross (not necessarily the incarnation),[5] covenant,[6] human rebellion,[7] and surrender.[8] This language, as well as that of "kingdom," "reign," and the "lordship of Christ,"[9] repeatedly returns to the "obedience" narrative of following Jesus, which conveys a collegial rather than intimate relationship with God,[10] the kind of relationship that Jesus both modeled and initiated. Mennonite missiology would benefit from a story of Jesus that emphasizes "God with us" instead of "Jesus is Lord," a story of God's mission that is motivated by relationship instead of politics, love instead of ideology.

Mennonite missiologists are correct when they suggest that following Jesus can be costly; many have suffered because of their decision to live and

2. Harder, "Postmodern Suspicion," 279. See my discussion in ch. 2.

3. Mark Van Steenwyk suggests that we "can get wrapped up in beliefs and ideas and somehow remain aloof from the things those beliefs and ideas point toward. We can care about poverty but not the poor woman on the corner. We can care about the idea of love but leave it fundamentally unexpressed" (*UnKingdom of God*, 44–45).

4. Augsburger, *Robe of God*, 42.

5. Augsburger, *Robe of God*, 102.

6. Augsburger, *Robe of God*, 13. See also Shenk, *Write the Vision*, 87.

7. Augsburger, *Robe of God*, 14 and 107.

8. Augsburger, *Robe of God*, 54. He calls this surrender/discipleship "solidarity with Jesus."

9. This vocabulary is particularly prevalent in the work of John Howard Yoder, as seen in *Theology of Mission*.

10. While David Shank describes Jesus in service to God not as a relationship of slave to master or subject to royalty but as an "intimate parent-to-child-to-parent relationship of mutual love," he still uses the language of "willful, active, and obedient" as the core of how Jesus responded ("Jesus the Messiah," 64).

share the good news of God's Dream on earth. Mennonite emphasis on suffering may be more shaped by our narrative of Anabaptist origins than by our theology, however; or, rather, our theology has been shaped by the early Anabaptist experience of persecution and suffering. While this theology may have been an important survival resource for early Anabaptists, who were facing fear and uncertainty, it may not be as relevant today for Mennonites living in the relative safety of religious plurality in the United States.

In looking back on Anabaptist and Mennonite history, we must remain aware of the Mennonite tendency to see early Anabaptism as a golden age, against which everything should be measured. Similarly, "Anabaptist" can become code for the ideal, while "Mennonite" describes the less than desirable reality.[11] Feminist Mennonite theologian Malinda Berry warns how easy it is to allow "our favorite sixteenth-century Anabaptist(s)" to dictate our current theology instead of paying attention to the experiences of those on the margins of today's Church.[12] In reflecting on the past in this book, I am not suggesting that we try to duplicate it but to learn from it. By understanding the underlying values and motivations of our spiritual ancestors, we may be able to better understand ourselves. Thus we hold these stories lightly and evaluate them through the same lens that we use to evaluate other conversation partners. Some of the stories from our past will be helpful in today's context and others will not.[13]

This is especially true when we bear in mind that not all the risks that the early Anabaptists took were healthy, productive, or God-honoring. In an attempt to follow Jesus, some early Anabaptists took his command to "become like a child" literally, babbling like babies and playing with toys.[14] Other early Anabaptists tried to establish God's kingdom on earth by violently overthrowing a city government, practicing polygamy and capital punishment, and physically enforcing adult baptism.[15] Menno Simons himself was known for outlandish positions on the celestial flesh of Jesus and church discipline.[16] These stories of failure are not the ones Mennonites frequently tell nor are they stories of which we are proud. Often, we do everything that we can to distance ourselves from stories that do not meet our

---

11. Brown, *Black and Mennonite*, 96.

12. Berry, "Needles Not Nails," 272–73 and 278.

13. "To simply claim Anabaptism for one's position is to obscure one's real reasons for accepting some views but not others" (Finger, *Contemporary*, 394–95).

14. Klaassen, *Anabaptism*, 2.

15. Horsch, "Rise and Fall."

16. Roth, *Practices*, 54 and Estep, *Anabaptist Story*, 250–51.

current ethical standards.[17] Yet acknowledging and learning from mistakes can be a pivotal part of risk-taking.[18]

Our Anabaptist past further challenges contemporary risk-taking through the narrative of martyrdom. The story of the early Anabaptist martyrs who followed Jesus to the point of death is a founding narrative for the Mennonite Church, one that is repeatedly told in publications and sermons, one that has been passed down through the generations. This heritage was institutionalized when, in 1660, Dutch Mennonite pastor Theilem J. Von Bracht was concerned that his congregation was becoming too much like "the world" in dress, occupation, and values. In response, he gathered more than 800 stories of Anabaptist martyrs (including predecessors to the Anabaptist movement throughout history) to encourage his congregation to keep the faith. This publication, now called "The Martyrs Mirror," was translated into German by the Franconia Mennonites in 1745 "with the definite purpose of strengthening the nonresistant faith of the church in the face of the rising threat of war."[19] *The Martyrs Mirror* has been repeatedly used for this purpose throughout Mennonite history; the Anabaptist history of martyrdom (at the hand of both Protestant and Catholic magistrates) has been a badge of pride.[20] For centuries, most Mennonite families owned a copy of *The Martyrs Mirror* and passed it down to the next generation alongside the family Bible. "The martyr has become a central archetype in collective Mennonite identity," writes Mennonite ethnographer Stephanie Krehbiel. "We're at the point where the way we repeat these stories says far more about who we are than do the histories themselves."[21]

Yet the narrative of martyrdom portrays an incomplete understanding of risk. Martyrs are represented as confident, convinced of their righteousness.[22] They have unfailing strength in going to their deaths because they are sure of the outcome: eternal life and vindication. Martyr stories leave no room for uncertainty or doubt. Martyrs never fail (except for those who recant, whose

17. Harold Bender is a prime example of this (see ch. 2).

18. These stories are not limited to the distant past; Mennonites also have more recent stories of racism, the cover-up of sexual abuse, schism, and positive relations with the Nazi government, among others. See *The Mennonite*, "Mennonite Church USA"; Sanchez, "Hope for the Future;" Huber, "Lancaster Conference;" and Goossen, "How to Radicalize."

19. Van der Zijpp et al., "Martyrs' Mirror."

20. Stutzman, *From Nonresistance to Justice*, 270.

21. Krehbiel, "Staying Alive." I, too, have been disheartened by the inadequacy of my faith tradition's level of passionate commitment (Ralph, "Baptized Again") but discovered that our obsession with martyrdom has blinded us to the current realities of oppression, marginality, and identity (Ralph Servant, "Gentrification").

22. Goering, "Dying to be Pure," 13.

stories are rarely told) and, thus, the true Church of the martyrs remains pure. Martyrdom is never experimental. The suffering and death are themselves celebrated, not the behaviors that led to suffering and death. In the martyr stories, risk becomes equated with death. Is it possible this narrative might confuse the Church when discerning future endeavors? Do we assume that we face no risks because our choices may not lead to death?

The insistence of Anabaptist theologians and missiologists on the necessity of suffering in following Jesus suggests both that those who experience suffering should celebrate the witness of faithfulness and that those who do not experience suffering because of their witness must not be faithfully living the gospel. These stories of suffering suggest that submission to suffering is a virtue. This association of suffering with risk-taking in mission undermines the Church's call to struggle for wholeness, life, and liberation, to resist suffering whenever possible, and to stand with those who are suffering when suffering cannot be avoided.[23] When suffering is equated with faithfulness in mission, those who are not suffering may either question whether their efforts are Spirit-led or intentionally provoke suffering under the conviction that only in suffering can they reflect the true character of Jesus. This does not reflect the nature of the God of Life, who birthed the world into existence and is actively working to resist suffering and bring about life, abundantly.[24] Does the focus on suffering and death allow us to avoid the real risks of vulnerable relationship that we might face when we engage in mission for the sake of love?

These real risks are often not a matter of life and death; they are instead a risk of reputation, a risk of embarrassment or humiliation, a risk of loss of resources, a risk of rejection or mockery, a risk of friendship, a risk of being wrong, or a risk of being changed. These last two are perhaps the most difficult for Mennonites, who have continued to be concerned with the purity of the Church: purity of theology, purity of ethics, purity of witness.[25] Throughout history, Mennonites have shown great caution about the ultimate risk of mission: the risk of closeness, the risk of letting people in, the risk of radical presence, the risk that the one evangelized will, in reality, be us.

23. See my discussion of suffering in ch. 6.

24. John 10:10. See my discussion of the difference between pain and suffering in ch. 8.

25. Martin, "Pure Church." See also chs. 1 and 2. Don Jacobs describes the dilemma facing the Mennonite Church as "Does God want us to build a pure church or a missionary church?" (*Pilgrimage in Mission*, 19). He suggests that it is possible to do both.

THE INCARNATED SPIRIT[26]

Seen as a test of faithfulness for those who desire to follow Jesus in community, the need to stay pure and somehow separated from the world remains strong for Anabaptists.[27] Mennonite theologian J. Denny Weaver contends that "the distinguishing marks of Anabaptism can all be organized under the rubric of the church distinguished from the world."[28] Missiologist Lois Barrett suggests that the Mennonite distinctive of separation from the world is "vitally connected" to the Mennonite vision for mission.[29] For several centuries, Mennonites have clearly identified the ways in which we are different from those around us: in the Reformation, adult baptism and nonviolent church discipline (the ban) set us apart; as we settled in the American colonies, we clung to our German language and cultural heritages; as we encountered the unifying effects of revivalism, we emphasized simple dress and conscientious objection. Once all of these cultural distinctives began to fade away and as non-Mennonites (in both Christian and secular settings) began to accept Anabaptist emphases (such as adult baptism and anti-Vietnam war protests), we struggled to continue to articulate how we were different from those around us.[30] Mennonites are most comfortable when we are standing in opposition to someone or something, argues Melvin Goering. This is because Mennonites are "very good at saying 'no' to what is, but much less adept at establishing sound alternatives among those who do not accept their version of Christianity." This, describes Goering, "fosters a critical negativity without a corresponding sense of responsibility."[31]

This desire to remain separate from the world and uniquely Anabaptist has meant that Mennonites have focused on conservation, argues missiologist Wilbert Shenk:

26. Steven Bevans and Roger Schroeder suggest that "Jesus is, as it were, the 'face' of the Spirit, who is 'God inside out' in the world" (*Constants in Context,* 297). In re-storying language here, I am not suggesting that the Spirit was the Incarnated One, but that we consider what it meant for Jesus to be the living embodiment of something or someone and what it means for the Church to do the same.

27. According to Lydia Neufeld Harder, this has been a defining characteristic of Anabaptist/Mennonite theology from the beginning: "This perfectionist impulse expressed itself in strict criteria that could easily be used to judge other persons and institutions as unworthy of being the church" ("Power and Authority," 91).

28. Weaver, "Response," 30–31.

29. Barrett, "Anabaptist Vision," 304. She links this separation particularly to the call for peaceful, non-coercive evangelism, holiness, and witness from a minority posture.

30. See, for instance, Weaver, *Keeping Salvation Ethical.*

31. Goering, "Dying to be Pure," 11.

> Innovation was threatening, yet it did come. . . . Typically, some trusted individual who was able to stand on the margin of Mennonitism and interact with outside groups became the channel for mediating innovation within the Mennonite community. . . . Significantly, the Anabaptist legacy did not serve as the basis for renewal and change. Instead the early confessions of faith and *The Martyrs Mirror* were used to warn against innovations out of fear of compromise.[32]

These innovations have led to an identity crisis for North American Mennonites, maintains Shenk. When accommodating to the world, Mennonites have felt guilty and uncertain. New converts are unsure whether there is space within the Church for them and life-long Mennonites are afraid that change means surrender to the world.[33]

This dichotomy between the Church and the world does not recognize that God's Spirit is already active in the world. The Spirit's presence with Jesus allowed him to be fully present in the world without fear. Even more, Jesus became radically like the world, entering into the world for the sake of love. He lived for a purpose that was different than some of what he encountered in the world around him, but his difference arose not from a set-apart ideology but as a natural expression of his loving character and his desire for all those he met to experience God's healing and wholeness. Jesus lived *for* something; what he was *against* can be identified as that which gets in the way of what he was *for*.

How can Mennonites take risks for the sake of love when we see the world as the enemy and find our identity in standing in opposition to it? When we emphasize separation from the world and see the Church/world relationship as dualisms of light and dark, good and evil,[34] we are unable to recognize that these realities are true both in the world and in the Church. If the Church is only defined in its contrast with the world, then the Church can only exist if the world remains a place of harm. If, however, the Church is called to partner with God in bringing about God's salvation on earth, if God's Dream has already begun to come true, then we must be able to name God when we see the world living like Jesus. With God, we celebrate when the world embraces God's Dream in new and liberating ways. If we believe that

32. Shenk, *By Faith*, 112–13.

33. Shenk, *By Faith*, 116–17.

34. Beginning with the first Anabaptist confession of faith in 1527: "Truly all creatures are in but two classes, good and bad, believing and unbelieving, darkness and light, the world and those who have come out of the world, God's temple and idols, Christ and Belial; and none can have part with the other" (Yoder, "Schleitheim Confession," 12).

the Spirit is already at work in the world, then we must be open to identifying which voices in the world are speaking God's liberation while also identifying which voices (even voices in the Church) are not.[35] How can we love a world we hate enough to take risks for and in relationship with it?

Although the Spirit receives attention from most Mennonite missiologists and frequent mention in Mennonite theology, the Spirit is always overshadowed by the image and person of Jesus. Considering Anabaptism's christocentric hermeneutic, the centrality of following Jesus in Anabaptist tradition is to be expected. The two-fold tendency of Anabaptist theology, however, to focus on the teachings of Jesus and to describe the Spirit as the "Spirit of Jesus" can produce a pneumatology that is focused on what the Spirit has done instead of embracing what the Spirit is doing or is about to do. This routinizes the work of the Spirit, forgetting that "the Spirit can subvert our plans."[36] This fresh, creative, and surprising nature of the Spirit leads the Church into unexpected places; the Spirit is the source of movement but also the movement itself, a flexible and ever-changing inspiration and energy for risk-taking in mission.

In order to revitalize the Anabaptist theology of the Spirit without losing the christocentric emphasis essential to Anabaptist faith and practice, we must understand the life of Jesus as fully dependent on the activity of the Spirit. This interrelatedness, often referred to as Spirit-Christology,[37] brings to light the life-giving, creative, energizing person that is the Spirit. It is in relationship with the Spirit that the world lives and moves and finds our being.[38] In this way, Spirit-Christology brings together both the contemplative and charismatic experiences of the Spirit to show how awareness and receptivity to the Spirit forms us into creative, life-giving risk-takers. Like Jesus, we then become living embodiments of the Spirit. Rather than an act of obedience, through the Spirit, following Jesus flows out of relationship.

Mennonite pneumatology could benefit from a new embrace of the Spirit's provocative unpredictability. This calls for a discernment that is constant and vulnerable, willing to change direction mid-course as the Church remains in tune with the movement of the risk-taking Spirit. The work of the Spirit is creative and surprising—even, or perhaps especially, for the Church. While missiologists Alan and Eleanor Kreider and Paulus Widjaja

---

35. Luke Beck Kreider suggests that, instead of separating from culture, Mennonites should make "innovative uses and subversive transformations of common cultural elements" as faithful witness ("Mennonite Ethics," 465).

36. Shenk, "Essential Themes," 64.

37. Del Colle, *Christ and the Spirit*; Pinnock, *Flame of Love*; Yong, *Spirit Poured Out*; Hybets, *Anointed Son*; Dunn, *Jesus and the Spirit*; Lampe, *God as Spirit*.

38. Acts 17:28.

describe the peacemaking imagination of the Spirit[39] and church planter
Stuart Murray encourages creativity in mission and church planting,[40] creativity cannot simply be declared; it must be lived. Similarly, creativity cannot be contained only in the pages of a book; creativity is an outpouring of
the Spirit's movement from the imagination of God. Congregations cannot
join the Spirit in this work of creativity without connection to and communion with the Father through the Spirit.

Although this important work of connection is essential to risk-taking,
references to the Trinity in Mennonite theology tend to be in passing;[41] that
is, the Trinity is at times named as foundational without the implications
for that foundation being fleshed out.[42] The doctrine of the Trinity should
not be just a postscript to missional ecclesiology, however, but the source
of it. God is the lover and the loved; God is the sender and the sent; God
empowers and is empowered. The Trinity resists being reduced to a two-
dimensional image of God that can simply be followed instead of known
through risky, vulnerable relationship. The triune God's relational nature
forms God's Church into God's image. As a faith tradition that emphasizes
community, Anabaptists should embrace the way in which the Trinity challenges individualism; the Trinity is community in mission.[43] In contrast to
years of sending individuals to the frontiers for solitary risk-taking, new
waves of risk-taking need to become a community endeavor—this is essential for fostering security and courage, for nurturing creativity, for dealing
with failure, and for ethical accountability. As the Mennonite Church continues to seek a deeper understanding of what this means for congregational
life, it will be important for us to think more deeply about the Church as an
outpouring of God's mission. The Church, an agent of God's mission, is first

39. Kreider et al., *Culture of Peace*, 124.

40. Murray, *Church Planting*, 42.

41. One exception to this would be John Howard Yoder's engagement with trinitarian doctrine in *Theology of Mission*, in which he makes the missional argument that the
economic Trinity is the immanent Trinity (131–37).

42. Some examples include: team ministry as a reflection of the Trinity (Murray, *Church Planting*, 41; Shenk and Stutzman, *Creating Communities*, 42–43); the
Church's sending in mission is a reflection of the Trinity and the God who created the
world is "triune" (Kreider and Kreider, *Worship and Mission*, 44–45); the Apostles'
Creed (Krabill, *Is it Insensitive*, 97). Perhaps one of the most thorough engagements
with the Trinity is a short section of *God's Call* in which David Shenk discusses how
the loving relationship of the Trinity models love for the Church and invites the world
to participate in that love; this invitation is a reflection of God the sender and God
the sent (68–70).

43. Bevans and Schroeder suggest the phrase "communion-in-mission" instead of
community in mission (*Constants in Context*, 298).

and foremost a community of people who have been reached, redeemed, and restored by God's mission. God's mission toward us has not ended with our commitment to follow Jesus in life.

The doctrine of the Trinity has further impact on Anabaptist missiology, however. The gospel of reconciliation holds a central place in Mennonite theology and missiology; through Jesus, humans are reconciled to God, to one another, to themselves, and to creation. Many Mennonite resources are focused on outward reconciliation, bringing *shalom* and flourishing to all of creation. But what does it mean to be reconciled with God?[44] Reconciliation among people is crucial to a holistic understanding of the gospel; like the theology it seeks to correct, however, it too falls short of the fullness of the gospel message: reconciliation is not simply an act of following Jesus. The triune God is a relational God who desires vulnerable relationship with humans. God's love is not an abstract idea but a relational way of knowing and being known. Just as the Father, Son, and Spirit are in communion with one another in the Trinity, so reconciliation with God leads to communion, the experience of loving and being loved, forming a secure base for risk-taking.[45] The implications of reconciliation with God as relationship, therefore, will further enrich Mennonite understandings of *shalom*, wholeness, and flourishing. Just as knowledge of her parents' love allows a young child to experiment and explore,[46] the communion of God's unequivocal love becomes the security from which the Church can venture out—experimenting, taking risks, and allowing the energy of the Spirit to flow through them.

Risk-taking in mission begins with the intimacy of sharing in the life of the Trinity. Without the secure base formed by the communion of the Trinity and the Church, Jesus-followers will not have the support system they need to venture out. This shared life provides courage and creativity to work for liberation, nurture and "survival resources" for facing vulnerability and danger, and a redemptive welcome that breathes new life into mistakes and failures. Sharing in the life of the Trinity creates a miracle where "the whole is greater

---

44. In "Shalom for Shepherds," Gary Yamasaki argues that *shalom* includes a holistic vision that incorporates spiritual, material, and political well-being. Even so, he stops short of exploring what reconciliation with God actually looks like (160).

45. Boccia, "Human Interpersonal Relationships," 23. While Boccia uses the term "secure base," she spends more time on God as a haven of security to which people run when they are experiencing crisis. Her exploration of trinitarian theology at the end of the article includes references to human relationality in reflection of the Trinity but does not consider the day-to-day reality of sharing in God's life in communion with the Church.

46. Grossmann et al., "Universal," 80.

than the sum of its parts." This miracle of reunion with God is, as Frederick Buechner says, "where one plus one equals a thousand."[47]

THE RESURRECTED FATHER

The Mennonite tendency to focus solely on following Jesus results in a scarcity of stories about the first person of the Trinity. By not developing a more nuanced story, this lack of attention portrays God the Father as far away and irrelevant. If humans only experience the Father in the Son and Spirit, then does the Father really matter for the life of the Church, and, even more importantly for this book, does the Father really matter for risk-taking in mission?[48] Can God the Father be legitimately folded into our understanding of the Trinity? An Anabaptist theology of risk-taking requires a resurrection of the Father by developing the narrative that God the Father is still active in our world and can be experienced by the Church as the creative Source and Imagination for risk-taking.

As the Source of risk-taking in mission, God the Father models and fosters the motivation for missional engagement: an overflowing of love. This is particularly important for a Church that struggles to find the motivation for taking risks in mission. It seems entirely possible that contemporary Mennonites may never experience the same level of risky engagement as the early Anabaptists, simply because we are not a first-generation Church. "The original Anabaptists were all first-generation people—people who in becoming Anabaptists consciously rejected their backgrounds, including their religious heritage, as being part of the 'world,'" suggests Mennonite mission worker Robert Ramsayer.[49] For that very reason, the modern Church will never be able to completely duplicate the Church of the early Anabaptists. The only possible way to foster a first-generation consciousness would be

> to become so vitally engaged in mission that a large proportion of our group will always in fact be first-generation Christians. It means becoming so open in listening for God to speak to us through our brothers and sisters, regardless of how long they have been committed to following Christ, that our group decision-making will always reflect the consciousness of having moved from the world to the people of God.[50]

47. Buechner, *Alphabet of Grace*, 60.

48. See, for instance, Wilbert Shenk's four elements necessary for the *missio Dei*: Jesus the Messiah, the Holy Spirit, the messianic community, and the eschatological framework of mission ("Relevance," 31).

49. Ramseyer, "Anabaptist Vision," 179.

50. Ramseyer, "Anabaptist Vision," 181.

Yet this demands the question: how? If the Church needs a majority of first-generation Christians in order to be motivated to take the risks necessary to connect with and integrate a majority of first-generation Christians, how will this cycle be broken in today's Church? It seems as if nothing short of the miraculous could make this much of an impact on our congregations.

A lack of first-generation motivation may not be solely to blame for fading motivation for risk-taking in mission, however; the decline in evangelistic urgency may also have resulted from a loss of eschatological vision. The early Anabaptists felt compelled to evangelize so that their friends and neighbors could enter God's kingdom before the time of judgment arrived. These early martyrs also felt emboldened to take the risks of evangelism, believing that, when Jesus returned, they would be vindicated before all those in the State Churches who condemned them.[51] Yet many of these early Anabaptists also believed that the Kingdom of God had already begun; God's day of mercy was already at hand.[52] Anabaptist witness incorporated much more than simply forgiveness for sins or the Lutheran assurance of grace in depravity; Anabaptists believed that salvation began in the present: "Anabaptists connected regeneration more with the subsequent new life in Christ—'life' not in a mystical but a here-and-now, day-to-day sense. Where Reformers looked mostly to the sin that went before, Anabaptists looked mostly to the new creature whom regeneration created."[53] Thus, while Anabaptists were motivated by the hope of Christ's return, they were also driven by the desire to see people experiencing a regenerated, Jesus-like life *now*. The hope of salvation was not just a future occurrence; the end had already begun.[54]

This understanding of eschatology could impact contemporary Mennonite congregations with the same urgency that the Anabaptists felt: the call to mission is a call to bring regeneration, transformation, and salvation *now*. Yet this issue faces the same challenge regarding cycles of motivation as that of first-generation faith: how does the Church experience eschatological urgency without those who are deeply in touch with their own regeneration? How might the need for a deep awareness of one's own regeneration resulting in eschatological urgency determine the mode and importance of formation? If our congregations do not already desire to see those in their neighborhoods and families encounter this transformational change and salvation as soon as possible, what will motivate them to take the risks necessary to bring that message and reality into their communities? How might a shift away from

51. Barrett, "Rethinking," 162.

52. Finger, *Contemporary*, 534.

53. Schlabach, *Gospel*, 25.

54. Finger, "Is 'Systematic Theology' Possible," 51.

a story of regeneration as a life of obediently following Jesus to a story of regeneration as a life of transformation in relationship with God allow Jesus-followers to experience eschatological urgency in mission?

Only in communion with God the Father, the Source of Life and the end to whom all life will return, can we experience the transformation needed to break the motivational cycle. As we are reconciled to God, we become formed into a people who love deeply, who will become vulnerable and take risks in response to loving relationships with others. When we believe that the Creator God is still active in our world, bringing new life out of death, inspiring exploration, experimentation, and creative problem solving, we can endure failures and anticipate redemption. In community with the trinitarian God through the Spirit, we know that we are never alone.

CONCLUSION

I have argued that the emphasis on following Jesus in the stories we tell in the Mennonite Church do not form us into risk-takers in mission but, instead, may undermine our efforts to encourage congregations to take the risks and make the changes essential to mission. These stories have led to the elevation of suffering and martyrdom, the portrayal of discipleship or mission as obedience (or duty), the importance of purity and separation from the world, and the collapsing of Jesus with the Spirit. The dominance of these stories also highlights some gaps in Anabaptist storytelling around themes like the Father and the Trinity, motivation for mission (eschatology and regeneration), and the redemption of failure.

Research into risk-taking identifies the fundamental nature of risk as vulnerability. When congregations engage in the risk of vulnerable relationship with those around them, they find that the courage for risk emerges from a secure and loving community, the energy for risk is expressed through creativity, the consequence of risk is often failure, and the ethics for risk arise from love and a desire for justice. Theologies of risk ground themselves in a loving God who risks everything in order to live in relationship with humanity. Anabaptist theology's christocentric emphasis suggests that the most complete expression of this loving risk-taking is the incarnation, life, death, and resurrection of Jesus. While mission literature's focus on God the Son is primarily around the salvific work of Jesus and risk literature's focus is on the risk of the incarnation, neither take the further step to evaluate what the vulnerability of the incarnation means for the Church in mission. None of the literature explores the role of the Spirit in the transformation of humans into God's image or how relationship with a loving God provides the security Christians need to explore and experiment. None of the literature explores the redemptive creativity of God the Father in response to failure as the Church takes risks in mission. These inadequacies leave ample space for the development of a christocentric, formational, and practical Anabaptist theology of risk-taking in mission, a theology which will be explored in the next three chapters.

6

The Human One

INTRODUCTION

THOSE WHO SEEK TO take risks in mission will necessarily engage in vulnerable relationships. This vulnerability reflects God's own vulnerability in creating and relating to our world. This chapter tells the story of creation and humanity, as God risks creating a world in which vulnerability opens up possibilities for both harm and transformation. Into this vulnerability, God the Expression risks becoming the fully Human One,[1] embracing the vulnerability of human life without seeking to protect himself by hoarding resources or harming other vulnerable people. Jesus is not simply the perfection of God in human form and, therefore, an ideal model because of his divinity, but is a human being with human limitations who models both the vulnerability of relationships with others and the need for connection with God's Community in order to take those risks. In his incarnation, Jesus becomes radically present to humans, even to the extent of death, a death that is witness to his ultimate risk—the risk of rejection and harm that can result from engaging in vulnerable human relationships. God's motivation for this risk is an all-consuming love built on the foundation of radical presence.

THE VULNERABILITY OF CREATION

The first line of Genesis describes how "in the beginning, God created the heavens and the earth."[2] God birthed the cosmos as a mother gives birth

---

1. Green, "Human One."
2. Gen 1:1.

from her own body.[3] "All of us . . . are born from the bodies of our mothers, all of us are fed by our mothers," argues white feminist theologian Sallie McFague. "What better imagery would there be for expressing the most basic reality of existence: that we live and move and have our being in God?"[4] The cosmos was formed and nurtured from God's very being. Just as a baby is his own person, yet still vulnerable without the love and nurture of a caregiver, the cosmos was birthed into its own existence, yet still dependent on God for sustenance, nurture, love, and relationship. The God who birthed creation is passionately connected to her "offspring" as only a parent can be. Thus the act of creation, the act of giving birth to the world, was a vulnerable act for God.[5]

After God created, "the earth was without shape or form, it was dark over the deep sea, and God's wind [Spirit] swept over the waters."[6] The Spirit hovered over the deep, the chaos,[7] the creative possibilities out of which something new and brilliant could be made. The imagination of God the Father became reality through the expression and embodiment of the Son.[8] The Spirit's energy brought creation to life. The fullness (Community) of God was present at the creation of the world:[9] God the Source (Father);[10] God the Expression (Son); God the Energy (Spirit).[11] Creation could not exist without the fullness of the trinitarian community: creative source and imagination must be expressed; expression without energy is lifeless. In this way, the roles of the Trinity within the world cannot be so easily differentiated; each is

---

3. While the doctrine of *creatio ex nihilo* has long been accepted in Christian tradition, contemporary scholars are beginning to question its validity, suggesting that it was developed as a defense of God's impassibility, creates a false dichotomy between God and creation, and does not make sense within the whole of the biblical witness. Sallie McFague argues for a creation out of God's body, in *Models of God* (62), while Thomas Reynolds suggests that the "nothing" was actually "chaos," in *Vulnerable Communion* (155).

4. McFague, *Models of God*, 104–5.

5. See ch. 8 for a deeper discussion of God's birthing of creation.

6. Gen 1:2.

7. The chaos out of which God created the world is rarely seen as creative possibility (see, for instance, Tucker, "Creation," 110). In contrast, Reynolds suggests that "order is not opposed to chaos but emerges from it" (*Vulnerable Communion*, 155).

8. Col 1:15–20 draws parallels between Jesus as the source of the world and the source of the Church.

9. Gen 1:1–2; John 1:1–3; Eph 3:9.

10. In the next three chapters, I will use "Source" and "Imagination" interchangeably.

11. Wilbert Shenk uses similar imagery in *Changing Frontiers*, calling God the "Source," Jesus the "Embodiment," and the Spirit the "Power" of mission (106–7).

completely dependent on the others.[12] The act of creation flowed out of God's Community as a result of God's lavish love.[13]

Among the creation that God birthed were human beings, made in the image of God to be like God.[14] In imagining creatures in God's image, God (Source) impressed on them the essence (Expression) of who God was and breathed into them the breath of life (Spirit).[15] Interrelationship was at the heart of God's desire for the world (as reflected in the trinitarian community), so God designed humans with a certain level of dependency. Not only do humans need each other, but they also need other creatures, plants, trees, water, and oxygen; the whole of creation is an interdependent system created to support one another.[16] "Each part of creation is differentiated, unique and fruitful, multiplying after its own kind. And yet, each part is incomplete without the whole; everything exists in interdependent relationships," describes Keetoowah (Cherokee) pastor and theologian Randy Woodley. "Everything is in harmony, in balance with each other and with the Creator. It is a picture of a creation in community."[17]

The world that God created was not homogenous and predictable; it was a world of chaotic possibility,[18] full of endless creativity because of its endless diversity.[19] In designing a persistently creative world of interdependence and interrelationship, mutuality and need, God risked the possibility of tragedy. In freedom, God's first act for humans was a creative act, giving them the right to choose whether to respond to community with mutuality or domination, argues womanist theologian Kelly Brown Douglas.[20] "Diversity and variety, while inherently good, also yield conflicts as creatures pursue varied and sometimes opposing ends," describes disability theologian Thomas Reynolds. "Beings are contingent and fragile in their interdependence. Their dance with one another contains the potential for compatibility and cooperation along with incompatibility, alienation, and conflict."[21] This interdependency sustains life, but it also means that humans

12. Manohar, "Spirit Christology," 284. See Elizabeth Johnson's discussion of mutuality and friendship in *She Who Is*, 218, and "being in communion constitutes God's very essence," 227.

13. Pinnock, *Flame of Love*, 31.

14. Gen 1:26–27.

15. Gen 1:27 and 2:7.

16. Johnson, "For God so Loved," 18.

17. Woodley, "Early Dialogue," 97–98.

18. Reynolds, *Vulnerable Communion*, 155.

19. Reynolds, *Vulnerable Communion*, 160.

20. Douglas, *Stand Your Ground*, 159.

21. Reynolds, *Vulnerable Communion*, 162.

cannot always determine our own fate or that of those we love, nor can we "predict with certainty the outcomes of our choices, regardless of how good our intentions may be," suggests white feminist theologian Elizabeth Gandolfo. "Try as we might, our efforts to do good are always vulnerable to failure, distortion, and demise."[22]

The diversity and interdependency of humans with each other and the world can cause great joy as well as great suffering. Yet the vulnerability of life is a gift, suggests Gandolfo, since "the features of human life that expose us to misfortune are precisely those dimensions of our condition that make possible our experience of love and joy, beauty and truth. Our embodied, relational, (inter)dependent, changing, and ambiguous condition makes us vulnerable, but it also makes available to us a life of great power and possibility."[23] Vulnerable humans are open to the possibility of love[24] but "with great love comes great vulnerability."[25]

In creating a world of people with the freedom to choose, the Community of God took an enormous risk: the risk that people would choose isolation and domination instead of interdependence and mutuality.[26] Even after humans chose a path of separation from God,[27] the Community of God never stopped working for wholeness and union, dreaming of a day when all will be reunited with God.[28] God the Source is still imagining. God the Spirit is still energizing. God the Expression is still embodying. The fullness of God has not ceased to be present in the world. The chaos has never disappeared. The world is still ripe with possibilities, opportunities for creative imagination. The Spirit of God is still hovering over the world, ready to breathe new life and new ideas.[29] God "vivifies, knits together, and upholds the world in pervading and unquenchable love."[30]

THE VULNERABILITY OF INCARNATION

God's desire for abundant life is reflected in humanity. Humans are vulnerable by nature, an expression of the vulnerable, interdependent God who

22. Gandolfo, *Power and Vulnerability*, 94.

23. Gandolfo, *Power and Vulnerability*, 96.

24. Reynolds, *Vulnerable Communion*, 186.

25. Gandolfo, *Power and Vulnerability*, 99.

26. Pinnock, *Flame of Love*, 74.

27. Gen 3:1–10.

28. Rev 21. Pinnock, *Flame of Love*, 57.

29. Johnson, *She Who Is*, 134.

30. Johnson, *She Who Is*, 135.

created us.[31] In the incarnation, Jesus came face to face with the vulnerability of the human condition. Just as God created humans in God's own image, God's Image became human.[32] This human frailty was not just a "phase" of God, briefly manifested between God's true expression as ruler and king, but, rather, the essence of God revealed.[33] "Incarnation does not involve the mystery of God merely dressing up like a human being and living a physically and psychologically truncated charade," argues white feminist theologian Elizabeth Johnson. "Jesus [was] born to a life of creaturely finitude marked by the pleasures and pains of the body, nescience and growth in wisdom, and freedom with the need to risk."[34] Although the incarnation was a new, never-before-seen creative expression, what humanity experienced as an "A-ha!" moment was actually another piece of God's on-going imaginative interaction with God's people. God's vulnerability in creating the cosmos and in initiating relationship with humanity came to its fullest expression in the incarnation, God With Us: fully human, fully vulnerable.

"When divine love enters into the human condition in the Incarnation, there is no supernatural exemption from the perils of existence," maintains Gandolfo.[35] Natality is, in itself, a risky endeavor, dependent on "maternal health, nutrition, social networks, and access to assistance or intervention during a complicated childbirth."[36] Although the adult Jesus could choose his risks and respond to his vulnerability, the infant Jesus could not.[37] His survival and wholeness depended on circumstances beyond his control, on the interdependency of nature, humanity, and social constructs. In his vulnerability, Jesus was carried away to Egypt to protect him from a savage king, even as other vulnerable infants were unable to escape.[38] Born into the underclass under Roman occupation in Galilee, he was at risk of the same illnesses, injuries, natural disasters, and political upheaval as other children of his time.

Not only did Jesus depend upon the care of his parents, extended family, and community as an infant and growing child, he also continued

31. Mitchell et al., "Mission," 159.

32. Col 1:15.

33. McFague, *Models of God*, 55. See also "I am contending that through the kenosis of God, 'God is truly God'" (Masao, "Kenotic God," 18). Sarah Coakley makes a similar point in *Powers and Submissions*: "Thus the human limitations of Jesus were seen as a positive expression of his divinity rather than as a curtailment of it" (22–23).

34. Johnson, "Redeeming," 130.

35. Gandolfo, "Truly Human Incarnation," 386.

36. Gandolfo, "Truly Human Incarnation," 386.

37. Gandolfo, "Truly Human Incarnation," 386.

38. Matt 2:13–18.

his interdependency into adulthood. The Gospels are clear that a group of women supported Jesus out of their own financial resources;[39] others fed Jesus and his disciples at their own tables;[40] some of the women disciples (including his mother) were present with him in his moments of agony on the cross, later preparing his body for burial.[41] Jesus seemed to be deeply invested in his friendships with Martha, Mary, and Lazarus;[42] in moments of great stress, Jesus sought solace in the company of his closest friends.[43] In his vulnerability, Jesus experienced the mutuality and interdependence of close human relationships.

The humanity of Jesus was not just an appearance, argues Gandolfo, but a very real experience of the divine. For God to be fully infinite and to experience the fullness of goodness and love, then God must also experience the vulnerable goodness and vulnerable love of humanity, which is ultimately risky. "Love is inherently unstable . . . . The 'safe' life of stable and eternal value is not really a human life, for it lacks the virtues only available in the realm of embodied and relational vulnerability," maintains Gandolfo.[44] Therefore, for God's goodness and love to be complete, God must redeem humanity through the vulnerability of human love. In Jesus, we discover the paradox of opposites: the invulnerability of divine love—a love from which humans can never be separated[45]—enfleshed in the vulnerability of human existence. This paradox empowers humans to overcome the need for control, a need that drives us to deny our vulnerability and to violate the vulnerability of others. For Jesus-followers, this means that our own incarnation of God's invulnerable love is vulnerable;[46] the radical "being-with" of mission is risky as we "relive" Jesus in our lives.[47]

While Jesus remained in compassionate solidarity with humanity, the term "solidarity" is not quite strong enough to describe the life of Jesus. Solidarity, at least in its contemporary usage, still carries the connotation that the one standing in solidarity, who usually comes from a position of privilege or supposed superiority, has the choice to walk away. While this

---

39. Luke 8:1–3.

40. Luke 10:38–42.

41. Matt 27:55–61; Mark 15:40 and 47; Luke 23:49–55; and John 19:25. See also Johnson, "Redeeming," 125.

42. Luke 10:38–42; John 11:1–44 and 12:1–11.

43. Matt 17:1–2 and 26:36–46.

44. Gandolfo, *Power and Vulnerability*, 213.

45. Rom 8:35–39.

46. Gandolfo, *Power and Vulnerability*, 214.

47. Chung, "Who is Jesus," 108.

agency is important, it carries the privilege of distance. In Philippians 2, Jesus is described as having "the form of God," yet not considering that equality as "something to exploit" but, instead, emptying himself and "becoming like human beings."[48] When mockers called to him that he should save himself by coming down from the cross,[49] Jesus refused to exploit his divine nature. Fully enfleshed in the human condition, Jesus gave up the privilege of walking away; in his "solidarity" with suffering humans, he became one of us. Thus, for Asians from a Buddhist background, for whom suffering is seen as an unavoidable experience of being human, describes Asian feminist theologian Kwok Pui Lan, "the fact that Jesus suffers shows that he is fully human, a co-sufferer with humanity. Jesus does not belong to the oppressors; he is one of the *minjung* (the masses)."[50]

What Kwok calls the *minjung*, Douglas calls the "crucified classes:" those who upset the law and order, the "peace," and the status quo.[51] Not only did Jesus intentionally associate with those on the margins of society, but he went out of his way to do so. He ignored the expectations of gender, ethnicity, and class, and, finally, on the cross

> Jesus fully divests himself of all pretensions to power, privilege, and exceptionalism, even as the incarnate revelation of God. What is clear is Jesus' free and steadfast identification with crucified bodies .... [When] understood in the context of Jesus' full ministry as it led to his crucifixion, this self-emptying indicates his "letting go" of anything that would compromise his absolute alliance with those of the crucified class.[52]

In his incarnation, Jesus did not only accept the vulnerability of his own human existence, but he overcame the anxiety it produces in order to be present to those whose vulnerability was regularly and violently violated. Jesus intentionally travelled through Samaria, conversing with a Samaritan woman and offering salvation to her whole village;[53] Jesus touched

---

48. Phil 2:6–7.

49. Matt 27:40–43.

50. Kwok, *Introducing*, 81.

51. Douglas, *Stand Your Ground*, 174.

52. Douglas, *Stand Your Ground*, 177. Douglas associates the "crucified class" during the time of Jesus with the lynchings of the twentieth-century American South and the recent victims of white privilege and "Stand Your Ground" laws throughout the US.

53. John 4:4–39.

the unclean and outcast: a leper,[54] a dead body,[55] and a bleeding woman.[56] "Scandalous though it may appear, his inclusive table community widens the circle of the friends of God to include the most disvalued people, even tax collectors, sinners, prostitutes."[57] In the face of human agony, Jesus is moved, claims Argentinian theologian Nellie Ritchie.

> Each time the Gospel speaks of Jesus' suffering compassion, it shows his complete identification with the other's situation; it shows his creative and active solidarity. Jesus' feelings precipitate changes—a search for the causes—that transform the pain-causing situation. This ability to "feel with others" leads Jesus to stop hunger, eradicate illness, and remove the burdens that hamper life.[58]

Instead of hoarding resources for resilience or self-protecting, Jesus risked relationships with hurting humans: moving closer, showing empathy, extending generosity, and encountering others intimately.

But why did Jesus risk vulnerability, relationship, and suffering? What was the purpose of the incarnation? What would lead God to give up the "form of God" and "become like human beings" even to the point of death?

THE VULNERABILITY OF ATONEMENT

In exploring these questions, we come face to face with the atonement. Do existing theories of atonement form a foundation for risk-taking in mission that accounts for the incarnation, the vulnerability of the human condition, and questions posed by feminist and liberationist theologians? J. Denny Weaver's popular Anabaptist nonviolent atonement theology[59] meets some of these needs but falls short of others; while the theory encourages the Church to act in counter-cultural opposition to systemic oppression, it lacks formational elements that would lend it to risk-taking in mission and encourages suffering for the sake of an ideology.[60]

---

54. Matt 8:1–3.

55. Mark 5:41.

56. Mark 5:28–30.

57. Johnson, "Redeeming," 123.

58. Ritchie, "Women and Christology," 86.

59. See, for instance, "Quickening," "Atonement," "Theological Implications," *Nonviolent Atonement*, "Forgiveness," and *Nonviolent God*.

60. In "Scoop up the Water," white feminist Catherine Keller argues that the "cross, when rendered normative rather than descriptive, can indeed work to create submissive martyrs rather than revolutionary risk-takers" (106).

Weaver's underlying assumption is two-fold. First, Mennonite christology insists that the character (nature) of Jesus and God are identical; therefore,
if Jesus taught and lived nonviolently, then God must also be fundamentally
nonviolent.[61] Second, Weaver insists that Mennonite theology has uniquely
emphasized nonviolence throughout its history and must recapture its nonviolent assumptions, especially in its theology of atonement.[62]

Weaver's narrative Christus Victor theory describes how Jesus did not
live on earth for the purpose of death but for the purpose of modeling the
reign of God. His life, teachings, and death are to show the world the nonviolent character of God and to illustrate the reign of God that is now but not yet.
The life and subversive message of Jesus so anger the powers and principalities of systemic evil in first-century Israel—represented by both governmen-
tal leaders as well as the mob of civilians—that he is put to death. God's plan
was never to accomplish salvation through the death of Jesus and his death
was not needed for salvation; humans and the powers of evil killed Jesus.[63]
His death was God's will only as much as it was God's will that Jesus stay true
to his mission, even to the point of death. Not only is the death of Jesus unneeded for salvation, claims Weaver, but the life and resurrection of Jesus are
what have salvific affect; in his resurrection, God defeats the ultimate enemy,
death, and initiates a new era of God's reign on earth.[64]

Humans make a decision to shift allegiances from the reign of evil and
join God's community, a community who, like Jesus, live God's reign on
earth.[65] "The resurrection reveals the true balance of power in the universe
whether sinners perceive it or not," argues Weaver. "Sinners can ignore the
resurrection and continue in opposition to the reign of God, but the reign of
God is still victorious."[66] This counter-cultural church community does not
seek death but knows that living nonviolently in opposition to the powers of
evil on earth may well result in death, even as it did for Jesus; they choose to
take that risk anyway. This historical matrix does not allow for the separation
of salvation and ethics; thus salvation is both personal and social.[67]

Traditional satisfaction, penal substitution, and moral influence theories of atonement identify God as the agent behind the death of Jesus, claims

61. Weaver, "Response to Reflections," 40.

62. Weaver, "Narrative Christus Victor," 2 and Keeping Salvation Ethical, 27.

63. Weaver, Nonviolent Atonement, 73–74.

64. Weaver, Keeping Salvation Ethical, 40.

65. Weaver, Nonviolent Atonement, 77–78.

66. Weaver, Nonviolent Atonement, 45.

67. Weaver, Keeping Salvation Ethical, 47.

Weaver, either to satisfy God's honor or law,[68] or to show God's love.[69] Asking the question "Who needed the death of Jesus?" highlights an important differentiation, since, for the narrative Christus Victor image "the closest thing to a need for Jesus' death is that powers of evil need his death in order to remove his challenge to their power."[70] If this is the case, then the death of Christ accomplishes nothing on behalf of either sinners or God.

Weaver's narrative Christus Victor has been challenged by other Anabaptists, even those who agree on the need for a nonviolent theory of atonement that is in harmony with the witness of the gospels. Peter Martens argues that Weaver's theory does an injustice to traditional atonement theories while also harboring its own forms of violence.[71] Christopher Marshall reflects on Scriptures related to the atonement that, he believes, Weaver ignores or misinterprets.[72] Tom Yoder Neufeld suggests that Weaver's emphasis on nonviolence above and beyond the narrative of the gospels creates a "canon over the canon"[73] and challenges Weaver's theodicy.[74] Sharon Baker, while generally supporting Weaver's work, is concerned that it is too subjective, with salvation depending on a responsive subject.[75] Mark Thiessen Nation is concerned that Weaver's theory negates the emphasis on costly discipleship and suffering love that has long been a "defining narrative" for the Anabaptist Church.[76] While she is appreciative of Weaver's creative and courageous confrontation of violence in Christian theology, Mennonite feminist Malinda Berry finds "that Weaver's work fails to lay bare issues of whiteness and sexism/male supremacy in Mennonite theology."[77] She wonders why he does not take the opportunity to question how Mennonites' attitudes toward theology reflect whiteness or racism. "Or what of our own systematic silencing of domestic and sexual abuse, issues of great concern to feminist and womanist theologians—including Mennonite women . . . ?"[78]

68. Weaver, *Nonviolent Atonement*, 19.

69. Weaver, *Nonviolent Atonement*, 18.

70. Weaver, *Nonviolent Atonement*, 72.

71. Martens, "Quest." See also Weaver, "Response to Peter Martens."

72. Marshall, "Atonement." See also Weaver, *Nonviolent Atonement*, 92.

73. Neufeld, "Weaver," 32. See also Weaver, "Response to Reflections."

74. Neufeld, "Weaver," 35.

75. Baker, "Don't Need No Satisfaction," 12. See also Weaver, "Response to Reflections."

76. Nation, "'Who Has Believed,'" 27. See also Weaver, "Response to Reflections" and Sider, "Critique."

77. Berry, "*Anabaptist Theology*." I question the implicit sexism and racism in Weaver's methodology in Ralph Servant, "Gentrification."

78. Berry, "*Anabaptist Theology*."

In addition to these critiques, Weaver's narrative Christus Victor continues to struggle to address the concerns of white feminist, Asian feminist, and womanist theologians when it comes to the atonement. If, as Weaver suggests, Jesus resisted the powers of evil throughout his life and ministry, why did he not resist his death to the end? To answer that resisting his death would have meant abandoning his "mission"[79] is unconvincing and does not adequately respond to feminist critique of passive submission.[80] Additionally, Weaver suggests that in response to the life, death, and resurrection of Jesus, humans decide to "switch teams" and join God in living God's reign. This assertion is similar to Michael Frost and Alan Hirsch's claim in *The Faith of Leap* that one can simply decide to take risks.[81] How does Jesus as a model of God's reign change humans? Where is the presence and work of the Spirit? When the risk of following Jesus in counter-cultural ways results in pain, what empowers the Jesus-follower to persevere? Both this objective decision to change allegiance and describing the death of Jesus as the result of dedication to his "mission" still seem to fall within a traditional theological paradigm that white feminist theologian Catherine Mowry LaCugna calls the "ultimate male fantasy,"[82] devoid of relationship and transforming, strengthening love.

These weaknesses point to the "spiritual poverty" of Weaver's nonviolent atonement theory:[83] his narrative Christus Victor reflects the "nonpassionate attention to the work of Christ and the work of the Spirit in the inner transformation of the person" that Stephen Dintaman describes.[84] While Weaver's theory rightly points to the systemic nature of sin and oppression,[85] it seems to forget that Jesus fought against evil and the "powers" by touching, engaging, and healing individual people.[86] The abstraction of Weaver's "reign of God" misses the relational nature of Jesus in his life, love, and ministry. While God's desire is well-being and peace for the whole world, the "wholeness" of that *shalom* is comprised of well-being and peace for each person; systemic oppression results from the harming of the vulnerability *of* individuals and groups of individuals *by* individuals and groups of

79. Weaver, "Narrative *Christus Victor*," 25.

80. See Brock, *Journeys by Heart*, 93–94, for one example.

81. Frost and Hirsch, *Faith of Leap*, 37.

82. LaCugna, "God in Communion," 91.

83. See my discussion of "spiritual poverty" in ch. 1.

84. Dintaman, "Spiritual Poverty," 205.

85. Weaver, *Keeping Salvation Ethical*, 47.

86. For instance, in Luke 8, we find Jesus casting out demons from a naked homeless man, healing a woman crippled by incurable bleeding, and raising a twelve-year-old child from the dead.

individuals.[87] This oppression, pain, and violence is very real for those who experience it. Commitment to a cause should never surpass commitment to the people affected by that cause.[88]

The relational nature of Jesus in his life and ministry highlights the difficulty of defining the foundational character of God as "nonviolent."[89] When "nonviolence" is the underlying criteria for God's actions and character, then the Good News is built upon a principle.[90] This principle becomes the "right thing to do," which could (and has) supported a narrative of progress that results in paternalism and moral superiority.[91] When, on the other hand, God's nonviolent behavior comes from the reservoir of God's love, the Good News is expressed relationally.

The difference between an atonement built on a foundation of nonviolence and one built on a foundation of love is substantial when it comes to risk-taking in the Church. Weaver is clear that Jesus took risks in his life—healing on the sabbath,[92] crossing ethnic and gender lines,[93] overturning tables in the temple[94]—but describes those risks as for the purpose of modeling the reign of God on earth.[95] This dedication to an abstract principle (nonviolence) suggests that living like this was a tremendous act of will for Jesus; the Gospel accounts, however, regularly refer to love as his motivating factor.[96] In his critique of Weaver's atonement theory, theologian T. Scott Daniels wonders "if the narrative Christus Victor theory would benefit from at least a hint of the moral influence theory in terms of a description of how the love of God—which is the source of divine

87. Ruether, *Sexism and God-talk*, 182.

88. Van Steenwyk, *UnKingdom of God*, 44–45.

89. Weaver suggests that violence is the root of all sin and oppression ("Violence," 141). Hans Boersma accuses Weaver of inconsistently defining and sometimes even advocating for violence ("Violence, the Cross," 57) while Peter Martens suggests that Weaver's theology actually *does* violence: to Weaver's "enemies" (those he theologically opposes), to humans in bondage to sin, and to God ("Quest," 304–7), claims which Weaver adamantly rejects in "Response to Hans Boersma" and "Response to Peter Martens," respectively.

90. Anablacktavist Drew Hart wonders if, by standing on the side of the oppressed, God is ever implicated in violence ("Peacemaking God?").

91. See Bowden, "In the Name," 43–44, and Graham, "Wrong Side." See also my discussion in ch. 8.

92. Matt 12:9–14; Mark 3:1–6; Luke 14:1–6.

93. Matt 9:18–25 and 26:6–13; Mark 7:24–30; Luke 10:38–42 and 13:10–13; John 4:4–42.

94. Matt 21:12 and John 2:14–16.

95. Weaver, *Nonviolent Atonement*, 40–41.

96. Mark 10:21; John 13:1; Matt 9:36; and John 11:5, for example.

victory—shapes not only Christ's mission but also the mission of his disciples."[97] Only if we understand God's purpose as love can we make sense of the incarnation, argues theologian Darby Ray:

> When one loves with infinite depth and divine ferocity, one . . . is compelled by the force of love itself to express it, to reach out to the other, and hence to risk rejection or misunderstanding. This is precisely what God does in Jesus. . . . God does not remain aloof or immune to the pain and struggle of finite existence but enters fully into it, experiencing the good and the evil, the ecstasy and the agony, that are part of real living.[98]

In Weaver's theory, God is a subversive idea that upsets the status quo or a power of good that models a different way[99] yet "the practice of loving involves more than obeying an ideal, applying a principle, or imitating a model," argue Asian American feminist theologian Rita Nakashima Brock and white feminist theologian Rebecca Parker. "Loving acts emerge from the grace we have come to know in the presence of one another."[100] The nonviolent atonement does not adequately express the relational nature of the atonement or articulate what makes change possible.

Additionally, if nonviolence is the ultimate goal, then nonviolent resistance becomes the only acceptable response to the threat of harm or oppression, resulting in self-sacrifice. This emphasis on self-sacrifice can be dangerous for all people, but can be particularly harmful to women and people of color who have lived under the shadow and expectation of self-sacrifice for the "greater good" for generations.[101] "Love requires courage for risk-taking and self-possession, not self-sacrifice," reflect Brock and Parker. "The more we love, the more loss carves into our souls. Pain is the risk of loving, not the basis of love."[102] White feminist theologian and ethicist Sharon Welch adds that there is no such thing as self-sacrifice: sacrifice expected by others does not originate in the self; a self-emptying that comes from within the self is not a loss of self, but rather an enlarging of self.[103] If love is the motivation for risk, self-sacrifice is not considered the only or even ultimate response, but rather the interweaving of love of self and love of the other in

---

97. Daniels, "Response," 44.

98. Ray, *Incarnation*, 45.

99. Weaver calls Jesus an "activist" (*Nonviolent Atonement*, 49).

100. Brock and Parker, *Proverbs of Ashes*, 110.

101. Kwok, *Introducing*, 80; Brock and Parker, *Proverbs of Ashes*, 25.

102. Brock and Parker, *Proverbs of Ashes*, 158.

103. Welch, *Feminist Ethic*, 165.

self-giving.[104] Risk-taking, therefore, does not have the goal of suffering, but the goal of relationship, liberation, and redemption.

This brings into question Weaver's assertion that obedience to his mission could only be accomplished by Jesus through his self-sacrificing death. If Jesus had given in to the powers of violence by responding violently instead of by nonviolently submitting to death,[105] Weaver argues, he would not have fulfilled his mission: "Since saving his life would have meant abandoning his mission, his death was necessary in the sense that faithfulness required that he go through death."[106] This claim seems to identify only two options for Jesus: to respond violently or to give himself over to death. While Weaver does not disagree with feminist and womanist critiques that traditional theories of atonement amount to divine child abuse,[107] he still states that "Jesus died for them—as the manifestation of the reign of God offered to sinful humankind, while the nonviolent response to death expressed his Father's great love for sinful humankind, a love great enough to give up the Son in order to make the gift of the rule of God visible."[108] In this analysis, Weaver elevates the principle of the rule of God over the life of the Son of God; if this is truly God's priority, then God's mission to make God's reign visible will always take precedence over the life and well-being of God's people.

What if, instead, we were to understand the suffering of Jesus on the cross not as staying true to his "mission" but as a result of the divine decision to become human? The vulnerability of humanity is reflected in the cycle of life: humans are born, they live, and they die. In the incarnation, Jesus opted into this cycle of life, with all its risks and vulnerabilities. Jesus then spent his life radically present to those around him, resisting everything that makes humanity less than whole: healing, casting out demons, accepting the outcasts, rejecting systems of oppression, raising the dead back to life, and even escaping attempts on his own life.[109] Eventually, his resistance to the powers of evil and death was no longer possible. Without calling down angels from heaven to rescue him, death was inevitable. In choosing not to supernaturally

---

104. "Self-giving," as opposed to "self-sacrifice," does not indicate a loss of self in the process of sacrifice; thus it is not the sacrifice or giving that feminists challenge but sacrifice at the expense of self instead of sacrifice as an extension of self.

105. Weaver describes this as submitting to God (*Nonviolent Atonement*, 65).

106. Weaver, "Narrative *Christus Victor*," 25 and "Response to T. Scott Daniels," 153.

107. Weaver, "Violence," 155.

108. Weaver, *Nonviolent Atonement*, 43.

109. The story of when the crowds in Nazareth attempted to throw Jesus off a cliff (Luke 4:14–30) is an interesting counterpoint to the cross: Jesus resisted his death and moved to prevent it in that case, so why not later in Jerusalem?

avoid his death (thus "exploiting" his divinity),[110] Jesus showed his love in the ultimate risk of "being-with:" accompanying humans in their suffering, even to the point of death. Thus the death of Jesus is an act of creation, suggests white feminist theologian Mary Grey; just as God birthed a new vulnerable relationality in the creation of the world and God was radically present to vulnerable humans in the birth of Jesus as the fully Human One, so is Jesus giving birth to a new form of mutuality in his death,[111] a "tremendous affirmation of connection and presence."[112]

While Asian feminists strongly reject innocent suffering and sacrifice, Kwok suggests that many "Christian women in Asia identify with such a compassionate God who suffers in solidarity with them, listens to their cries and responds to their pleas."[113] Womanist theologian Karen Baker-Fletcher identifies the act of Christ as threefold: liberation, solidarity, and redemption.[114] Jesus is the one who liberates from suffering (in his life and ministry), the one who provides "survival resources" in suffering and risk (in his death), and the one who redeems suffering to new life (in his resurrection). While womanists join other liberation theologians in celebrating God's liberating power, they also see themselves as more realistic, acknowledging that the experience of black women has been that God does not always liberate, but instead is present with those who are oppressed in their suffering and resistance, risking *with* them.[115]

The depth of God's love led to incarnation, the act of "being-with." Jesus chose to become a vulnerable human, to be radically present with vulnerable humans. This being-with continued through his death on the cross, where Jesus not only joined humanity in the suffering of death, but where he experienced the radical presence of God the Source and God the

---

110. Phil 2:7. See Douglas, *Stand Your Ground*, 177.

111. Grey, *Redeeming the Dream*, 139.

112. Grey, *Redeeming the Dream*, 149. Cherokee scholar Laura Donaldson argues that what matters about Jesus is not his death, but "the way his crucifixion extends and strengthens the world's web of relations" ("Native Women's Double Cross," 107).

113. Kwok, *Introducing*, 81. Matthew Eaton believes that the incarnation should be described as God entering into the frailty and vulnerability of the enfleshed state, and therefore, redeeming and relating to all materiality. He goes on to suggest that "we encounter the incarnate God of Jesus insofar as we encounter material vulnerability within the cosmos regardless of the form it takes" ("Enfleshed in Cosmos," 245). While I would agree that the vulnerability of the cosmos reflects the nature of God, I would argue that the incarnation of Jesus is more than just paradigmatic.

114. Baker-Fletcher and Baker-Fletcher, *My Sister, My Brother*, 79.

115. Baker-Fletcher and Baker-Fletcher, *My Sister, My Brother*, 75 and Baker-Fletcher, *Dancing with God*, 135 and 143. Karen Baker-Fletcher describes Weaver's narrative Christus Victor as a legitimate alternative to traditional atonement theories (136–37).

Spirit. Jesus was never abandoned by either his heavenly or earthly parent: just as Mary's blood was also shed on the cross,[116] so Mary was present with her son as he suffered an agonizing death.[117] In the words of Karen Baker-Fletcher, the presence of both his divine and human communities were "survival resources" for Jesus as his risk led to death. While the presence of his communities did not lead to his liberation from death, they did give Jesus courage and strength to persevere. Intimacy, claims Brock, not self-sacrifice, is the greatest form of love.[118]

Intimacy is cultivated by presence, by proximity and "being-with." It was loving concern for the well-being of others as well as his awareness and confidence of the love of God that made intimacy possible for Jesus. This loving Community of God and people nurtured an environment in which Jesus could take risks. The support, strength, and love of the divine community does not undermine each person's agency, as Brock and Parker have long been concerned.[119] Instead, communion with God changes the paradigm of mission: the Church is not sent as the actor working on the subject of the world, a posture that produces paternalism and an inability to see how the Church has contributed to the world's problems;[120] "being-with" makes both the Church and the world actors and subjects together.

THE VULNERABILITY OF BELONGING

To genuinely love someone, argues Reynolds, we must encounter them up close. Distance only leads to pity, which allows us to remain aloof while appearing to show compassion and sympathy.[121] This often results in charity, which is a disinterested giving out of one's abundance to a generalized other. With charity, "I give to the other not out of an experience of the other's own value, but because of some external criterion of measurement by which value is conferred upon the other and by which I am directed to forget myself and attend to it," describes Reynolds. This leaves no space for mutual vulnerability and relationship but is "directionless, often inappropriately deemed 'blind.' It does not take account of the uniqueness of

116. Baker-Fletcher, *My Sister, My Brother*, 82.

117. John 19:25.

118. Brock, *Journeys by Heart*, xii. Brock considers the community formed around Jesus to be the essence of God (52). While I value Brock's insights into community and erotic love, I am not ready to dismiss Jesus as just another human in community.

119. Brock and Parker, *Proverbs from Ashes*, 156.

120. Brock, *Journeys by Heart*, 8.

121. Reynolds, *Vulnerable Communion*, 114. Reynolds uses the word "sympathy," but his understanding of the term is similar to Brené Brown's "empathy."

another, nor does it receive from another the distinctive gifts she or he may have to offer."[122] Traditional definitions of *agape* love as "disinterested" and "self-less" have only furthered the divide between the lovers and the objects of their love, argues McFague, by stressing that *agape* loves despite the unworthiness of the object.[123] Instead, she suggests, *agape* should be understood as basic in affirming its delight in the existence of the other:[124] "It says, I love you just because you are you, I delight in your presence, you are precious beyond all saying to me. . . . Perhaps for the first time in one's life one realizes that one might be lovable."[125]

Because of human limitations, both proximity and resemblance allow humans to empathize with one another and therefore work toward another's relief, describes Gandolfo. "Some form of contact, and even direct sight of the object, are necessary for the imagination to do its job in the production of sympathy and compassion. The imagination needs such contact in order to have an idea of the other person's suffering; without such an idea, there is nothing for the imagination to work with."[126] Therefore, charity from a distance will never measure up to genuine love: the kind of love that inspired God the Source to imagine the world and love humans into existence; the kind of love that drew God the Expression to enter into the human condition; the kind of love that sent God the Energy to break down barriers to life and wholeness. Genuine love is close and personal.

Love is the connection between two people, a way of belonging together, according to Reynolds. It shows that we have become vulnerable to one another, involved and invested in the well-being of the other.[127] Personal wholeness "is found not through ability but through an acknowledgment of vulnerability that is made concrete in relations of dependence upon others."[128] This kind of particular love is risky: it risks rejection, embarrass-

122. Reynolds, *Vulnerable Communion*, 115.

123. McFague, *Models of God*, 102.

124. McFague, *Models of God*, 117.

125. McFague, *Models of God*, 128. Despite the similarity of language and concept between Reynolds and McFague, McFague insists that salvation and God's love are general—"For God so loved the *world*"—and through the general become particular (*Models of God*, 86). In this way, she can account for evolutionary concepts like survival of the fittest within her paradigm of God's love (*Models of God*, 104). Although she would argue that her theology is meant to be liberating for the "last and the least" (for example, *Models of God*, 70), I am concerned that its implications could be dangerous for those with disabilities and others on the margins of society.

126. Gandolfo, *Power and Vulnerability*, 127.

127. Reynolds, *Vulnerable Communion*, 119.

128. Reynolds, *Vulnerable Communion*, 107. Womanist Linda Thomas suggests that we change the paradigm of mission away from a Matthean model of colonization (Matt

ment or humiliation, missteps and misunderstanding, confusion and a lack of control. Most of all, particular love, the radical "being-with" of vulnerable relationship, puts us at risk of being changed.

Many churches, however, continue to attempt to practice love from a distance.[129] With sweeping generalizations of love toward groups of people (refugees, those with disabilities, veterans, or even "enemies"), churches pray that their love would increase. This is where many congregations miss an important step. Desire to love is truly the seed of love, but love grows through proximity and relationship. If we want to love who God loves, we need to go where God goes, or, more accurately, be where God is—in vulnerable relationship. Prayer from a distance will not do. Once we have discerned the seed of love planted by the Spirit, we must position ourselves where we can build the relationships needed for real love to grow. Otherwise, church programs risk becoming mere charity from a position of superiority, a paternalistic mission "for" strangers instead of a mutual mission "with" friends.

CONCLUSION

Jesus promised that where people are engaged in vulnerable relationships of radical "being-with," he would be present among them.[130] In this way, the Expression of God is still embodied in our world, in vulnerable humanity that reflects not only the image of God, but seeks to be imitators of God.[131] This imitation of God is not simply following the *idea* of Jesus or shaping one's life around the ethics of his teachings, but instead understanding his embrace of human vulnerability and human relationships as foundational to his purpose; he did not come only to die, but to live in community with us. Congregations who desire to join Jesus in taking risks in mission will embrace their vulnerability, a vulnerability that is both open to harm and to transformation. By connecting with others, particularly those in today's "crucified class," those who seek to follow

---

28) to a Lukan model of dependence (Luke 9–10): "In the parabolic way Jesus prefers to teach, the disciples go to new towns and meet new people not to change but to be changed, not to tell but to listen, not with power but helpless" ("Anthropology," 130).

129. Dorothy Day identifies the difficulty of breaking the motivational cycle when she suggests that love "casts out fear, but we have to get over the fear in order to get close enough to love them" ("Peace Is My Bitterness").

130. Matt 18:20.

131. Reynolds, *Vulnerable Communion*, 179.

Jesus become like him in his true expression of the ultimate humanity, as "humankind's creaturely possibility in full bloom."[132]

Jesus lived in his vulnerability by being present to others, loving and receiving their love in return. His willingness to become fully human was a natural expression of the radical "being-with" that he experienced in the Community of God. In his life and death we see his awareness of God's Community manifested in earthly existence. Through his experience and expression of God during his life, we can better understand God's nature. In the next chapter, we will explore how Jesus was able to live a radically vulnerable life, taking risks for the sake of love, because of his connection to the Community of God through the Spirit; through the energy of the Spirit, we, too, can share in the life of God, taking risks in the way of Jesus, in an expression of love.

132. Reynolds, *Vulnerable Communion*, 202.

7

Jesus of the Spirit

INTRODUCTION

IN CHAPTER 6, I developed a theology of vulnerability, suggesting that, in the incarnation, Jesus lived as the fully human one who experienced the vulnerability of interrelatedness without seeking to hoard resources or harm others. This chapter further explores the incarnation by telling the story of his dependence on God the Energy for his connection to divine power and community. As the fully human one, Jesus needed the Spirit's energy to break down barriers to wholeness so that he could take the risk of vulnerable relationship. The Spirit was not just the "Spirit of Jesus," but was a distinct other with whom Jesus lived in relationship. Through the Spirit's radical presence, Jesus experienced the creative, energizing, often surprising life of God's Community. This connection to the Community of God formed a "secure base" for Jesus from which to take risks in his mission to bring all of creation into union with God. This same energy is available for the Church, connecting us to the Community of God, and enabling us to be radically, creatively, and vulnerably present with those around us, offering transformation to others and consenting to transformation ourselves.

THE SPIRIT "HOVERS" IN THE WORLD

"I love the Holy Spirit," declares *evangélicas* theologian Zaida Maldonado Pérez. "She is like the wild child of the Trinity, anywhere and everywhere moving, calling forth, and stirring things up. She is wonderfully illusive yet also fully present. She is untamable, full of possibility and creative potential."[1] Korean Canadian feminist theologian Grace Ji-Sun Kim adds that the Spirit "has infinite possibilities and is the boundless source of change."[2] In the Church, we are tempted to simply think about instead of experience the Spirit, Kim suggests, causing us to forget that "God the Spirit is present and in our midst."[3]

The Spirit gives life; creation "emerges out of the powers and energies of God's own Spirit."[4] Just as the Spirit hovered over the chaos in the beginning, bringing new life from fathomless possibility, life-giving is so essential to the character of the Spirit that anything that interferes with life cannot be from the Spirit. "Rather, where there is Spirit, there is healing: that which is broken, sick, and mangled by the powers and principalities of sin is resisted and overcome when the Spirit moves in our midst. Spirit transforms," say *evangélicas* theologians Elizabeth Conde-Frazier and Loida Martell-Otero.[5] In other words, God's Spirit can be "described in terms of life-giving potential, preferring everything that prizes life over death."[6] This is why, Kim suggests, the Church has ignored the Spirit for so long: because when we acknowledge and open ourselves to the Spirit, we have to move—to participate in healing, whole-making activities.[7] In this way, humans participate in God's creativity, thus sharing in the Spirit's inner life, which means sharing in the life of God's Community.[8]

Kim uses the Chinese term "Chi" to describe the Christian Spirit. Understood as Chi, the Spirit is the energy[9] which gives life to all of creation; the Spirit is present everywhere, producing "life and liveliness in all things."[10] If God were to withdraw God's Spirit, the world would cease to exist.[11] Our

1. In Martell-Otero et al., "Dancing," 14.

2. Kim, *Holy Spirit*, 17. Kim draws parallels between the "Spirit" in Christian scriptures and the "Spirit" in other cultures and religions in order to open avenues for dialogue.

3. Kim, *Holy Spirit*, 37–38.

4. Kim, *Holy Spirit*, 45.

5. In Martell-Otero et al., "Dancing," 27.

6. Kim, *Colonialism*, 69.

7. Kim, *Holy Spirit*, 52–53.

8. Kim, *Holy Spirit*, 45 and *Colonialism*, 69.

9. While traditional Christianity has used "power" to represent the Spirit's activity, I prefer to use "energy" whenever possible. "Power" is often used to describe domination and force, while the Spirit's energy provides strength, perseverance, and companionship. When I do use the word "power" in this chapter, I define it as Martin Luther King Jr. did: "Power, properly understood, is the ability to achieve purpose. . . . Power at its best is love implementing the demands of justice" (*Where Do We Go*, 37–38).

10. Kim, "In Search," 123.

11. Johnson, *She Who Is*, 134.

very breath is an "icon" of God's presence with and in us,[12] reminding us that God's Spirit is not only universal (filling and sustaining the world) but personally near, giving each one of us life, abundantly. "One's encounter with the Spirit is an encounter with God's interiority at the deepest level of one's self," describes Indian theologian Christina Manohar. "It is the meeting of the Spirit or the depth of God with the spirit or depth of the soul."[13] The work of the Spirit is to break down the barriers that keep humans and all of creation[14] from experiencing this abundant life in union with God.[15] When humans lash out in our vulnerability and harm others, we block the Spirit's energy from flowing. Our sin can build barriers to the Spirit's flow within ourselves or in someone else. Sin can also construct obstacles through societal structures and systems. These barriers prevent people from experiencing the abundance of life that the Spirit desires for them. The Spirit's energy can also be blocked by illness or injury, a reflection that the "Chi" Spirit within someone has been kept from moving freely.[16] The Spirit's mission is to break the barriers that sin and brokenness create and bring all people into wholeness and union with God.[17] "Chi embraces life and makes it whole," declares Kim, therefore "it is essential that humanity recognize this Chi and affirm it in their lives. . . . Chi will keep us stronger and help build bridges between humanity. . . . Chi's creating essence will bring forth new life. . . . If

12. "Remembering the breath, and returning to the breath, becomes a way of remembering and returning to the presence of God" (Kim, *Holy Spirit*, 43).

13. Manohar, "Spirit in Mission," 142.

14. Manohar argues that "the relationship between humans and nature is not one of human dominating nature but participating in nature," seeking to help the earth "live abundantly" and fruitfully ("Spirit Christology," 318). In the same way, when we take risks in our space/communities, our goal is to help our neighborhood live abundantly and fruitfully.

15. Hawthorne, *Presence*, 187. "The goal of human beings and the whole of creation is to be united with God" (Manohar, "Spirit Christology," 333). Contrast this with Norman Kraus's assertion that "In the biblical perspective, the human family (community) living under God's covenant of peace (*shalom*) is the goal of creation" (*Community*, 38), and Myron Augsburger's claim that "God's program in the world is to make saints out of sinners" (*Quench Not*, 62).

16. Kim, "In Search," 128, and "Global Understanding," 23. This understanding that illness or injury *can* block the Spirit's movement should be differentiated from the idea that it *always* does. When illness or injury results in suffering, or when suffering is experienced because of others' response to our illness or injury, the Spirit can break down barriers to wholeness; this is evidenced in the healing ministry of Jesus. See my discussion of the difference between suffering and pain in ch. 8.

17. Thomas Finger describes the Spirit's movement as needing to "clear out that channel, opening it toward God" (*Contemporary*, 358). He suggests that the powers of the world "blocked the Spirit from transforming" God's people (359).

God dwells within us, it makes a difference in how we live, treat others and view the world."[18]

Conde-Frazier describes the movement of the Spirit as resurrection. "When we are built up from the inside out, we are resurrected at every level of our personhood. We are empowered, and each time we give ourselves to the overflowing of the Spirit we are transformed," she suggests. "The transforming flow eventually brings us to an insight about ourselves, our circumstances, and God—an insight that is catalytic of new patterns of thinking and acting. This is not only a holy moment or religious phenomenon but a way to release life from within."[19] This transforming flow is a result of the Spirit's constant presence and activity in our lives. Humans do not have to ask God's Spirit to come because the Spirit of God is already present, sustaining us; instead we simply need to "reclaim the spirit that is within us," argues Kim.[20] "We want God to open us to the presence of the Spirit so that we may be transformed. We believe that this openness to God's transforming presence will make us more truly alive."[21]

We are transformed from the inside out, Kim suggests. "Where the Spirit is present, God is present in a special way, and we experience God through our lives, which become holy living from within. We experience whole, full, healed, and redeemed life."[22] This process is what has traditionally been called sanctification, or, in the Anabaptist experience, divinization or new birth.[23] The Spirit is "God for us because She is God in us. She is God's ¡presente!" delights Pérez. The Spirit's presence in us "affirms our personhood [as] instruments of God's reign in whatever way God deems. The Holy Spirit is divine presencia. Since She is Holy, we are made holy."[24] The personhood of God as Spirit reaffirms the personhood of humans. If we turn the Spirit into a non-person (an impersonal force or simply the love between the Father and Son),[25] we turn God into an object, therefore turning ourselves into objects.[26] "When God is spoken of as Spirit, the human relationship with God is interpreted with this most intimate relationship of one person to another,"

18. Kim, "In Search," 129, and "Global Understanding," 29.

19. In Martell-Otero et al., "Dancing," 23.

20. Kim, Holy Spirit, 144.

21. Kim, Holy Spirit, 136.

22. Kim, Holy Spirit, 47.

23. Reimer, Mennonites, 264.

24. In Martell-Otero et al., "Dancing," 17.

25. As first articulated by Augustine (On the Trinity, XV.17.24).

26. Kim, Holy Spirit, 110.

Kim affirms. "God's penetration[27] and knowledge of one's being is not from the outside, something external, but it is from within . . . . God is never far but exists within us and within our community."[28]

The Spirit incorporates us into God's life, drawing us into intimate relationship with God, energizing us to take risks, not only for the sake of love, but for the sake of life. The person of the Spirit invites us into the Community of God and breaks down the barriers that keep us out. Our invitation into God's life, the life of the Trinity, brings us re-union with God, so that we experience the radical presence of God with us, God for us. It is from within the security of that loving community that we find strength and courage to venture out and risk.

THE SPIRIT "HOVERS" IN THE COMMUNITY OF GOD

White Roman Catholic feminist theologian Catherine Mowry LaCugna suggests that the invitation to share in the life of the Trinity has been forgotten over nearly two millennia of theological development,[29] which has separated the work of God in the world from the essence of God's nature, making trinitarian theology irrelevant to the everyday Christian.[30] By rediscovering that God can only be understood as "God for us," not as "God in God's self," argues LaCugna, we return to the heart of the Christian life, which is an "encounter with a personal God who makes possible both our union with God and communion with each other."[31] It is only through this union and communion that we can risk the vulnerability of radical presence with others.

In *God for Us: The Trinity and the Christian Life*, LaCugna describes the essence of the Trinity (ontology) as relational.[32] In response to and building

27. For survivors of sexual trauma to feel safe within the loving, mutual relationship of the Trinity, language other than "penetration" will need to be developed to articulate the intimacy of mutual indwelling; perhaps the language of embracing, receiving, and enveloping the Spirit may be more appropriate. See Maltz, *Sexual Healing Journey*, 300.

28. Kim, *Holy Spirit*, 47.

29. LaCugna argues that this happened because of the separation of *theologia* from *oikonomia* in the fourth century. See *God for Us*, 31. Raith criticizes LaCugna for improperly appropriating the theology of the Cappadocian fathers in, "Ressourcing [*sic*] the Fathers." David Cunningham accuses LaCugna of "historical scapegoating" in *These Three Are One* (31).

30. LaCugna, "Trinitarian Mystery," 177. Kwok Pui Lan argues that, in a context where many people are struggling for basic necessities, Asian feminist theologians rarely begin with abstract conversations about doctrines like the Trinity (*Introducing*, 66).

31. LaCugna, "Trinitarian Mystery," 155.

32. Groppe, "Catherine," 730–31. See also LaCugna, "Re-Conceiving the Trinity"; "Relational God"; "Philosophers and Theologians"; "Baptism"; "Returning," with Kilian McDonnell; and "Baptismal Formula."

upon the work of Karl Rahner,[33] LaCugna suggests that the very vocabulary of the "immanent" Trinity (God as God's self) and "economic" Trinity (God as expressed in creation) are troublesome for meaningful theology.[34] The use of the term "immanent" is problematic, according to LaCugna, because one cannot talk about God as God *is*: God is not defined by God's "substance" or "essence," but as "persons in communion with other persons."[35] LaCugna suggests that trinitarian theology would be better understood as the distinction between and harmony of the *theologia* (the mystery and being of God) and the *oikonomia* (God's plan of salvation, expressed from the creation of the world to its consummation).[36] To LaCugna, "God as revealed in the covenant with Israel, in the Incarnation of Jesus Christ and in the gift of the Holy Spirit is God as God eternally is," summarizes Roman Catholic theologian Elizabeth Groppe, "and hence the ultimate ground and foundation of reality is not an "in itself" or a "by itself" or a "for itself" but rather a person (God) turned toward another in ecstatic love,"[37] what womanist Karen Baker-Fletcher calls the "divine whirlwind."[38] The life of God is not "intradivine," LaCugna argues: "God is not self-contained, egotistical and self-absorbed but overflowing love, outreaching desire for union with all that God has made. The communion of divine life is God's communion with us in Christ and as Spirit."[39]

Because creation has come from the Source and is returning to union with the Source, discussion of who God is apart from God's involvement in the economy is unnecessary, argues LaCugna.[40] The starting point of theology should always be the economy[41] and any assertions made about God should always be checked against the witness of the Christian scriptures, God's self-revelation.[42] We can only understand the relational, social Trinity by how we see the Trinity expressed in the economy. "By emptying ourselves of concepts and images of God, or of expectations about what God is or should be or should be doing," LaCugna states, "we

33. Rahner, *Trinity*. LaCugna also draws on the work of John Zizioulas, particularly *Being as Communion*.

34. See LaCugna's engagement with Rahner in *God for Us*, 209–17.

35. LaCugna, *God for Us*, 225.

36. Groppe, "Catherine," 742.

37. Groppe, "Catherine," 748.

38. Baker-Fletcher, *Dancing with God*, 55.

39. LaCugna, *God for Us*, 15.

40. LaCugna, "Trinitarian Mystery," 177. This resonates with Weaver's argument that atonement must be based on the historical incarnation of Jesus.

41. LaCugna, "Trinitarian Mystery," 157 and *God for Us*, 3–4.

42. LaCugna, "Trinitarian Mystery," 162.

become free to know and love the real living God instead of the God of our projections."[43] The result of the theological enterprise, therefore, is not mastery of knowledge, but relationship: "One does not speculate about God but is transformed by God."[44]

For many years, the Church has been obsessed with developing theology that defines who God is in God's self, which LaCugna calls a "self-defeating fixation."[45] She suggests, instead, "contemplating the mystery of God's activity in creation, in human personality and human history, since it is there in the economy and nowhere else that the 'essence' of God is revealed."[46] In the economy, God and humans meet; it is a place of encounter. Like the African concept of *ubuntu*, which, in essence, means, "I am because we are,"[47] LaCugna defines "to be" as "to-be-a-person-in-communion."[48] Kwok Pui Lan describes this as the "radical relationality" of human existence. "A person does not exist in isolation, but in the web of relationship in which she finds herself," describes Kwok. "Asian cultures see a person-in-relation."[49] Likewise, in contrast to Enlightenment definitions of personhood that emphasize independence, autonomy, and self-sufficiency, LaCugna suggests that personhood is defined instead by equality, interdependence, and fellowship.[50] A person's character is defined by what he does in relation to other persons:[51] "God's To-Be is To-Be-in-relationship, and God's being-in-relationship-to-us is what God is."[52] Even so, we will never completely understand God—not because God is distant or unknowable, but because God is a person. No one person can know the depths of another. "As a partner in love, God permanently remains Mystery to us, no matter how advanced is our intimacy."[53] This is why it remains of utmost importance, according to LaCugna, to remember as we seek to know God, that the object of our knowledge is another "subject," the "God who relentlessly pursues us to become partners in

43. LaCugna, "Trinitarian Mystery," 157.

44. LaCugna, "Trinitarian Mystery," 159.

45. LaCugna, *God for Us*, 225.

46. LaCugna, *God for Us*, 225.

47. The widespread understanding of *ubuntu* beyond the African continent came about through the writings of Desmond Tutu (Tutu Foundation).

48. LaCugna, *God for Us*, 250.

49. Kwok, *Introducing*, 78.

50. Or, as I suggested in ch. 6, vulnerable, radical presence.

51. LaCugna, *God for Us*, 258–59 and "Practical Trinity," 681.

52. LaCugna, *God for Us*, 250.

53. LaCugna, *God for Us*, 323.

communion. God who is Love chooses to be known by love, thus theological knowledge is personal knowledge."[54]

Because of God's relentless pursuit, describes LaCugna, God's life does not belong to God alone: *Trinitarian life is also our life.*"[55] There are not divine and earthly distinctions in which the Trinity serves as a model for the community of the Church but, instead, humans "are made sharers in the very life of God, partakers of divinity as they are transformed and perfected by the Spirit of God."[56] The Community of God forms not only a secure base from which to venture out in mission but also accompanies the exploration and experimentation and offers a haven of security that is already present at any destination. The Community of God sends, goes, and receives. God is for us and God is with us.

Communion with God shapes Jesus-followers into God's image, the image of a community of love constantly inviting others to share in that communion, courageously venturing out and taking risks in order to make that invitation known. Sharing in the life of the Community of God builds intimacy, security, and relationship, leading to transformation. This divine-human community could also be called the "household of God," or Martin Luther King's "beloved community," suggests Baker-Fletcher.[57] The challenge of being near to God is that it requires "being-with" others. Many earthly communities are "antithetical to divine life," claims LaCugna, and "destroy or inhibit full personhood."[58] Communities who share in the life of God are being transformed into something more: "The church is a partial historical realization as well as an eschatological sign of the destiny of all persons for communion with God and with each other," LaCugna argues. "Ecclesial persons are eschatological, pointing beyond themselves to their future when they will be what they were destined to be."[59] Asian American feminist theologian Rita Nakashima Brock describes the pursuit of such community as a search for a love that "breaks isolation, that heals the wounded soul, and that opens the self to the warmth of mutuality, respect, and intimacy." It is a quest, she suggests, for "the capacity to love without barriers."[60]

Love without barriers, birthed out of the Community of God, can only be experienced through the creative energy of God's Spirit. The Spirit that

54. LaCugna, *God for Us*, 332. See also LaCugna and McDonnell, "Returning" 204.
55. LaCugna, *God for Us*, 228, italics hers.
56. LaCugna, *God for Us*, 228.
57. Baker-Fletcher, *Dancing with God*, 46.
58. LaCugna, *God for Us*, 264.
59. LaCugna, *God for Us*, 264.
60. Brock and Parker, *Proverbs of Ashes*, 74.

gives and sustains our life is present within us (for a Spirit-less person is dead), but many people are not aware of it. When Jesus-followers realize that the Spirit is within us and receive the energy of the Spirit at work in and through us, we break down the walls within us that keep the energy of the Spirit from moving. Then, empowered by the Spirit, we join Jesus in his work of destroying the barriers that hold others hostage to death, oppression, and sin. This experience of being filled with the Spirit is not a one-time occurrence, but a daily consent, a continual saying "yes" to the Spirit's energy.

The life of Jesus perfectly models what it looks like when a human perpetually says yes to the Spirit. As fully God, Jesus was truly open to the experience of the Spirit within him, the only person to have no barriers to the full movement of the Spirit's energy, and therefore no barriers to full participation in the life of the Community of God.[61] As fully human, Jesus was able to minister—preaching good news to the poor, bringing freedom for the captives, giving sight to the blind, liberating the oppressed, taking risks to draw others into God's life and love—only because the Spirit of God was upon him.[62] In addition to calling the Spirit the "Spirit of Jesus,"[63] then, it is also accurate to talk about "Jesus of the Spirit."[64]

THE SPIRIT "HOVERS" IN JESUS

Philippians 2 describes the movement of God-the-Expression toward incarnation: "Though he was in the form of God, he did not consider being equal with God something to exploit. But he emptied himself by taking the form of a slave and by becoming like human beings" (vv. 6–7). New Testament scholar Gerald Hawthorne suggests that in becoming human, the "emptying" of Jesus was actually a "filling:" his "self-giving was accomplished by taking," by becoming, by being formed.[65] White feminist theologian and ethicist Sharon Welch describes this emptying-by-filling as an enlarging of one's self; that is, becoming more one's self by the act of giving of one's self.[66] The act of vulnerable incarnation did not make God less like God but instead made God

61. Hawthorne, *Presence*, 219.

62. Luke 4:14–21. Finger uses similar imagery in *Contemporary*, 360.

63. "In the New Testament alone there are over 300 references to 'Spirit.' Of these, 220 speak simply of Spirit or the Spirit; . . . 19 references are made to the Spirit of God, of the Lord, or of the Father; only 5 times does the phrase the Spirit of Christ appear" (Johnson, *She Who Is*, 294n18, cited from Dusen, *Spirit, Son and Father*, 52).

64. Lucy Peppiatt suggests speaking of how Christ is "of the Spirit" ("Spirit Christology," 253), but, as far as I have seen, the phrase "Jesus of the Spirit" has not been used before.

65. Hawthorne, *Presence*, 207.

66. Welch, *Feminist Ethic*, 165.

even more God-like; incarnation was how God was true to God's character. In taking on the limitations and vulnerability of humanness, Jesus opened himself up to the Spirit in a new, energizing expression of the eternal trinitarian mutuality, interdependence, and community.[67]

While traditional theology emphasizes the Spirit's role in divinization, for *evangélicas*, the incarnation of Jesus evidences the "redemptive power of Spirit to humanize. That is to say, the Spirit is the One who gives us a vision of what life is, and exposes the lies of the nonlife that have been constructed for us by oppressive social structures."[68] This Spirit is always "going native,"[69] always "present to the reality and lives of flesh-and-blood people. Spirit is not theory."[70] In the humanity of Jesus, the Spirit enabled him to do what he could not have done on his own. "The Holy Spirit in the life of Jesus is but one additional proof of the genuineness of his humanity," reflects Hawthorne. "The significance of the Spirit in his life lies precisely in this: that the Holy Spirit was the divine power by which Jesus overcame his human limitations, rose above his human weakness, and won out over his human mortality."[71] It was only through the Spirit that the limits of his human mind could come to grasp the fullness of his divinity.[72]

The intimate relationship that Jesus had with the Spirit was evidenced in his conception. Luke 1 says that Mary was given the invitation to participate in God's risk-taking love. When she accepted that invitation (v. 38), the Spirit's energy filled her, making it possible for her to do what she could not have done on her own:[73] not only conceiving (v. 31), but conceiving the incarnated God (v. 32). With humans such a thing is impossible, but "nothing is impossible for God" (v. 37). The Spirit can take what exists and rearrange it into what has not yet been, the ultimate creative act.

As Jesus grew, he became more and more aware of the energy of the Spirit within him. The Spirit, who had been with him since before conception,

---

67. Thomas Finger agrees that Jesus no longer acted in some divine ways and was empowered by the Spirit working through his humanity (*Contemporary*, 462) but argues that the God-like character we see in Jesus came from his divinity, instead of the work of the Spirit in him (414).

68. Martell-Otero, in Martell-Otero et al., "Dancing," 20.

69. Pérez, in Martell-Otero et al., "Dancing," 28.

70. Martell-Otero, in Martell-Otero et al., "Dancing," 21.

71. Hawthorne, *Presence*, 35. Hawthorne's book continues to be the only one that fully evaluates the relationship of Jesus with the Spirit in his ministry (Pinnock, *Flame of Love*, ch. 3, n1). Damon So explores the trinitarian reality of Jesus's ministry in *Forgotten Jesus* but focuses more on his relationship with the Father (see also So, "Christianity and Trinity").

72. Hawthorne, *Presence*, 132.

73. Hawthorne, *Presence*, 67; Kim, *Holy Spirit*, 40.

was filling him with wisdom and strength.[74] The Spirit did this formationally, using the social structures around him, taking "advantage of every educational instrument that was thus readily available—home, parents, school, Scriptures, life and worship of the synagogue, and so on—to mold the intellectual and spiritual dimensions of this developing personality,"[75] as well as supernaturally, astonishing all who heard him speak at the temple with his insight.[76] During his developing years, Jesus grew in his knowledge of his culture and society as well as his spirituality, domains that would later prove valuable in his creative process.[77]

The incarnated Jesus had to be formed into who he had always been: the Expression of God. His understanding sometimes came gradually, and other times came suddenly. At his baptism, the Spirit landed upon him in the form of a dove and brought with her a message from God the Source, the Ultimate Imagination: *"You are my Son,"* *the fullest expression of my creative essence. I love you and I am delighted with you.*[78] Just as the creator God said of God's world in the beginning, "It is good that you exist!,"[79] so now God the Source, through God's Spirit, reminded Jesus of who he was—his value, his purpose, and his Community.[80] Spirit gives life, suggests Kim, but it also provides "a place of safety for those who need a haven, a space to be liberated and free."[81] Once Jesus was assured of his participation in the divine Community, he could begin to engage with the powers of the world that were interfering with the wholeness and union with humanity that God so desired.[82] The more Jesus understood his identity and place within God's Community, the more he was able to take risks.

Jesus broke down the barriers to wholeness that kept those around him from experiencing the entirety of God's aliveness. He faced down temptation through the energy of the Spirit within him.[83] He preached the coming of God's Dream on earth, declaring that the Dream was coming to fruition through him because of the energy and anointing of the

---

74. Luke 2:40; Hawthorne, *Presence*, 99.

75. Hawthorne, *Presence*, 101.

76. Luke 2:47; Hawthorne, *Presence*, 107–8.

77. Sawyer, *Explaining Creativity*, 94.

78. Luke 3:21–22.

79. Johnson, *She Who Is*, 179.

80. Hawthorne, *Presence*, 135–36.

81. Kim, *Holy Spirit*, 40.

82. Acts 10:37–38.

83. Luke 4:1–14; Matt 4:1–11; Mark 1:12–13.

Spirit.[84] He freed people from the oppression of demons and healed those who were sick and injured through the overflowing life of the Spirit.[85] Through the guidance of the Spirit, Jesus escaped an angry mob that was determined to kill him.[86] He touched the undesired—lepers, women, and children[87]—and ate with the unloved[88]—Gentiles, tax collectors, and prostitutes[89]—because of the overflowing love of the Spirit. Jesus brought the dead back to life[90] and fought systems of economic oppression and greed,[91] standing up to civil and religious leaders who were trying to control and dominate the people.[92] Through the energy of the Spirit, Jesus saw into the minds of those around him and understood their deepest needs.[93] The energy of the Spirit flowed through him without barriers, filling him as he continually said "yes" to the Spirit's presence.

Connecting to the energy of the Spirit comes through relationship with a person, not just an impersonal force.[94] White feminist Elizabeth Johnson argues that, rather than destroying one's autonomy and personhood, in healthy love relationships, "the stronger the bond, the more creative of personhood the relationship is."[95] In relationship with the Spirit, Jesus became more fully himself; as Jesus became more fully himself, his intimacy with the Spirit grew.[96] As his intimacy with the Spirit grew, the Spirit also fostered his sense of connection to and place in the Community of God. Even in his humanness, through the Spirit, he was able to experience the union with the Source that was the essence of his experience of divinity.[97] Jesus often took

---

84. Luke 4:14–27.

85. Luke 4:31–41; Matt 12:9–14; Mark 1:21–34.

86. Luke 4:28–30.

87. Mark 1:4–45; Matt 9:18–26; Luke 8:40–56.

88. Kraus suggests that terms like "unlovable" make one a benevolent giver and the "Other" an object of benevolence (*Community*, 153–55). As humans made in the image of God, the unloved do not lose their worth because others choose not to love them.

89. John 4:4–28; Luke 19:1–10; Matt 9:9–13.

90. John 11:1–44; Luke 7:11–17; Mark 5:21–43.

91. Matt 21:12–17; John 2:13–22.

92. John 8:1–11, Luke 11:46.

93. Mark 10:17–22; Luke 6:6–11; John 1:43–51. See also Hawthorne, *Presence*, 145–78.

94. In Martell-Otero et al., "Dancing," 19.

95. Johnson, *She Who Is*, 217. See also Manohar, "Spirit Christology," 281.

96. In discussing the "blurring of otherness," Kim suggests that "when we are unsure of our own self-differentiation, we can easily suffer intense anxiety when the boundaries blur; a healthy sense of self-identity actually makes intimacy possible" (*Holy Spirit*, 75).

97. John 14:10–11.

time to experience the divine Community, going off to solitary spaces for prayer and quiet[98] and even stopping in the midst of difficult situations to seek inspiration from the Source, through the Spirit.[99]

This meant that he was not only connected to the Source's creative imagination[100] but was also participating in the life of God's Community, his secure base.[101] Out of the security of those relationships, Jesus found courage to take risks: he purposefully went to dangerous places;[102] he challenged people in power;[103] he broke laws in order to bring people wholeness;[104] he introduced new teachings that challenged the status quo;[105] he loved people extravagantly, even when his love led to death.[106] The Spirit was present with him, in solidarity and strength. Through the Spirit, Jesus was inspired and energized for creative risk-taking.

The creative imagination of the Source did not end with the death of Jesus, however. Through the Spirit, God brought Jesus back to life.[107] The life-giving Spirit could not allow death to win. "As the water of life, the Spirit makes what is dying and withered to be living and fertile," Kim describes. "The Spirit is powerful enough to make changes and restore life. The Spirit continues to give life to us today."[108]

This "greening" Spirit[109] is still active, creating possibility in chaos. Not only will his disciples do the same work that he did, Jesus said, but they will do even greater things, because of their connection to the Spirit.[110] Jesus had to go to be with the Source so that the disciples would stop depending on him for inspiration and courage and become aware of the Spirit available to them, within them.[111] Only after Jesus was gone could they start saying "yes" to the Spirit. Thus, argues Hawthorne,

98. Luke 5:15–16 and 6:12; Matt 14:13 and 23; 17:1–3; and 26:36.

99. John 8:1–8.

100. John 14:24–26.

101. John 15:9–13.

102. Luke 9:51–53.

103. Mark 7:1–15; Matt 23:1–39; Luke 22:66–71.

104. Mark 3:1–6; Luke 13:10–17; John 5:1–18.

105. Matt 5:1—6:36; Mark 10:1–45.

106. John 13:1, Matt 26:6–16.

107. Luke 24:1–12; Rom 8:11; 1 Cor 6:14.

108. Kim, *Colonialism*, 69.

109. Johnson, *She Who Is*, 135.

110. John 14:12–20.

111. John 16:7.

Jesus demonstrated clearly that God's intended way for human beings to live . . . is in conjunction with God, in harmony with God, in touch with the power of God, and not apart from God, not independent of God, not without God. The Spirit was the presence and power of God in Jesus, and fully so.[112]

THE SPIRIT "HOVERS" IN THE CHURCH

God the Source is still imagining, inspiring, creating. God the Spirit is still energizing, encouraging, giving life. God the Expression is still embodying, incarnating, "going native."[113] In light of this reality, the book of Acts can be read as the story of the Church incarnating and embodying God's Expression in the pattern already described in Luke.[114] The author of Luke-Acts seems determined to draw parallels between the Spirit-filling of Jesus and the Spirit-filling of the Church. "It is difficult to believe that Luke did not intentionally use parallel language when he spoke of the Spirit's work in preparing the human body of the historical Messiah and in preparing a new human body for the resurrected Lord," argues Mennonite theologian Norman Kraus. "According to his account the angel told Mary, 'the Holy Spirit *will come upon you*, and the *power* of the Most High will overshadow you . . .' (Luke 1:35, emphasis added). In Acts 1:8 Jesus told his disciples, 'You shall receive *power* when the Holy Spirit *has come upon you*. . .' (emphasis added). In both cases the body of Christ is formed."[115] Johnson draws the parallel even further, describing how "the Spirit mothers Jesus into life at his conception in Mary's womb, empowers him into mission at his baptism, and brings believers to birth out of the watery womb of the baptismal font."[116]

Both Jesus and the Church became aware of the Spirit's energy in a break-through moment.[117] The Church, filled with the energy of the Spirit,

---

112. Hawthorne, *Presence*, 234. Thus, Jesus-followers are called not so much to emulate the behavior of Jesus but to emulate his dependence on the Spirit, which energized and made possible his behavior. See also Peppiatt, "Spirit Christology," 257.

113. Pérez, in Martell-Otero et al., "Dancing," 15.

114. The genre of Luke-Acts is still the subject of debate. Of all these theories, I find that Luke-Acts as a two-part biography is the most practical for the life of the Church: the book of Acts continues the biography of Jesus by showing how his followers lived as his resurrected body in the world. For an overview of scholarship related to the genre of Acts, see Penner, "Madness."

115. Kraus, *Community*, 15, italics his. It should be noted, however, that Kraus's high christology causes him to lean toward modalism, such as when he calls the Spirit "Christ's alter ego" (180).

116. Johnson, *She Who Is*, 86.

117. Luke 3:21–22; Acts 2:1–4.

then began to preach the coming of God's Dream on earth,[118] to free people from the oppression of demons and heal those who were sick and injured,[119] to escape death,[120] to touch the undesired and eat with the unloved,[121] to bring the dead back to life,[122] to fight systems of economic oppression and greed,[123] to stand up to civil and religious leaders,[124] and to understand the deepest needs of those around them.[125] By the energy of the Spirit flowing through them, the Church took risks: they purposefully went to dangerous places,[126] challenged people in power,[127] broke laws in order to bring people wholeness,[128] introduced new teachings that challenged the status quo,[129] and loved people extravagantly, even when their love led to death.[130]

The experience of both Jesus and the Church shows that the Spirit is always doing something new, risking change and transformation. Despite acknowledging the Spirit's creativity, the Church often resists the Spirit's movement. "The church is the dwelling place of the Spirit and is to be directed by the Spirit," suggests Mennonite theologian Myron Augsburger. "In a living, dynamic church there are always new issues to be faced, especially on the growing edge" but, because of fear, "we safeguard the status quo and quench the Spirit. The thrilling thing about the Jerusalem conference was not that they had a conference 'platform,' but that they ascertained the Spirit's program."[131] When working with the Spirit, the outcome can never be predicted,[132] maintains theologian Lucy Peppiatt, and "allowing spontaneity and creativity is a far more challenging pursuit than following programs and patterns decided on beforehand."[133] Mennonite theologian James Reimer adds that a genuine doctrine of the Spirit calls the Church

118. Acts 2:14–40 and 28:30–31.

119. Acts 9:32–35 and 14:8–10.

120. Acts 12:1–10 and 28:1–6.

121. Acts 8:26–40; 10:1–48; and 16:11–15.

122. Acts 9:36–43 and 20:7–10.

123. Acts 5:1–11 and 16:16–24.

124. Acts 4:5–20; 23:1–11; and 24:10–23.

125. Acts 3:1–10.

126. Acts 21:1–6.

127. Acts 22:25–30.

128. Acts 18:12–17.

129. Acts 19:23–40.

130. Acts 6:8—7:60.

131. Augsburger, *Quench Not*, 52–53.

132. Peppiatt, "Spirit Christology," 236.

133. Peppiatt, "Spirit Christology," 237.

to make "genuinely new decisions" because to "say that the Holy Spirit is very God is to open history to God's continuing dynamic and new action in the name of Christ."[134] The Spirit "always means something living compared with something dead, and something moving over against that which is rigid and petrified," describes Kim.[135] In resisting or denying the work of the Spirit, the Church commits what Jesus called the "unforgivable sin:"[136] attributing the energy of the Spirit to the forces of evil.[137] A risk-averse Church resists a creative, dynamic God.

The same Spirit that energizes the Church is also present within the world.[138] "The dove's flight is the image of the Spirit's freedom, which is not tethered to the church," Kim stresses. "This freedom of the Spirit needs to be realized and emphasized. Too often we want to tie down and limit the Spirit's work. It is the Spirit's freedom that nurtures creativeness and life."[139] While the Spirit is a "wild child," that cannot be tethered, she can always be recognized by her fruit, say Martell-Otero and Conde-Frazier.[140] "Spirit is in agreement with the Son and agrees with what he said and did," describes theologian Clark Pinnock. "The reciprocity is clear—Spirit births the Son in Mary's womb, and the Son identifies the ways of the Spirit."[141] This does not mean, however, that the Spirit is "pointing to any worn-out interpretations of Christ or baptizing everything that the church's tradition has said about him. Spirit also convicts the church where it has gone wrong and helps us grasp old truths in new ways."[142] The Spirit never stops evangelizing the Church.[143] Evaluating the activity of the Spirit by the example of Jesus is not the same as expecting the Spirit to do only what the

---

134. Reimer, *Mennonites*, 371.

135. Kim, *Holy Spirit*, 38.

136. Matt 12:22–37.

137. Hawthorne, *Presence*, 172.

138. Johnson, *She Who Is*, 139.

139. Kim, *Holy Spirit*, 41.

140. In Martell-Otero et al., "Dancing," 27.

141. Pinnock, *Flame of Love*, 209. See also Manohar, "Spirit Christology," 298.

142. Pinnock, *Flame of Love*, 211. See also Kim, *Holy Spirit*, 132. Manohar calls this the "Spirit of revolution" ("Spirit Christology," 324 and 328).

143. "If we take the idea of dialogue seriously, then mission will involve risk and the possibility of change, not just on the part of the hearers of the gospel but also for the church" (Peppiatt, "Spirit Christology," 243). See also: "The church's mission, as given to the Spirit, is as much about being evangelized by the cosmos, the earth, and other human beings as it is about a commitment to their welfare and cultivation" (Bevans, "God Inside Out," 104).

Spirit has done before (i.e. during the life of Jesus); through the Spirit, the Church should always expect surprises.

Today's Church can partner with the Spirit in seeking to break down barriers that block the energy of the Spirit from flowing within and between people—anything that keeps people from living abundant life in union with God and, as a result, with others. The Church can offer spaces of refuge and healing for inner brokenness caused by sin, illness, or abuse; the Church can dismantle systems and structures of oppression, racism, and economic inequality; the Church can actively work toward reconciliation, both in the Church and in the world; the Church can foster diversity as an opportunity for creativity and authentic love;[144] the Church can care for the earth and everything in it. All of this is genuine mission, bringing about God's Dream on earth: union with God. None of this is possible without a willingness to risk vulnerability, relationship, and change.

Understanding Jesus as the ultimate Expression of the Spirit's energy (not simply a historical model) allows us the flexibility we need to interpret the work of the Spirit in our own time and context. "The Spirit stirs within us to make a difference within our community, society, and world," describes Kim.[145] The Spirit drives us to work for justice, to realize the gift of the Spirit within is purposed for love and service.[146] The Spirit is "paradoxical and impish, appearing where we least expect as it is caught between life and death. Its energy emerges in the tension that brings contradictions together."[147]

The dualisms of Western Christianity are extinguished in light of the Spirit's energy: there is no contradiction between divinity and humanity,[148] universality and particularity,[149] creativity and continuity,[150] spirit and matter,[151] past and future.[152] Within the "tension that brings contradictions together," the Spirit creates hybridization and "the formation of hyphenated, fractured, multiple, and multiplying identities."[153] This balance of yin

144. "Diversity is a boundless resource" (Johnson, *She Who Is*, 156).

145. Kim, *Holy Spirit*, 53.

146. Kim, *Holy Spirit*, 51.

147. Kim, *Holy Spirit*, 53.

148. Manohar, "Spirit Christology," 277.

149. Manohar, "Spirit Christology," 280.

150. Glaveanu, "Unpacking," 14–15.

151. Kim, *Holy Spirit*, 140 and Manohar, "Spirit Christology," 319.

152. Kim, *Colonialism*, 83.

153. Kim, *Holy Spirit*, 97. See also Isasi-Díaz, *En La Lucha*, 15, on the concept of *mestizaje*.

and yang, apparent dichotomies or irreconcilable differences in the Western mind,[154] combine into "other ideas, concepts, and beliefs, to come up with a new and different understanding of self, context, and the world. It lifts up the reality that we are not pure, pristine, and simplistic, but rather, complex, chaotic, interdependent, and complicated."[155] The hybridity creates a third space where creativity and innovation can be born.[156] The Spirit is the great harmonizer, always seeking balance; thus unity is possible.[157]

"Breath and fire belong together as intertwining images of the Spirit. The Spirit guides us into a life in which these moments of stillness and of action, of silence and of energy, are balanced," suggests Kim.[158] Action cannot replace relationship. "Knowing and experiencing this wild child is indispensable," argue Martell-Otero and Conde-Frazier. "It is the repeated and intimate encounter with Spirit that ultimately aids in recognizing her presence in [our] midst."[159] It is within this "third space" of action and reflection, knowledge and relationship, innovation and formation, that creativity can thrive.

If the Church is the embodiment of Jesus, the Expression of God,[160] then we, too, can experience the energizing movement of the Spirit as we take risks for the sake of love. As we join with the Spirit in removing barriers that prevent people from experiencing abundant life in union with God, we are energized and inspired with God's own creativity. We are formed as we gain knowledge and experience and as we connect in ever-deeper ways with God and one another. We are willing to take chances because we have experienced the loving Community of God and we want others to participate in the life of the Trinity in ways that transform them as well. We continually say "yes" to the energy of the Spirit within us, allowing the Spirit to fill and form us into the image of Jesus.

In opening his human limitations to God, Jesus opened himself to the energy of the Spirit. His humanity was not the full story, however; through his relationship with the Spirit, he was able to break down barriers that kept those around him from the wholeness and abundance of

154. Kim, "In Search," 122. See also Donaldson, "Native Women's Double Cross," 106.

155. Kim, Holy Spirit, 92.

156. Kim, Holy Spirit, 99 and Martell-Otero, "Introduction," 5.

157. Kim, "In Search," 129 and Holy Spirit, 145–46. See also Manohar, "Spirit Christology," 314.

158. Kim, Holy Spirit, 41.

159. In Martell-Otero et al., "Dancing," 27.

160. "The Spirit's mission is to reproduce Christ in ever-new ways" (Manohar, "Spirit Christology," 283).

life in relationship with God, others, themselves, and the earth. Through the Spirit's activity within, through, and around the Church, we can be energized by the Spirit within our humanness to bring healing and reconciliation to our communities.

CONCLUSION

God the Energy is prone to surprises. The "wild child of the Trinity, the Holy Subversive One,"[161] will not be tamed: she is a "tempest, a storm, a force in body and soul, humanity and nature."[162] She is bursting with creative energy, seeking to rearrange what *is* into what *could be*. She is strengthening the Church with courage in the vulnerability of risk-taking. Through the Spirit, we can break down the barriers to relationships with those around us even as we partner with the Spirit to sweep away anything that gets in the way of life, love, wholeness, and flourishing.

"The Spirit's dance comes into our own lives and bodies and makes us move around. It inspires us to become creative and liberating. It calls us to change and be movers. It requires us to do something about the injustices and inequality that are present in our world today," argues Kim.[163] "The Spirit is the very presence, the real presence of God, God with us. No matter how hard we try to ignore the presence of the Spirit, we cannot run away from it."[164] This Spirit is not just the predictable "Spirit of Jesus," but the provocative Energy of God already at work in the world, bringing God's imagination to life.

Through the Spirit, we are connected to God the Source, the creative imagination behind the Community of God's risk-taking and the one who responds to our own vulnerability and failures with creative redemption and endless ingenuity. In the next chapter, I will explore how God the Source continues to birth new possibilities in the midst of our vulnerable world, risking rejection, suffering, and failure for the sake of love and reunion.

---

161. Pérez, in Martell-Otero et al., "Dancing," 31.

162. Kim, *Holy Spirit*, 40.

163. Kim, *Holy Spirit*, 55.

164. Kim, *Holy Spirit*, 51.

8

God's Dream, Fulfilled

INTRODUCTION

SO FAR, I HAVE explored the nature of vulnerable relationship as the foundation of risk-taking in mission. In chapter 6, I suggested that God created the world to be vulnerably interrelated as a reflection of God's nature. God then entered into the world through the incarnation to live a vulnerable life and show humanity how to live in connection with one another and with God. In becoming human, Jesus took the risk of vulnerable relationship and radical presence. In chapter 7, I further developed this theology of vulnerability by describing how Jesus relied on God the Energy to connect him with the Community of God; through this relationship, Jesus was able to break down the barriers that kept others from union with God, wholeness, and flourishing. Connection with God's Community provided Jesus with a "secure base" from which to take the risks of vulnerability and relationship.

This chapter continues the story of the risk-taking God by exploring the death of Jesus and his resurrection. This resurrection was not triumphalistic, but a vulnerable redemption, the risk of new life coming from death and suffering. Jesus was sent from the Source and returned to the Source even as he was intimately connected to the Source throughout his life and ministry. In the same way, all of creation was imagined by the Source and is sustained by the Source; God's Dream is that all will be reunited with the Source—the final Judge and Redeemer. Knowing that God can redeem death or failure makes it possible for today's Church to continue to take risks even when confronted by overwhelming evil and hopelessness. Only through the love and creativity of the Source can we experience vulnerable resurrection as we take risks in mission for the sake of love. Our own experiences of resurrection and union motivate us to take risks for and with others, so that they, too, might be welcomed into God's Community of life and love.

THE COSMIC SOURCE

In the beginning, the cosmos was created from the loving Imagination of God. The creative Source dreamed up an interrelated world, with all that existed in loving communion with one another and with God. As the "fullness of being," however, God had to hollow out space for the world to exist, "without being swallowed up by God's overwhelming infinity." This meant that, in the act of creating, suggests white feminist Elizabeth Johnson, "divinity withdraws. God makes room for creation by constricting divine presence and power."[1] God made space within God's own self, in God's Community, for creation.[2]

Just as a child is fully herself, yet conceived from, nurtured within, and protected by her mother's body, all of creation is nestled within the life of God, shaped from the essence of God, meant to be at one with God. God the Source is deeply affected by what happens to God's offspring: God would not be "creator, vivifier, redeemer, liberator, companion, and future without it."[3] God is connected to God's creation; God hurts when God's creation hurts.[4] God established God's relationship with Israel on the foundation of this creative activity;[5] as the Source of all that exists, God cried out, "Even [a mother] may forget, but I won't forget you!"[6] Although God protected, cared for, and watched over Israel, God was pained that God's people "forgot the God who gave birth to [them]!"[7] God exhibits "power

1. Johnson, *She Who Is*, 233.

2. In New Testament times, the father was thought to be the one who brought forth life with his seed; the mother was an incubator for the developing child (Johnson, *She Who Is*, 174). Johnson suggests, however, that the "experience of originating others . . . is intensely female" since only women can make space in their bodies for someone else to "live and move and have their being" (Johnson, *She Who Is*, 175 and 234). Mennonite theologian John Miller argues the opposite in *Biblical Faith and Fathering*, suggesting that the Christian faith and the role of "father" in our secular culture will disintegrate if we use female imagery for God. He employs Freudian psychology to suggest that both men and women need the image of God as father to help them develop into fully-realized humans (119 and 135–36, for example).

3. Johnson, *She Who Is*, 232.

4. Johnson, *She Who Is*, 178.

5. Isa 42:5–9.

6. Isa 49:15.

7. Deut 32:18. The other imagery in this passage points to God as the Source: God as father and creator (v. 6), who made (v. 6), established (v. 6) and "sired" Israel (v. 18) as well as the metaphor of an eagle caring for its young (v. 11).

in the delivery of new life, warmth and strength in freely given love that bears responsibility to rear what one has created, and vulnerability in the ways a woman can be hurt by what damages her child."[8] God the Source is intimately connected with God's world, surrounding humanity and all of creation with God's overflowing compassion. "Accordingly, when God is spoken of as merciful, the semantic tenor of the word indicates that the womb is trembling, yearning for the child, grieved at the pain," suggests Johnson. "What is being showered upon the wayward is God's womb-love, divine love for the child of God's womb."[9] God and God's creation are intricately connected through the outpouring of God's love.

When Jesus called God his "Father," argues (Ana)baptist theologian James McClendon, he was describing God as both the one who liberates from bondage and as a friend who is intimately connected to the "cry of the human heart."[10] This *abba* father, claims Johnson, "connotes an intimacy of relation between Jesus and God, along with a sense of God's compassion over suffering, willing good in the midst of evil."[11] Yet Christian tradition has tried to distance God, to portray God as immutable, untouchable, and unrelated to the world, what Johnson calls the "ultimate patriarchal ideal, the solitary, dominant male."[12] Traditional theology has attempted to protect God from being impacted by God's world. As the early church assimilated and participated in Empire, the "Father" of Jesus came to be associated with a more Greek, Zeus-like "maintenance God of things-as-they-are."[13] This Father was not a parent[14] but a patriarch, contends white feminist theologian Sallie McFague, and "patriarchs act more like kings than like fathers:

8. Johnson, *She Who Is*, 178.

9. Johnson, *She Who Is*, 101.

10. McClendon, *Doctrine*, 292–93.

11. Johnson, *She Who Is*, 81. Damon So suggests that mission is only possible when the Church experiences the love of God the Father as Jesus did ("Christianity and Trinity," 127).

12. Johnson, *She Who Is*, 225. See Grey, *Redeeming the Dream*, 26.

13. McClendon, *Doctrine*, 293.

14. Catherine Mowry LaCugna suggests that the meaning of God the "Father" is not so much God the "Parent" as God the "Origin," and, therefore, we can understand the language of the Bible to describe God as the ultimate conceiver of creation (*God for Us*, 302–3). In exploring these metaphors for God, I am not attempting to replace "Father" with "Mother," but rather to flesh out the implications for "God the Source" as the Origin-Creator, and thus Parent. Sally McFague differentiates between the metaphors of God the creator/artist and God the creator/mother in *Models of God*, 104–5. In exploring these images, I hope to avoid what Johnson calls the "benevolent paternalism" that idealizes or romanticizes motherhood (*She Who Is*, 176–77); I would suggest that God's experience as a "giver of life," whether mother or father, creates a fierce, nurturing connection that draws God closer instead of keeping "him" at a distance.

they rule their children and they demand obedience."[15] This patriarchal parent was described with "masculine" attributes as the divine model of fatherhood—strength, sovereignty, rationality—while occasionally exhibiting his "feminine" side—compassion, mercy, and nurturing.[16]

The Church began to see God the Father as a judge, ruling over the world with an iron fist, much like the civil authorities. Like a king, God punished disobedience and put down rebellion;[17] God was to be feared. Yet seeing God as a kingly judge distorts our understanding of God's character, argues theologian John Sanders. God is not a "neutral, dispassionate decision-maker" but an advocate.[18] God "doesn't play favorites and doesn't take bribes. He enacts justice for orphans and widows, and he loves immigrants, giving them food and clothing."[19] God the Creator *is* a judge, contends McFague, but not one who metes out punishment; God is concerned with justice, with protecting God's creation. As the giver of life, God the Source is angry when the fulfillment of life is thwarted. Like a mother bear fiercely defending her young, "God is angry because what comes from her being and belongs to her" is threatened by a lack of resources, safety, or belonging. "Those who produce life have a stake in it and will judge, often with anger, what prevents its fulfillment."[20]

Thus compassion and justice are not opposites, but bound together as God seeks justice for the cosmos.[21] "As creative, life-giving mother of all that is, God has at heart the well-being of the whole world, its life-systems and all its inhabitants," declares Johnson.[22] God "freely gives life to all creatures without calculating a return, loving them inclusively, joyfully saying the basic words of affirmation, 'It is good that you exist.'"[23] The dichotomy between spirit and matter, God and creation, is false, suggests Korean Canadian feminist theologian Grace Ji-Sun Kim.[24] This very present God is active in the world, communicating God's imaginative love to all of creation.[25] "Creation is indeed the fruit of divine love and freedom," argues white feminist theologian

---

15. McFague, *Models of God*, 66.

16. Johnson, *She Who Is*, 49.

17. McFague, *Models of God*, 113–14.

18. Sanders, *God Who Risks*, 65.

19. Deut 10:17.

20. McFague, *Models of God*, 113–14. See also Hos 13:8.

21. Johnson, *She Who Is*, 185.

22. Johnson, *She Who Is*, 184.

23. Johnson, *She Who Is*, 179.

24. Kim, *Embracing the Other*, 130.

25. LaCugna, *God For Us*, 303.

Catherine Mowry LaCugna, but "to be in relation to creation as the Creator, is not a relation added on to the divine essence, ancillary to God's being. To be God is to be the Creator of the world."[26]

God's divine nature as Creator-Source means that God's act of creation was not a one-time occurrence; God is characterized by creative fertility.[27] God the Source's ingenuity[28] and "scrappy resourcefulness"[29] means that God is at work in the midst of the brokenness and vulnerability of this world, bringing new life out of death, and making a way where there is no way.[30] God the Source is characterized by "relentless compassion and audacious creativity"[31] and can bring about restoration from "the shards of human tragedy and suffering, the twisted remains of shattered dreams," and "the scraps of resistance and rebellion." This God "can make do with what is on hand."[32] God's creativity was not just revealed once in the past, but is true about God's ongoing character and activity, suggests theologian Darby Ray. "God was, is, and will be ingeniously divine and divinely ingenious not for the sake of innovation itself or even divinity itself but in order to heal that which is broken, redirect that which has gotten off course, and love into new being that which has lost its vitality."[33] God's work of creation is thus also God's work of redemption. White feminist Mary Grey suggests that "redeem" can mean to "'extricate from futility or meaninglessness,' 'reclaim,' 'liberate,' 'fulfill,' or 'realize.'"[34] Redemption has been God's activity in the world, "always creating and offering new possibilities which are at the same time redeeming ones."[35] God's creative and redemptive work brings all of creation to wholeness and flourishing in relationship with God's Community so that "those who are separated are brought near, what is distorted is untwisted, and what is broken is mended and made whole;" God's redemption leads to at-one-ment.[36]

---

26. LaCugna, *God For Us*, 355.

27. LaCugna calls this "fecundity," in *God for Us* (355 and throughout).

28. Ray, *Deceiving the Devil*, 138–39.

29. Ray, *Incarnation*, 14.

30. Womanist Monica Coleman describes how this phrase summarizes the way black women have experienced God's liberation in their struggle against oppression (*Making a Way*, 9).

31. Ray, *Incarnation*, 33.

32. Ray, *Incarnation*, 99.

33. Ray, *Incarnation*, 156.

34. Grey, *Redeeming the Dream*, 2.

35. Grey, *Redeeming the Dream*, 5.

36. Ray, *Deceiving the Devil*, 2.

God the Source's redemptive activity does not mean that redemption is only done to us or for us, however; humans are called to participate in God's "task of transforming the world."[37] God's creative redemption leaves God vulnerable to the world that God redeems, as humans have rejected God's "redemptive possibilities."[38] Yet when humans choose to participate with God in redemption, accepting our own vulnerability in the process, God's creativity can take on "flesh;" this, argues Grey, "is the joy of God spilling into the world, as people participate in greater and greater forms of fullness."[39] If we are made in the image of God, then surely "part of what it means to be human is to be imaginers, people of vision who refuse to let each other perish," Ray argues. As such, it is not enough to simply engage in ideological games, suggests Ray; we need to incarnate our imaginations: "We've got to put flesh on those bones"[40] in the pattern of the ultimate "Ingenuity Incarnate," Jesus.[41]

THE CREATIVE SOURCE

To be open to participating in God's redemptive possibilities means con- senting to the work of the Spirit in the vulnerability of our humanity. In the incarnation, Jesus modeled a life of openness to God the Source's cre- ative imagination.[42] Everything he knew and taught, Jesus said, he received from the Source. He trusted what he heard, because he knew that God was the source of life.[43] His decisions about what to do, how to behave—his acts of healing and liberation—came from the Source and reflected the character of the Source.[44] *When you see me, you see God*, he declared to his skeptical disciples.[45]

During his earthly ministry, Jesus received the inspiration of God the Source through the Spirit. Jewish feminist Judith Plaskow suggests that Jesus did not always introduce unique teaching in his Jewish environment;[46] other Jews of his time were also challenging Rome, encouraging the inclusion of

37. Grey, *Redeeming the Dream*, 5.

38. Grey, *Redeeming the Dream*, 35.

39. Grey, *Redeeming the Dream*, 58.

40. Ray, *Incarnation*, 141.

41. Ray, *Incarnation*, 156.

42. Grey, *Redeeming the Dream*, 58.

43. John 12:49–50.

44. John 14:10–11. See also John 14:13; 15:8; 16:14; 17:1–5, 10, 22, and 24.

45. John 14:9.

46. Plaskow, "Feminist Anti-Judaism," 92–94.

women, and advocating justice.[47] Many rabbis, sects, and divisions among Judaism were claiming to represent the Dream of God; it was through the Spirit that Jesus learned to differentiate God's voice and God's Dream from the clamor of voices that surrounded him. This very connection to the Source of creativity, wisdom, and discernment was the promise Jesus made to his disciples when he assured them that they would benefit from his return to the Source.[48] Instead of receiving their teaching from Jesus, those that choose to follow Jesus and say "yes" to the Spirit would communicate directly with the Source and experience God's inspiration and resourcefulness.[49] God's Spirit "does help us in our weakness and can give us 'the ability to distinguish between spirits,'" argues white feminist Letty Russell. "With the inspiration of the Spirit we can seek out the signs of the times in a critical manner and find where our calling to action lies."[50] Even more importantly, stresses Kim, the Spirit "guides us into all truth and wisdom, but in the context of being part of a triune communion of love."[51] Just as Jesus was one with the Source who inspired him and the Spirit who energized him, so too are we drawn into the union of God's loving Community.[52]

Through the Spirit, the Imagination of God was present throughout the ministry of Jesus. The Source's ingenuity inspired Jesus to express spiritual truths in new ways ("The kingdom of heaven is like . . ."),[53] to creatively solve problems ("He knew they were trying to trap him so . . ."),[54] to imagine alternative outcomes ("He began to draw on the ground . . ."),[55] to challenge existing moral law ("You have heard it said, but I say . . ."),[56] and to believe that new ways of living were possible ("But he has already begun to smell . . .").[57] As this final example illustrates, his creativity was risky; in response to Jesus raising Lazarus from the dead, the religious leaders plotted to kill them both.[58] In relationship with the

47. Plaskow gives just a few examples, including the experience of women in the synagogue ("Feminist Anti-Judaism," 97).

48. John 16:7–15.

49. John 16:23.

50. Russell, *Human Liberation*, 35.

51. Kim, *Embracing the Other*, 135.

52. John 17:20–23; Kim, *Embracing the Other*, 135.

53. Matt 13:31–50.

54. Mark 12:13–17.

55. John 8:1–8.

56. Matt 5:17–48.

57. John 11:1–57 and Luke 8:40–56.

58. John 11:47–53; 12:9–11.

ultimate Imagination and creative Energy, however, Jesus grew confident in what he could accomplish, even in the face of opposition and at the risk of death. His boldness was a direct result of his knowledge of who he was and the creative energy to which he had access.[59]

Considering his dependence on God's creativity throughout his life and ministry,[60] it is no wonder that Jesus experienced a sense of forsakenness when he cried out for God the Source to creatively imagine another way as he faced the suffering of an unjust death. In the Garden of Gethsemane, he fell on his face and prayed, "My Father, if it's possible, take this cup of suffering away from me."[61] He knew that his inventive, creative Source was capable of imagining a different path or "untwisting" the one that he was on; yet nothing came to him. Even on the cross, white feminist theologian Rosemary Radford Reuther argues, as "his blood is poured out, he scans the sky looking for the hand of God. But the heavens remain closed. God does not reach down to draw his prophet out of many waters and deliver him from his enemies."[62] This cry of forsakenness resonates with all who experience the reality of evil, she contends, and we should not be quick to dismiss his experience of grief and loss in the light of the resurrection, but "let it continue to ring out from the cross, from all the crosses of unjust suffering throughout history, as a question mark about the nature of present reality."[63]

As Jesus hung on the cross, his sense of failure must have been acute, suggests Jesuit priest John Navone. Jesus "wept over Jerusalem which had not known the day of its visitation. His preaching failed to convert his people. His crucifixion was an act of rejection and public disgrace."[64] Although he had seen the individual successes of healed bodies and released spirits, his life and ministry had not accomplished his ultimate goal: to bring God's people back into union with God.[65] Relationally, his connection with his disciples was strained and broken—"there was a chasm between them"[66]—as one disciple had betrayed him, another had denied him, and most of the rest had abandoned him.[67] Jesus could not force or guarantee reciprocity when he took the

---

59. Luke 4:14–21.

60. See ch. 7 for a more thorough exploration of his ministry.

61. Matt 26:39 (CEB).

62. Ruether, *To Change the World*, 28.

63. Ruether, *To Change the World*, 29.

64. Navone, *Theology of Failure*, 1.

65. Navone, *Theology of Failure*, 6 and 9.

66. Navone, *Theology of Failure*, 14.

67. Navone, *Theology of Failure*, 6, 12, and 15.

risk of relationship; his failure was not his fault.[68] Yet failure was a defining feature of the cross as Jesus faced the failure of his God to rescue him from death. His cry of forsakenness was a bid for love, argues Navone; Jesus was calling out for a response from his Source: "Is there no love to respond to failure? Is there no compassion, no awareness, no concern? Does no one see or hear the misery of failure in its myriad agonizing forms?"[69] Would God's love surround Jesus, even after he had failed in his mission?

Yet in the midst of his suffering, God was present. God *is* a God of life, stress liberation theologians, but only if we understand that God is also a God of death, as death is an unavoidable part of life. For liberation theologians, to "claim that God is not somehow a God of death is to exclude God from the full gamut of life," suggests Ray; "it is to diminish God, to make God unreal, to consign God only to the happy times, to the times of growth and prosperity." For our understanding of God to be complete, we must see that "God's affirmation of life can and does occur even in death, even in experiences of suffering and injustice."[70] Death is a reality; even God incarnate did not escape it. Jesus was not alone on the cross, however; he was surrounded by his community: a remnant of his disciples (mostly women)[71] and the Community of God. Their presence gave him strength in the face of failure and suffering to continue to live God's character to the last. "Jesus refuses to allow evil to destroy who he is and thus to become somebody that he is not," argues womanist theologian Kelly Brown Douglas. "He does not succumb to narratives outside of himself, namely narratives of power. Most importantly, he does not allow them to compromise his bond with the powerless and oppressed."[72] Jesus stayed true to himself, even in the face of failure; he did not fail in taking the risk of love but failure came, nonetheless, in the rejection of the cross.

In response, God the Source poured out God's love on God's beloved child. As Jesus died a painful and unjust death, God the Source joined in his human community's grief—covering the world with darkness, splitting rocks, and tearing the temple veil from top to bottom[73]—a parent's agony over her child's suffering. A time of darkness and mourning had begun. Just as Jesus allowed time for grief and loss before he brought the dead back to

---

68. Navone, *Theology of Failure*, 5. See also Edmondson, "Strategies," 50.

69. Navone, *Theology of Failure*, 5–6.

70. Ray, *Deceiving the Devil*, 84–85.

71. John 19:25–26.

72. Douglas, "Crucifixion."

73. Matt 27:51; Mark 15:33; Luke 23:44–46.

life,[74] so now Jesus was laid in a tomb while his community—both human and divine—together felt the emptiness of loss and failure.[75]

In times of darkness and nothingness, we encounter the vulnerable God, claims Grey. As we stay present to the grief and loss, we discover that the darkness is not a time of evil but simply the winter "preparing for the birth of spring."[76] In the darkness, God is liberated for more redeeming possibilities.[77] The darkness of the birthing experience may feel like being torn apart, argues Grey. "We are in the dark, alone, in that primeval womb of chaos from which all life emerged. And yet, in that very darkness we can meet God as creative center. We are held by that nurturing center: from this being-torn-apart, this sense of loss, together You and I wordlessly create new life."[78]

As Jesus lay in the tomb, God the Source was working in the darkness of grief and loss: imagining, redeeming, creating new life. Along with other parents of children killed unjustly throughout time, God was declaring, "I'd rather have my child, but if I have to give him up, we're gonna make it count!"[79] This is the message of resurrection, argues Douglas. "It calls attention to the meaning of a life. Because of the resurrection, victims of the world's crucifying violence are able to overcome the 'absolute indignity' of their crucifying death. The resurrection is nothing less than a refusal to allow the final verdict on a person's life to be a crucifying verdict."[80] Because of God's vulnerable redemption, crucifixion does not get the last word.

THE REDEMPTIVE SOURCE

Out of the darkness of the tomb, the shadows of failure and loss, God the Source created life; new possibility was born out of suffering and death. The Jesus who emerged from the grave was not riding on a white horse or leading a conquering army, but rather the vulnerable Expression of God who was still in the flesh. His resurrection did not erase his suffering or heal his wounds; his disciples were still able to put their fingers into the holes in his hands and the gash in his side—his healing was still to come.[81] Liberation does not

74. Mark 5:35–43, Luke 7:11–15, John 11:38–44.

75. Luke 24:19–21.

76. Grey, *Redeeming the Dream*, 80.

77. Grey, *Redeeming the Dream*, 81.

78. Grey, *Redeeming the Dream*, 148.

79. Echoing the words of Susan Bor after her daughter Heather was killed while protesting white supremacy in Charlottesville, VA (Silverman et al., "'They tried to kill my child'").

80. Douglas, *Stand Your Ground*, 192–93.

81. John 20:24–29.

always mean a final triumph; sometimes it means a fresh start, movement in a new direction. "The resurrection moves humanity past suffering to pain and struggle," argues womanist theologian Emilie Townes. "The resurrection is God's breaking into history to transform suffering into wholeness—to move the person from victim to change agent. The gospel message calls for transformation."[82] For those who have experienced the pain of suffering and death, resurrection is not the end, but a beginning; resurrection is a promise that pain can be redeemed into new life.

"The secret to new life is in the compost," writes Mennonite pastor Isaac Villegas, "with the decomposing fruit, where the seeds of life abide. Compost shows us how fruit dies its way into the future."[83] Out of death and decay, new possibilities find root. The resurrection is God's creative redemption of the suffering and death of the cross, the new life growing out of the compost, the "scrappy resourcefulness" of God not allowing death to have the last word but initiating a renewed struggle toward life and wholeness.

The resurrection is a resounding "no!" to death-dealing social systems and those who would exclude the "outsiders" of our day, argues *evangélicas* theologian Loida Martell-Oterro.[84] In the face of a culture obsessed with death,[85] resurrection "fosters and nurtures a culture of life, even in the midst of death," suggests Douglas.[86] "It is a force that repudiates and virtually makes a joke of the crucifying powers in the world."[87] Resurrection is not just an other-worldly or eschatological experience, contends womanist pastor Irie Session, but something that happens in the present, which "affirms the value of living a purpose-filled life in the here and now."[88] Womanist theologian Karen Baker-Fletcher calls this "rehumanizing."[89] For those who are suffering or oppressed, resurrection means "giving up death" and the power that "death-producing ideologies" hold over us, argues Session. Only once we have given up death can we accept resurrection's offer "of the hope of new life."[90]

---

82. Townes, "Living," 84.

83. Villegas, "Fruit of the Vine." See also Donaldson, "Theological Composting."

84. Martell-Otero, "From *Satas* to *Santas*," 38.

85. Grey argues that two thousand years of death symbolism in the Church needs to now be balanced with birth imagery (*Redeeming the Dream*, 139).

86. Douglas, *Stand Your Ground*, 193.

87. Douglas, "Crucifixion."

88. Session, *Murdered Souls*, xxix.

89. Baker-Fletcher and Baker-Fletcher, *My Sister, My Brother*, 83. See also Baker-Fletcher, *Dancing with God*, 137.

90. Session, *Murdered Souls*, 87.

The reality of ongoing suffering and struggle, despite the historical resurrection of Jesus, is one reason that Anabaptist theologian Kate Eisenbise
is uncomfortable with Denny Weaver's emphasis on the resurrection as victory in his narrative Christus Victor model; the victory is often hard to see
at present. She reflects that the "whole notion of Christian victory seems
a bit odd, especially because winning never seemed to be a part of Jesus'
mission and ministry." She sees, instead, that "Jesus' mission was characterized by restoration . . . ; Jesus describes his mission in terms of releasing the
captives, restoring sight to the blind, and delivering the oppressed."[91] God's
resurrection victory in the world might just come in fits and starts, Eisenbise
suggests, in "slow, small actions" subtly growing into a movement that goes
unnoticed until it becomes too strong for the powers of evil to resist.[92] In
the vulnerability of the resurrection, we find a new revelation of God the
Source's creative ingenuity. Resurrection may not always be a triumphant
moment of victory but may instead unfold as a vulnerable redemption, a
hint of new life emerging tentatively from the wounding and pain of death
or failure. Out of our experiences of pain, God can creatively imagine new
possibilities that make possible a continuing struggle towards God's Dream
of wholeness, reconciliation, and union. This is why "the work of reconciliation begins with our wounds, which affect the deepest areas of our heart,"
suggests Kim. "If we are to work for justice and reconciliation, we need to
have the courage to enter the places of our greatest pain in order to be instruments of peace in the world."[93] The courage to face our experiences of
pain, failure, and suffering and thus open them to the redemptive possibilities of God creates space for new life to be born.

The resurrection holds all of these realities in tension: somehow God
liberates, yet in our vulnerable human existence we still encounter suffering,
oppression, or failure; in Jesus, God has initiated God's victory over evil
and death, yet every day we see evil and death triumph; God is a God of life
who struggles alongside us for flourishing and wholeness, yet, as vulnerable
humans, even those of us who acknowledge and strive to partner with God
hoard resources and harm one another in our efforts to protect ourselves
and those we love. Accepting the ambiguity of life and giving up our expectations of "final, complete victory" may aid us in the struggle toward liberation, suggests white feminist theologian and ethicist Sharon Welch. Utopian
expectations lead us to pursue immediate guarantees and absolute security,
which is really a distortion of God's Dream as we continue our search for

---

91. Eisenbise, "Resurrection as Victory?," 18.

92. Eisenbise, "Resurrection as Victory?," 19.

93. Kim, *Embracing the Other*, 152.

invulnerability.[94] Instead of embracing the positive impact of diversity and pluralism, as well as the benefits of productive conflict, this "pursuit of the absolute good, of final solutions," attempts to distance the "Other," enforce uniformity, and maintain total control.[95] This calls us "to an ethic of risk," argues Welch, "realizing that victories are always partial, their value resident in the matrix of possibilities created."[96] If we understand resurrection as the birth of a new struggle toward wholeness and freedom in which we receive assurance that creative redemption is possible, we find the courage and hope to risk. In the light of the resurrection, we work alongside God toward the elimination of suffering and evil, even when a final victory over "death-producing ideologies" seems impossible.

A RETURN TO THE SOURCE

The ideology of ultimate, eternal victory is the prevailing narrative in the Church, however. Traditional understandings of eschatology describe a climactic end in which evil is eviscerated and Jesus returns to reign on earth forever. White feminist Catherine Keller suggests that this "apocalypse script" has shaped both religious and secular culture and can be seen not only in theology, but in theater, environmentalism, and various manifestations of religious fundamentalism.[97] She describes how this pattern is built upon an either/or dichotomy of good versus evil. It identifies with the good and proceeds to purge itself from evil, "to feel that the good is getting victimized by the evil, [and] to expect some cataclysmic showdown in which, despite tremendous collateral damage (the destruction of the world as we know it), good must triumph . . . with the help of some transcendent power and live forever after in a fundamentally new world."[98] At its core, this apocalyptic script has suggested that "Our Father will make us a shiny new world when this one breaks,"[99] allowing Christians to ignore problems of justice and environmental destruction in the present by pointing to the (distant) future.[100]

---

94. Welch, *Feminist Ethic*, 33.

95. Welch, *Feminist Ethic*, 35–37.

96. Welch, *Feminist Ethic*, 47.

97. Keller, *Apocalypse*, 2–5.

98. Keller, *Apocalypse*, 11.

99. Keller, *Apocalypse*, 2.

100. Keller explores how theologies of hope, such as that of Jürgen Moltmann, continue to contribute to this separation of present from the future, although she admits that Moltmann's later work has become "less prone to neglect the present in favor of the future" (*Apocalypse*, 17).

Alongside these narratives developed the more optimistic "March of Progress" of late modernism.[101] Process theologians like Mary Grey see this movement as a continual progress toward perfection, in which "every situation may contribute to a new harmony, a new depth of relating."[102] Mennonite theologian Gordon Kaufman describes it as the development of humanness and a "cosmic trajectory."[103] Likewise, from the Enlightenment forward, modern mission efforts have been grounded in an optimistic belief in progress, argues missiologist David Bosch.[104] Christians believed that the Church was capable of "renovating the world"[105] and therefore "burdened themselves with a wide-ranging and comprehensive mission of renewing the face of the earth;" the Church invested in this mission because they believed that "the possibilities for realizing this were inherent in the present order."[106]

These optimistic understandings of eschatology as a perfect victory achieved either through a cataclysmic event or a trajectory of progress have not rung true with many feminists who see the continued presence of evil in the world and feel more pessimistic about either the divine intention or human ability to fully conquer it. Ruether prefers to think about eschatology from the perspective of Jubilee. She points to the Hebrew tradition, which also had a "sense of the trajectory of history," but which was shaped more around a combination of linear and cyclical patterns. In Hebrew tradition, society continually slipped away from God's intention for justice, balance, and freedom so that, every fifty years "there must be a revolutionary conversion."[107] During this time of conversion, or Jubilee, injustices were righted, and balance restored. Ruether describes this cyclical pattern as paradigmatic for the Church:

> To be human is to be in a state of process, to change and to die. Both change and death are good. . . . This return to harmony within the covenant of creation is not a cyclical return to what existed in the past, however. Each new achievement of livable,

---

101. Keller, *Apocalypse*, 6.

102. Grey, *Redeeming the Dream*, 36.

103. Kaufman, *In Face of Mystery*, 339. He also suggests that humanity only became aware of this trajectory of progress in the late nineteenth century (387).

104. Bosch, *Transforming Mission*, 334.

105. Bosch, *Transforming Mission*, 335.

106. Bosch, *Transforming Mission*, 339.

107. Ruether, *Sexism and God-Talk*, 254–55.

humane balances will be different, based on new technologies
and cultures, belonging to a new moment in time and place.[108]

Jesus himself seemed to base his ministerial vision more on a Jubilee pattern
than an apocalyptic end, argues Ruether.[109] Faithfulness to that vision requires
that every generation is called to "correct the distortions and violations of life
that have arisen in their time" so that the world is not passed on to the next
generation in worse shape than when we began.[110] Believing in the "tyranny
of impossible expectations of final perfection" keeps us from seeing what we
can do to bring about justice in our time, she contends.[111] Final perfection is
simply not possible and therefore we must accept the limits of our power as
well as the tragic reality of finite life.[112]

Keller has surveyed these myriad understandings of eschatology and
wonders how the Church can find a path forward without falling into the
ditches of optimism or pessimism. That is, she asks, "how can we acknowledge the apocalyptic dimensions of the late-modern situation in which we
find ourselves entrenched without either clinging to some millennial hope
of steady progress or then flipping, disappointed, back to pessimism?"[113]
These questions are not just theoretical, because our views of eschatology
affect our actions, argues Keller. Within the US context, for example, "there
is a traditional tendency to get active, to get enraged, and then to give up,
surrendering to the lull of the comforts and conveniences extracted from
the tribulations of the rest of the planet."[114] In light of God the Source's creative resourcefulness and ingenuity, God the Expression's vulnerability and
radical presence, and God the Energy's movement to break down barriers to
wholeness, flourishing, and union, how can the Church resist these pitfalls
and instead partner with God in bringing about God's Dream on earth, taking risks in mission for the sake of love, and witnessing to the world that
death-producing ideologies do not get the last word?

Martell-Otero suggests that, rather than focusing on the *when* of
eschatology, we should understand eschatology as about the *who, what,*
and *where.* Eschatology is not just about the future or the return of Christ,
she argues, but is intimately related to creation and redemption. Eschatology is the reign of God, "the fulfillment of God's vision—one that began

108. Ruether, *Sexism and God-Talk,* 255.

109. Ruether, *Sexism and God-Talk,* 256.

110. Ruether, "Eschatology and Feminism," 121.

111. Ruether, *Sexism and God-Talk,* 256.

112. Ruether, "Eschatology and Feminism," 122.

113. Keller, *Apocalypse,* 14.

114. Keller, *Apocalypse,* 14.

at creation. This vision is related to the holistic formation of community and responds to God's command for justice and mercy."[115] The obsession in theological circles with time and debates about whether God's reign is (ever) coming or is already realized reveal a Western anxiety about time or finitude, she claims; this question is irrelevant for those whose existence is tenuous and for whom the connection between eschatology and justice is essential.[116] "It is interesting that *Parousia* does not really mean 'second coming' as so many define the term, but rather is a Greek term meaning 'presence,'" Martell-Otero explains. "The issue is not whether Jesus is coming a second time but that he was and is the embodiment of the reign." When Jesus was asked about timelines, he "would wave away the question;" instead, he focused on the *what* and the *who*:

> "In my [Parent's] house there are many dwelling places. If it were not so, would I have told you that I go to prepare a place for you?" The reign is *parousia*, for those who have been told they have no place. There is a place at the table, a place at the inn, a place at the synagogue, a place at the banquet. *Hay fiesta con Jesús* [There is a feast/celebration with Jesus].[117]

Eternity is not about time, Martell-Otero argues, but about place: "Eternity is where God is." Eschatology, then, is "the border crossing of God's eternity with our creation space."[118] We live God's Dream on earth as it is in heaven: "creating a sacred space, a home for those whose lives have been continuously threatened. It is about making a room for everyone. . . . It is about justice, mercy, love, and grace. Above all, eschatology is about bringing life—full and abundant—to this place."[119] By bringing together body and spirit, human and divine, present and future, eschatology is *mestizaje* (a hybrid in which all are equally true): incarnational. As we live God's Dream now, we leave timelines up to God and instead live in union with God and one another, an act of at-one-ment.[120]

This incarnational understanding of eschatology as drawing all of creation into union with God is reflected in scriptural accounts of Jesus "coming." Christian tradition has lumped all of these passages together into a composite description of Jesus returning at the end of time, argues McClendon, but these varied images in scripture are rarely so straightforward: sometimes they

115. Martell-Otero, "Neither 'Left Behind,'" 109.
116. Martell-Otero, "Neither 'Left Behind,'" 111–12.
117. Martell-Otero, "Neither 'Left Behind,'" 114 (Martell-Otero's translation).
118. Martell-Otero, "Neither 'Left Behind,'" 120.
119. Martell-Otero, "Neither 'Left Behind,'" 124.
120. Martell-Otero, "Neither 'Left Behind,'" 123–24.

refer to appearances of the resurrected Jesus, to the transfiguration, to the gift of the Spirit, to the death of believers, or even to the Eucharist. These present a picture, not of a single "coming" at the end of time, but of multiple and diverse "comings." The multiplicity of his comings incorporate a promise: the Jesus who has come, is coming, and will continue to come is not yet done with his work in the world.[121] If eternity is where God is and God the Expression is continually coming into our world, then we can live as though "new creation is already present to our lives."[122]

Just as Jesus was radically, vulnerably present in the world through the incarnation, God the Expression is still radically present to us now. This is the story of creation, argues Russell: what we call "tradition" is the mission of God:

> God's handing over of Jesus Christ into the hands of all genera-
> tions and nations until Christ hands all things back to God. . . .
> The means by which people participate in the traditioning is by
> sharing in the receiving and passing on of Christ. The location
> of God's concern and action in sending Christ is the world, in
> order to bring a "new creation." When the end and goal of the
> traditioning action is completed, Christ will hand himself and
> all things back to God.[123]

There is only one "dynamic movement" of God, suggests LaCugna, and that is "outward, a personal self-sharing by which God is forever bending toward God's 'other.'"[124] This is an outward ecstatic movement by which all things originate from God the Source "through Christ in the power of the Holy Spirit, and all things are brought into union with God and returned to God."[125] God's vision for the "end of time" is not eternal punishment, but at-one-ment; "[W]hat if the power in us, that which gives us our very existence, is not primarily judging individuals but calling us back," questions McFague, "wanting to be more fully united with us. . . ?"[126] This Dream, imagined by God the Source, embodied by God the Expression, and enabled by God the Energy is the reconciliation of all creation, sharing in the life of God's Community: a reunion.[127]

---

121. McClendon, *Doctrine*, 81–82.

122. Russell, *Human Liberation*, 42.

123. Russell, *Human Liberation*, 77 (emphasis hers).

124. LaCugna, *God for Us*, 222.

125. LaCugna, *God for Us*, 223.

126. McFague, *Models of God*, 101.

127. Damon So suggests that mission is "drawing more people into the network of loving relationships in the church (through faith in Christ and the power in the Spirit)"

Focusing on the *who*, *what*, and *where* of reunion with God presents an image of eschatology that is not a timeline in any form—whether trajectory toward progress or cycle of Jubilee—but is a web of connections. This web originates from God the Source and is ever-increasing, making more space and growing more complete as it includes more and more of the cosmos. God's Dream does not reach fulfillment in the right timing, but when those who need a home and a place are drawn back toward the center, sharing in God's Community of life.

For this reunion to happen, however, all of creation must be transformed. This is the purpose of the final "Judgment," argues Niels Gregersen: protection and transformation. "Divine judgment liberates"[128] because we come face to face with the divine gaze of God, the "gaze of reinstatement,"[129] not one of condemnation. God's "judgment" is a learning process in which we see ourselves as God sees us and in which we are shaped into the character of Jesus, restored to the one in whose image we are made.[130] God the Source is passionately committed to bringing all of humanity and creation into reconciliation with God and with one another; as McFague argues, the one who created the cosmos has a vested interest in its survival and flourishing.[131] If we are all to live in union with God and one another—oppressors and the oppressed, victims and perpetrators—then transformation is required for justice to be done. In the transformative gaze and embrace of God, we lose our shameful or guilt-ridden identities as evil is transformed into love.[132] Thus the "day of judgment" begins now[133] as each person says "yes" to the energy of the Spirit and is drawn into the Community of God.

"In and through Jesus' life, ministry, death, and resurrection—empowered by the Spirit—we have been brought into God's space and time," describes Martell-Otero. "In this sense, eschatology has begun. It is not coming to us; it is here among us. It has taken place. But it is also 'promise.' It is the

---

while "the church is in turn drawn by the Spirit into the holy and loving communion within the Trinity" ("Christianity and Trinity," 133).

128. Gregersen, "Guilt," 110.

129. Gregersen, "Guilt," 112.

130. Gregersen, "Guilt," 113. Gregersen uses the language of purgation and suggests that the "fire" is not for punishment but for refinement. While I appreciate his insights into the learning and transforming functions of God's judgment, I struggle with the harshness of this imagery.

131. McFague, *Models of God*, 113–14. See my discussion earlier in this chapter.

132. See Gregersen's reference to Moltmann on page 118, "It is a source of endlessly consoling joy to know, not just that the murderers will finally fail to triumph over their victims, but that they cannot in eternity even remain the murderers of their victims" (*Coming of God*, 255).

133. McClendon, *Doctrine*, 81.

vision of what will be when all powers and principalities are destroyed, when death is completely overcome, and when we are living fully cognizant that everything is 'God-space.'"[134] As we join with God in taking risks for the sake of love, all our experiences of death, forsakenness and failure will be swept into God's life, love, and embrace. Then, as we are all drawn into reunion with God's Community, God our Source will wipe away the tears from our eyes, a final "no!" to suffering, death, and grief.[135]

CONCLUSION

Risking vulnerable relationships in mission comes from a desire to see the world reunited with God, even as we are in union with God's Community. As we consent to the Spirit's energy and participate with Jesus in bringing God's Dream on earth, our hearts are at rest in God's presence.[136] Just as Jesus modeled the character of God the Source, we will recognize God at work in the world when God "comes" among us, because we are being transformed into God's image.[137]

The Church takes risks in mission in order to invite all people to join in God's Dream, to hear God's good news of radical presence and creative redemption. Our attempts to reach the whole world are not because we believe that all nations must hear the gospel before Jesus can return or because we believe that we are on a trajectory of progress toward a future perfection, but because God's desire is to be in union with all people and all of creation. God's transforming love in our lives will not allow us to give up or to stop trying, even in the face of suffering and failure.

For Jesus to be fully and finally present, embodied among us, we need to recognize God's Expression as incarnated in the diversity of all of humanity. Only when all people have been drawn into the divine embrace will the Church truly reincarnate the Body of Jesus. Only when the fullness of God's Expression is manifest in our world will God's Dream come true on earth as it is in heaven, so that all of creation, all of the cosmos, is reunited with God's Community of love and life.

---

134. Martell-Otero, "Neither 'Left Behind,'" 125.

135. Rev 21:3–4: "In an incredibly tender gesture most often observed in the interaction of a mother with her child or lovers with each other, she will wipe away every tear from their eyes" (Johnson, *She Who Is*, 138–39).

136. 1 John 3:18–19.

137. 1 John 3:2.

Conclusion

BORN OUT OF THE fiery evangelism and bold risk-taking of the Radical Reformation, today's Mennonite Church has become increasingly risk-averse in local, congregational mission. Rather than promoting risk-taking in mission, some of the stories that Mennonites tell about God in our theology, ecclesiology, and missional literature may have undermined the efforts of pastors and leaders as they have encouraged congregations to make changes and take risks essential to mission.

In order to change those stories, I have listened to voices from outside and on the margins of the Mennonite tradition so that our stories can be reshaped through critique and dialogue. Voices that lead to liberation and wholeness provide valuable insight into the Dream of God, guiding us to re-story our theology to be shaped into risk-takers for the sake of love. Research into the best practices for risk-taking has shown that, for congregations to engage in risk-taking in mission, we must invest in vulnerable relationships. We are challenged to foster cultures of safety and creativity while providing accountability and learning from failure. For risk-taking to be ethical, we must engage in it from a posture of love and justice, in relationship with diverse individuals and communities, with an openness to being changed. In exploring the stories currently being told about God and mission in the Mennonite Church, we have discovered the tendency in Mennonite story-telling to allow our emphasis on following Jesus in community to valorize suffering and martyrdom, to champion a dualistic separation of Church and world, and to prioritize the mission/ideology of God over the relationality of God. The literature on risk has highlighted the importance of changing some of these stories by expressing how the essence of risk arises out of God's loving nature; in taking risks for the sake of love, we expand our sense of self, becoming more truly humans made in the image of God.

The theological stories that arose out of this research reflect new ways of conceiving God, the world, and the Church. In the incarnation, God became radically present to vulnerable human beings by sharing in our vulnerable human life. As the fully Human One, Jesus experienced the interdependence of our world, yet was able to embrace his vulnerability without harming the vulnerability of others. Jesus resisted the powers of evil and destruction, remaining fully present with humanity, even to the point of death. In doing so, Jesus introduced a new way of relating, in which the Church can be radically present to others, working together for liberation, solidarity, and redemption. This closeness risks the vulnerability of rejection, humiliation, and harm as well as the possibility of being changed; therefore, we can engage only through the cultivation of a deep love and friendship with those around us.

Jesus did not attempt to take these vulnerable risks on his own, however; as the fully Human One, Jesus was inspired and directed by the Imagination of God and energized by God's Spirit. Through his radical "being-with" in the incarnation, Jesus made re-union with God possible. Jesus lived the reality of God: a community of life, overflowing in love, with a desire to create space for others to belong. In becoming human, Jesus lived vulnerably and yet was also secure in his participation in the divine community and energized beyond his human capacities through relationship with the Spirit. These relationships made it possible for Jesus to live as humans were created to live: taking risks, exhibiting creativity, inviting others to participate in God's Dream, all for the sake of love.

God's Dream is reunion with God. God the Source birthed creation into being and thus is intimately connected with it, desiring the wholeness and flourishing of all. As the endlessly creative and fertile one, God the Source is still birthing new possibilities out of experiences of suffering, death, and failure. As a grieving parent, God the Source refused to let a crucifying death have the last word, bringing about vulnerable resurrection and initiating a new struggle to end death-producing ideologies. Through God the Source's ingenuity, we too can birth new life and redeem the failure that results from risk-taking as we say "yes" to God's Spirit and are transformed into God's image. As we reflect God's character and God's heart, we join God in desiring that all people will be drawn with us into God's Community of love and life, returning to the God who gave us birth.

My research into congregational risk-taking in mission has been focused on an overview of the Mennonite Church, its history, and its current practice. I have proposed theories based on these patterns that need now to be considered in the context of real congregational life. This study could be continued with field research into specific congregational practices that seem to foster environments of safety and creativity, where vulnerability and failure are accepted. Further investigation of how congregations pursue creative action, evaluate risky options, and respond to both perceived successes and failures or mistakes would provide valuable information on risk-taking in real congregational life. Interviews with pastors, congregational leaders, and church members would provide insight into how they are attempting to change their narratives about God and whether those changes are resulting in the transformation of their congregational culture and practice.

This book could only briefly explore the theological implications of risk-taking in mission. In addition to ongoing field research, this theology would benefit from a more thorough development of the interactions among the Community of God during the life and ministry of Jesus, particularly during the crucifixion and resurrection. Other important points in the life of Jesus could also be explored through the lens of risk-taking, vulnerability, creativity, and community, including the temptation, transfiguration, post-resurrection appearances, and ascension. Dialogue with other voices on the margins of the institutional Church, including more men of color, sexual minorities, immigrants, survivors of sexual trauma, Indigenous populations, people with disabilities, children, and the elderly would continue the process of transforming our theology through encounters with the "Other."

As I described in chapter 2, the stories we repeatedly tell and hear shape our reality. For congregations who desire to take the risk of vulnerable relationships in mission, changing the stories used in congregational life will be a first step in experiencing the transformation of encounter with the "Other." In congregational settings, storytelling happens in public and private moments. Stories are told from the pulpit and during Sunday School lessons or Bible studies. Stories are shared in books and denominational periodicals. Stories are passed down from one generation to the next, revisited around kitchen tables, and remembered next to hospital beds. Stories are explicit and implicit in the songs that we sing, the prayers that we pray, and the shape of our programs and activities.

Changing these stories begins with congregational leaders. Many leaders learn to interpret Scripture and tell biblical stories in seminary classrooms or from the pages of theological books. The Mennonite Church would benefit from evaluating the theological stories told in its seminaries and published through its press. Once aware of the nature of the stories being told, these stories can be shifted by intentionally drawing on sources from outside of the Mennonite Church or voices on the margins of the institutional Church to help us re-story our theology. As pastors and other leaders experience these shifts, they can then turn to evaluate the ways in which they tell theological stories in their own congregations: preaching, teaching, pastoral care, vision-casting, and through the witness of their lives. Congregational leaders are not the only storytellers, however; part of their responsibility is to help their community members to recognize the stories that they themselves tell and to explore the possibility of new ways of talking about God, the Church, and mission.

The story of a risk-taking God who entered a vulnerable world and took on the vulnerability of humanity in order to enter into relationship with us suggests that the purpose of mission is not programs, but relationships; even as God gave the gift of God's self, so we, too, have a personal stake in mission. Mission cannot just be about promoting ideals like nonviolence, justice, enemy-love, or simple living (as important as these values are). Congregations are called to step out from behind the safety of programming to vulnerably offer who we are as advocates, companions, and, most importantly, friends. Just as Jesus gave to and received from others, risk-taking in mission involves mutual relationships in which we are not only teachers but students, in which we acknowledge weakness and ask for help, and in which we take the risk of being changed by our encounter with others.

The story of an active Spirit who breaks down the barriers to wholeness, flourishing, and relationship fosters an attitude of expectation and openness. If the Spirit is truly at work in our world, then we view our communities with new eyes, watching for glimpses of God's Dream coming true and then joining the Spirit in that work. This suggests that the Church may not have all the answers, but, if we remain open to learning and change, we could find ourselves being transformed even more into the image of God. Openness and transformation require being involved with our communities, up close and personal, while staying connected to one another and to the Community of God through regular spiritual practices. We cannot take risks in mission alone, just as we cannot be ethical alone. We need one another and we need the energy of God's Spirit, who makes connection to God and others possible.

The story of a creative Source who is continually birthing and redeeming offers space to hope. When past experiences of mission seem ineffective and current plans for mission seem futile, we can believe that God the Source is passionately seeking to be reunited with the world that God made. Even in response to failure (or to the possibility of failure), we can have courage to try, to risk, to learn, or to be changed because we know that God redeems suffering, failure, and loss. We might not experience glowing moments of triumph, but we will see God bringing new life out of death as God refuses to give up, continuing to pursue the wholeness and flourishing that come from all of creation being united with God.

A shift in these stories in congregational life could have a significant impact on a congregation's way of being, doing, and relating. Instead of telling stories that undermine our call to mission, we can tell stories that challenge us to see the nature of mission differently and, therefore, call for a different level of participation and encounter. Instead of seeing mission as a duty or simply an act of obedience for those who follow Jesus, mission becomes an outpouring of regenerated lives; as we have experienced the loving Community of God, so we desire for others to be united with God as well. Instead of equating risk-taking in mission with extreme calls to suffering and martyrdom reserved for the heroic among us, we find the courage for ordinary acts of vulnerability in relationship with our community. Instead of pursuing a set-apart, pure Church, we expect the Spirit to draw us into Jesus-like relationships with our neighbors so that we can break down the barriers to justice, flourishing, and wholeness together. Instead of keeping it safe in order to avoid the risk of failure, we embrace that vulnerability can lead to transformation as well as harm, and—together—we try.

I have seen glimpses of God's Dream coming true as congregations take the risks of vulnerable relationship in mission:

- members of a mission outpost in the city's poorest neighborhood eating weekly meals together, playing basketball in the parking lot, sharing a garden, and supporting one another through births, deaths, and all of life in between

- a congregation of Indonesian immigrants building relationship with the local Muslim community, offering sanctuary and a meeting space, and partnering together to fight against unjust immigration policies

- a team of urban church planters building relationships with people in their community who are poor, homeless, battling addictions, and struggling with violence

- a congregation impacted by the opioid epidemic sponsoring a community training so that concerned individuals can learn how to save the life of someone who has overdosed

- an aging congregation in the middle of cornfields, who allowed themselves to be transformed by an influx of refugees from Burma

These congregations have all been transformed through relationships with the "Other." Their commitment to take risks with their finances, property, theology, church traditions, and even their physical bodies arises out of the vulnerable relationships they have built together; they are committed not to a cause or an ideal, but to living, breathing people.

Change has traditionally been resisted by many in the Mennonite Church as we have striven to maintain our uniqueness and separation from the world; yet encountering the "Other" in mutual relationships of care and transformation will be essential for the renewal of the Church in mission. The vulnerability of radical presence with others will mean sharing in their pain and struggle as well as coming face to face with our own complicity in their suffering. Getting close to those outside of our Anabaptist communities opens congregations to the possibility of doubt, uncertainty, rejection, and failure. We may begin to see ourselves and our traditions differently. We may grow uncomfortable and restless. We may find that we can no longer support or maintain the status quo. If, however, we truly are a Church devoted to following in the way of Jesus, vulnerable presence will need to be our defining posture. To join with God in God's Dream of cosmic reunion, we will need to be radically present to those who God loves. We will need to risk everything that we hold valuable and trust that God is bringing new life out of each death-producing ideology that we release.

When we embrace our vulnerability and join Jesus, the fully Human One, in being radically present to others, we discover who we were created to be: reflections of God's image, yearning to be reconciled to all people and all of the cosmos, whatever the cost. In the security of God's Community of Life, energized by God's Spirit, inspired by God's Imagination, and incarnating God's Expression, we step out in faith, taking risks for the sake of love.

Bibliography

Abe, Masao. "Kenotic God and Dynamic Sunyata." In *The Emptying God: A Buddhist-Jewish-Christian Conversation,* edited by John B. Cobb et al., 3–65. Maryknoll, NY: Orbis, 1990.

Abelard, Peter. *Commentary on the Epistle to the Romans.* Translated by Steven R. Cartwright. Washington, DC: The Catholic University of America Press, 2011.

AMBS. "Spiritual Life." https://www.ambs.edu/about/Spiritual-life.cfm.

Amundson, Jon K. "Why Narrative Therapy Need Not Fear Science and 'Other' Things." *Journal of Family Therapy* 23 (2001) 175–88.

Anabaptist Wiki. "The Holy Spirit in the Life of the Church (Mennonite Church, 1977)." http://www.anabaptistwiki.org/mediawiki/index.php/The_Holy_Spirit_In_the_Life_of_the_Church_(Mennonite_Church,_1977).

Anabaptist World, "Theologian's ministerial credential terminated." *Anabaptist World* (October 21, 2020). https://anabaptistworld.org/theologians-ministerial-credential-terminated/.

Anselm. *Why God Became Man.* Translated by Jasper Hopkins and Herbert Richardson. Toronto: EMellen, 1974.

Asheervadham, I. P., et al. *Churches Engage Asian Traditions.* Intercourse, PA: Good, 2011.

Athanassoulis, Nafsika, and Allison Ross. "A Virtue Ethical Account of Making Decisions about Risk." *Journal of Risk Research* 13 (2010) 217–30.

Augsburger, Myron S. *Quench Not the Spirit.* Scottdale, PA: Herald, 1961.

———. *The Robe of God: Reconciliation, the Believers Church Essential.* Scottdale, PA: Herald, 2000.

Augustine. *On the Trinity.* Translated by Stephen McKenna. Cambridge: Cambridge University Press, 2002.

Aulén, Gustaf. *Christus Victor.* Translated by A.G. Hebert. New York: Macmillan, 1931.

Bainton, Roland. "The Anabaptist Contribution to History." In *The Recovery of the Anabaptist Vision,* edited by Guy F. Hershberger, 317–26. Eugene, OR: Wipf & Stock, 2001.

Baker, Sharon L. "Don't Need No Satisfaction: Rolling the Stone Away with J. Denny Weaver." *CGR* 27 (2009) 7–16.

Baker, Vaughn W. *Evangelism and the Openness of God: The Implications of Relational Theism for Evangelism and Missions.* Eugene, OR: Pickwick, 2013.

Baker-Fletcher, Garth Kasimu, and Karen Baker-Fletcher. *My Sister, My Brother: Womanist and Xodus God-Talk.* Maryknoll, NY: Orbis, 1997.

Baker-Fletcher, Karen. *Dancing with God: The Trinity from a Womanist Perspective.* St. Louis: Chalice, 2006.

Barrett, Lois Y. "The Anabaptist Vision and Modern Mission." In *Anabaptist Currents: History in Conversation with the Present,* edited by Carl S. Bowman and Stephen L. Longenecker, 303–9. Camden, ME: Penobscot, 1995.

————. *Building the House Church.* Scottdale, PA: Herald, 1986.

————. "Defining Missional Church." In *Evangelical, Ecumenical, and Anabaptist Missiologies in Conversation: Essays in Honor of Wilbert R. Shenk,* edited by James Krabill et al., 177–83. Maryknoll, NY: Orbis, 2006.

————. "Rethinking Anabaptist Apocalypticism." In *Apocalypticism and Millennialism: Shaping a Believers Church Eschatology for the Twenty-First Century,* edited by Loren L. Johns, 156–72. Kitchener, ON: Pandora, 2000.

————. "Taking Risks as a Contrast Community." In *Treasure in Clay Jars: Patterns in Missional Faithfulness,* 74–83. Grand Rapids: Eerdmans, 2004.

Barto, Andrew, et al. "Novelty or Surprise?" *Frontiers in Psychology* 4 (2013) 1–15.

Bauman, Harold E. *Presence and Power: Releasing the Holy Spirit in Your Life and Church.* Scottdale, PA: Herald, 1989.

Beck, Richard A. "God as a Secure Base: Attachment to God and Theological Exploration." *Journal of Psychology and Theology* 34 (2006) 125–32.

Beck Kreider, Luke. "Mennonite Ethics and the Ways of the World." *MQR* 86 (2012) 465–92.

Becker, Palmer. "What is an Anabaptist Christian?" In *Fully Engaged: Missional Church in an Anabaptist Voice,* edited by Stanley W. Green and James R. Krabill, 133–43. Harrisonburg, VA: Herald, 2015.

Behar, Ruth. *The Vulnerable Observer: Anthropology That Breaks Your Heart.* Boston: Beacon, 1997.

Bender, Harold S. *The Anabaptist Vision.* Scottdale, PA: Herald, 1944.

————. "Perfectionism." *GAMEO* (1959). http://gameo.org/index.php?title=Perfectio nism&oldid=83810.

————. "'Walking in the Resurrection': the Anabaptist Doctrine of Regeneration and Discipleship." *MQR* 35 (1961) 96–110.

Berry, Malinda Elizabeth. "Anabaptist Theology in Face of Postmodernity: A Proposal for the Third Millennium and The Nonviolent Atonement." *Mennonite Life* 59 (2004). https://ml.bethelks.edu/issue/vol-59-no-1/article/anabaptist-theology-in-face-of-postmodernity-a-pro/.

————. "Mission of God: Message of Shalom." In *Anabaptist Visions for the Next Millennium,* edited by Dale Schrag and James C. Juhnke, 167–73. Scottdale, PA: Herald, 2000.

————. "Needles Not Nails: Marginal Methodologies and Mennonite Theology." In *The Work of Jesus Christ in Anabaptist Perspective: Essays in Honor of J. Denny Weaver,* edited by Alain Epp Weaver and Gerald J. Mast, 263–68. Telford, PA: Cascadia, 2008.

Bevans, Stephen B. "God Inside Out: Toward a Missionary Theology of the Holy Spirit." *International Bulletin of Missionary Research* 22 (1998) 102–5.

Bevans, Stephen B., and Roger P. Schroeder. *Constants in Context: A Theology of Mission for Today.* Maryknoll, NY: Orbis, 2004.

Biesecker-Mast, Gerald J. "The Persistence of Anabaptism as Vision." *MQR* 81 (2007) 21–42.

———. "Recovering the Anabaptist Body (To Separate It for the World)." In *Anabaptists and Postmodernity,* edited by Susan L. Biesecker and Gerald J. Biesecker-Mast, 193–213. Scottdale, PA: Herald, 2000.

———. "Reply to 'Narrative Theology in an Anabaptist-Mennonite Context,' by J.D. Weaver." *CGR* 12 (1994) 330–34.

Birkey, Del. *The House Church: Model for Renewing the Church.* Scottdale, PA: Herald, 1988.

Blough, Neal. "Messianic Mission and Ethics: Discipleship and the Good News." In *The Transfiguration of Mission: Biblical, Theological and Historical Foundations,* edited by Wilbert R. Shenk, 178–98. Scottdale, PA: Herald, 1993.

Boccia, Maria L. "Human Interpersonal Relationships and Love of the Trinity." *Priscilla Papers* 25 (2011) 22–26.

Bochner, Arthur P. *Coming to Narrative: A Personal History of Paradigm Change in the Human Sciences.* Walnut Creek, CA: Left Coast, 2014.

Boers, Arthur P. *On Earth as in Heaven: Justice Rooted in Spirituality.* Scottdale, PA: Herald, 1991.

Boersma, Hans. "Violence, the Cross, and Divine Intentionality: a Modified Reformed View." In *Atonement and Violence: A Theological Conversation,* edited by John Sanders, 47–69. Nashville: Abingdon, 2006.

Bosch, David J. *Transforming Mission: Paradigm Shifts in Theology of Mission.* Maryknoll, NY: Orbis, 1991.

Boshart, David W. *Becoming Missional: Denominations and New Church Development in Complex Social Contexts.* Eugene, OR: Wipf & Stock, 2011.

Bowden, Brett. "In the Name of Progress and Peace: The 'Standard of Civilization' and the Universalizing Project." *Alternatives* 29 (2004) 43–68.

Boyd, Greg A. "Can Traditional Anabaptists Change to Embrace Neo-Anabaptists?" AMBS (November 21, 2014). http://www.ambs.edu/blog/10152/7403.

Brock, Rita Nakashima. *Journeys by Heart: A Christology of Erotic Power.* New York: Crossroad, 1988.

Brock, Rita Nakashima, and Rebecca A. Parker. *Proverbs of Ashes: Violence, Redemptive Suffering, and the Search for What Saves Us.* Boston: Beacon, 2001.

Brown, Brené. *Daring Greatly: How the Courage to Be Vulnerable Transforms the Way We Live, Love, Parent, and Lead.* New York: Gotham, 2012.

———. *The Gifts of Imperfection: Let Go of Who You Think You're Supposed to Be and Embrace Who You Are.* Center City, MN: Hazelden, 2010.

———. *I Thought It Was Just Me (but It Isn't): Telling the Truth about Perfectionism, Inadequacy, and Power.* New York: Gotham, 2007.

———. "My Response to Adam Grant's New York Times Op/ED: Unless You're Oprah, 'Be Yourself' Is Terrible Advice." *LinkedIn* (June 5, 2016). https://www.linkedin.com/pulse/my-response-adam-grants-new-york-times-oped-unless-youre-bren%C3%A9-brown?trk=hp-feed-article-title-like.

———. *Rising Strong.* New York: Spiegel & Grau, 2015.

Brown, Hubert L. *Black and Mennonite: A Search for Identity.* Scottdale, PA: Herald, 1976.

Browning, Don S. *A Fundamental Practical Theology: Descriptive and Strategic Proposals.* Philadelphia: Fortress, 1991.

Buechner, Frederick. *The Alphabet of Grace.* New York: Seabury, 1981.

Burrell, Stephen D. "A Study Developing a Biblical View of Success and Assessing the Grief Process After Amoral Failure in Order to Prepare the Minister for Courageous Involvement in Future Ministry Opportunities." DMin diss., Grace Theological Seminary, 2011.

Bush, Perry. "Anabaptism Born Again: Mennonites, New Evangelicals, and the Search for a Useable Past, 1950–1980." *Fides et Historia* 25 (1993) 26–47.

Caneday, A.B. "Putting God at Risk: A Critique of John Sanders's View of Providence." *Trinity Journal* 20 (1999) 131–63.

Cannon, Mark D., and Amy C. Edmondson. "Confronting Failure: Antecedents and Consequences of Shared Beliefs about Failure in Organizational Work Groups." *Journal of Organizational Behavior* 22 (2001) 161–77.

Carlson, Vivian J. and Robin L. Harwood. "The Precursors of Attachment Security: Behavioral Systems and Culture." In *Different Faces of Attachment: Cultural Variations on a Universal Human Need,* edited by Hiltrud Otto et al., 278–303. New York: Cambridge University Press, 2014.

Carr, Anne E. "The New Vision of Feminist Theology: Method." In *Freeing Theology: The Essentials of Theology in Feminist Perspective,* edited by Catherine Mowry LaCugna, 5–29. New York: HarperOne, 1993.

Chopp, Rebecca S. "Eve's Knowing: Feminist Theology's Resistance to Malestream Epistemological Frameworks." In *Feminist Theology in Different Contexts,* edited by Elisabeth Schüssler Fiorenza and Mary Shawn Copeland, 116–23. London: Orbis, 1996.

———. "Practical Theology and Liberation." In *Formation and Reflection,* edited by Lewis S. Mudge and James N. Poling, 120–38. Philadelphia: Fortress, 1987.

———. *The Praxis of Suffering: An Interpretation of Liberation and Political Theologies.* Maryknoll, NY: Orbis, 1986.

Chung, Hyun Kyung. "'Han-Pu-Ri': Doing Theology from Korean Women's Perspective." *The Ecumenical Review* 40 (1988) 27–36.

———. "Who is Jesus for Asian Women?" In *The Strength of Her Witness: Jesus Christ in the Global Voices of Women,* edited by Elizabeth A. Johnson, 103–19. Maryknoll, NY: Orbis, 2016.

Cleveland, Christena. *Disunity in Christ: Uncovering the Hidden Forces that Keep us Apart.* Downers Grove, IL: InterVarsity, 2013.

Coakley, Sarah. *Powers and Submissions: Spirituality, Philosophy, and Gender.* Oxford: Blackwell, 2002.

Coggins, James R. "Toward a Definition of Sixteenth-Century Anabaptism: Twentieth-Century Historiography of the Radical Reformation." *JMS* 4 (1986) 183–207.

Cohen-Rottenberg, Rachel. "Connection Takes More Than Courage: More Thoughts on Systemic Oppression and Brené Brown's 'The Power of Vulnerability.'" *The Body is Not an Apology* (September 25, 2013). http://thebodyisnotanapology.tumblr.com/post/62241269026/connection-takes-more-than-courage-more-thoughts.

———. "Shame and Disconnection: The Missing Voices of Oppression in Brené Brown's 'The Power of Vulnerability.'" *The Body is Not an Apology* (January 9, 2015). https://thebodyisnotanapology.com/magazine/shame-and-disconnection-the-missing-voices-of-oppression-in-brene-browns-the-power-of-vulnerability/.

Coleman, Monica A. *Making a Way Out of No Way: A Womanist Theology.* Minneapolis: Fortress, 2008.

Collins, Robin. "A Defense of Nonviolent Atonement." *Brethren in Christ History and Life* 35 (2012) 185–213.

———. "Girard and Atonement: An Incarnational Theory of Mimetic Participation." In *Violence Renounced: René Girard, Biblical Studies, and Peacemaking,* edited by Willard Swartley, 132–56. Scottdale, PA: Herald, 2000.

Corbett, Steve, and Brian Fikkert. *When Helping Hurts: How to Alleviate Poverty without Hurting the Poor—and Yourself.* Chicago: Moody, 2014.

Cramer, David. "Mennonite Systematic Theology in Retrospect and Prospect." *CGR* 31 (2013) 255–73.

Crites, Stephen. "The Narrative Quality of Experience." *Journal of the American Academy of Religion* 34 (1971) 291–311.

Culp, Kristine A. *Vulnerability and Glory: A Theological Account.* Louisville: Westminster John Knox, 2010.

Cunningham, David. *These Three Are One: The Practice of Trinitarian Theology.* Oxford: Basil Blackwell, 1997.

Daniels, T. Scott. "Response to J. Denny Weaver." In *Atonement and Violence: A Theological Conversation,* edited by John Sanders, 42–46. Nashville: Abingdon, 2006.

Day, Dorothy. "In Peace Is My Bitterness Most Bitter." *The Catholic Worker* (January 1967). http://www.catholicworker.org/dorothyday/articles/250.html.

Del Colle, Ralph. *Christ and the Spirit: Spirit-Christology in Trinitarian Perspective.* New York: Oxford University Press, 1994.

Denck, Hans. "Whether God is the Cause of Evil." In *Spiritual and Anabaptist Writers,* edited by George Williams, 88–111. London: Westminster John Knox, 2006.

Dintaman, Stephen. "The Spiritual Poverty of the Anabaptist Vision." *CGR* 10 (1992) 205–8.

Donaldson, Laura E. "Native Women's Double Cross: Christology from the Contact Zone." *Feminist Theology: The Journal of the Britain and Ireland School of Feminist Theology* 29 (January 2002) 96–118.

———. "Theological Composting in Romans 8: An Indigenous Meditation on Paul's Rhetoric of Decay." In *Buffalo Shout, Salmon Cry,* edited by Steve Heinrichs, 142–48. Harrisonburg, VA: Herald, 2013.

Douglas, Kelly Brown. "Crucifixion, Resurrection, and the Reversal of Power." *Feminism and Religion* (April 15, 2014). https://feminismandreligion.com/2014/04/15/cruci fixionresurrectionandthereversalofpowerbykellybrowndouglas/.

———. "Marginalized People, Liberating Perspectives: A Womanist Approach to Biblical Interpretation." *Anglican Theological Review* 83 (2001) 41–47.

———. *Stand Your Ground: Black Bodies and the Justice of God.* Maryknoll, NY: Orbis, 2015.

Driver, John. *Images of the Church in Mission.* Scottdale, PA: Herald, 1997.

———. *Kingdom Citizens.* Eugene, OR: Wipf & Stock, 1998.

Dunn, James D. G. *Baptism in the Holy Spirit; a Re-Examination of the New Testament Teaching on the Gift of the Spirit in Relation to Pentecostalism Today.* Naperville, IL: A.R. Allenson, 1970.

———. *Jesus and the Spirit: A Study of the Religious and Charismatic Experience of Jesus and the First Christians as Reflected in the New Testament.* Philadelphia: Westminster, 1975.

Durnbaugh, Donald. *The Believers' Church: The History and Character of Radical Protestantism.* Scottdale, PA: Herald, 1985.

Dusen, Henry V. *Spirit, Son, and Father: Christian Faith in the Light of the Holy Spirit.* New York: Scrubner's, 1958.

Dyck, C. J. *An Introduction to Mennonite History: A Popular History of the Anabaptists and the Mennonites.* Scottdale, PA: Herald, 1993.

Eaton, Matthew. "Enfleshed in Cosmos and Earth." *Worldviews: Global Religions, Culture and Ecology* 18 (2014) 230–54.

Edmondson, Amy C. "Strategies For Learning From Failure." *Harvard Business Review* 89 (2011) 48–55.

———. *Teaming to Innovate.* Hoboken, NJ: John Wiley & Sons, 2013.

Eisenbise, Kathryn. "Resurrection as Victory?: The Eschatological Implications of J. Denny Weaver's 'Narrative *Christus Victor*' Model of Atonement." *Brethren Life and Thought* 53 (2008) 9–22.

Elliot, Matthew A. "The Emotional Core of Love: The Centrality of Emotion in Christian Psychology and Ethics." *Journal of Psychology and Christianity* 31 (2012) 105–17.

———. *Feel: the Power of Listening to Your Heart.* Carol Stream, IL: Tyndale, 2008.

Enns, Fernando. "The Challenge of Diversity." *Canadian Mennonite* (January 13, 2016). http://www.canadianmennonite.org/stories/challenge-diversity.

Escobar, Samuel. "Present and Future Realities for Anabaptist Mission." In *A Relevant Anabaptist Missiology for the 1990s,* edited by Calvin E. Shenk, 35–41. Elkhart, IN: Council of International Ministries, 1990.

Estep, William R. *The Anabaptist Story: An Introduction to Sixteenth-Century Anabaptism.* Grand Rapids: Eerdmans, 1996.

Fessenden, Tracy. "'Woman' and the 'Primitive' in Paul Tillich's Life and Thought: Some Implications for the Study of Religion." *Journal of Feminist Studies in Religion* 14 (1998) 45–76.

Field, Tiffany. "Attachment and Separation in Young Children." *Annual Review of Psychology* 47 (1996) 541–62.

Finger, Thomas N. "Christus Victor and the Creeds: Some Historical Considerations." *MQR* 72 (1998) 31–51.

———. *A Contemporary Anabaptist Theology: Biblical, Historical, Constructive.* Downers Grove, IL: InterVarsity, 2004.

———. "Is 'Systematic Theology' Possible from a Mennonite Perspective?" In *Explorations of Systematic Theology from Mennonite Perspectives,* edited by Willard Swartley, 37–56. Elkhart, IN: IMS, 1984.

Fiorenza, Elisabeth Schüssler. "To Follow the Vision: The Jesus Movement as *Basileia* Movement." In *Liberating Eschatology: Essays in Honor of Letty M. Russell,* edited by Margaret A. Farley and Serene Jones, 123–43. Louisville: Westminster John Knox, 1999.

Frantz, Nadine Pence. "The (Inter)Textuality of Our Lives: An Anabaptist Feminist Hermeneutic." *CGR* 14 (1996) 131–44.

———. "Theological Hermeneutics: Christian Feminist Biblical Interpretation and the Believers' Church Tradition." PhD diss., University of Chicago Divinity School, 1992.

Freedman, Jill, and Gene Combs. *Narrative Therapy*. New York: W. W. Norton: 1996.

Frei, Hans. *The Eclipse of the Biblical Narrative*. New Haven, CT: Yale, 1974.

Fretz, J. Winfield. "Newly Emerging Communes in Mennonite Communities." *International Review of Sociology* 6 (1976) 103–12.

Friesen, Abraham. *Erasmus, the Anabaptists, and the Great Commission*. Grand Rapids: Eerdmans, 1998.

Frost, Michael, and Alan Hirsch. *The Faith of Leap: Embracing a Theology of Risk, Adventure and Courage*. Grand Rapids: Baker, 2011.

Gallardo, José. "Ethics and Mission." In *Anabaptism and Mission*, edited by Wilbert R. Shenk, 137–57. Scottdale, PA: Herald, 1984.

Gandolfo, Elizabeth O. *The Power and Vulnerability of Love: A Theological Anthropology*. Minneapolis: Fortress, 2015.

———. "A Truly Human Incarnation: Recovering a Place for Nativity in Contemporary Christology." *Theology Today* 70 (2014) 382–93.

George, Timothy. *Theology of the Reformers*. Nashville: Broadman, 1988.

Gingerich Stoner, Andre. "Our Victim Mentality." *MWR* (May 28, 2012). http://www.mennoworld.org/archived/2012/5/28/our-victim-mentality/.

Glaveanu, Vlad P. "Developing Society: Reflections on the Notion of Societal Creativity." In *Creativity, Culture, and Development*, edited by Ai-Girl Tan and Christoph Perleth, 183–200. New York: Springer Science + Business, 2015.

———. "Unpacking the Triad of Creativity, Culture, and Development: an Exercise in Relational Thinking." In *Creativity, Culture, and Development*, edited by Ai-Girl Tan and Christoph Perleth, 13–28. New York: Springer Science + Business, 2015.

Gocłowska, Malgorzata A., et al. "Whether Social Schema Violations Help or Hurt Creativity Depends on Need for Structure." *Personality and Social Psychology Bulletin* 40 (2014) 959–71.

Godwin, Colin. *Baptizing, Gathering, and Sending: Anabaptist Mission in the Sixteenth-Century Context*. Kitchener, ON: Pandora, 2012.

Goering, Melvin. "Dying to be Pure: The Martyr Story." *Mennonite Life* 47 (1992) 9–15.

Goossen, Benjamin W. "How to Radicalize a Peaceful Minority." Princeton University Press Blog (February 7, 2017). http://blog.press.princeton.edu/2017/02/07/benjamin-w-goossen-how-to-radicalize-a-peaceful-minority/.

———. "Mennonite Privilege." *The Mennonite* (March 9, 2017). https://themennonite.org/feature/mennonite-privilege/.

Graham, David A. "The Wrong Side of 'the Right Side of History.'" *The Atlantic* (December 21, 2015). http://www.theatlantic.com/politics/archive/2015/12/obama-right-side-of-history/420462/.

Grant, Adam. "Unless You're Oprah, 'Be Yourself' Is Terrible Advice." *The New York Times* (June 4, 2016). https://www.nytimes.com/2016/06/05/opinion/sunday/unless-youre-oprah-be-yourself-is-terrible-advice.html?smid=fb-nytimes&smtyp=cur&_r=1.

Grant, Jacquelyn. *White Women's Christ and Black Women's Jesus*. Atlanta: Scholars, 1989.

Green, Joel. "The 'Human One' Explained." https://vimeo.com/31602853.

Green, Stanley W. "Cultivating a Spirituality that Sustains Missional Engagement." In *Fully Engaged: Missional Church in an Anabaptist Voice*, edited by Stanley W. Green and James R. Krabill, 155–62. Harrisonburg, VA: Herald, 2015.

Green, Stanley W., and James R. Krabill, eds. *Fully Engaged: Missional Church in an Anabaptist Voice*. Harrisonburg, VA: Herald, 2015.

Gregersen, Niels Henrik. "Faith in a World of Risks." In *For All People: Global Theologies in Context*, edited by Else Marie Wiberg Pedersen, et al., 214–33. Grand Rapids: Eerdmans, 2002.

———. "Guilt, Shame, and Rehabilitation: The Pedagogy of Divine Judgment." *Dialog* 39 (2000) 105–18.

———. "Risk and Religion: Toward a Theology of Risk Taking." *Zygon* 38 (2003) 355–76.

Grey, Mary. *Redeeming the Dream*. London: SPCK, 1989.

Grimsrud, Ted. *Instead of Atonement: The Bible's Salvation Story and Our Hope for Wholeness*. Eugene, OR: Cascade, 2013.

———. "Part of the Conversation? 'Neo-Mennonites' and Mennonite Theology." *Peace Theology* (March 2, 2014). https://peacetheology.net/2014/03/02/part-of-the-conversation-neo-mennonites-and-mennonite-theology/.

Groppe, Elizabeth T. "Catherine Mowry LaCugna's Contribution to Trinitarian Theology." *Theological Studies* 63 (2002) 730–63.

Grossmann, Klaus E., et al. "Universal and Culture-Specific Aspects of Human Behavior: The Case of Attachment." In *Culture and Human Development: The Importance of Cross-Cultural Research for the Social Sciences*, edited by Wolfgang Friedlmeier, et al., 75–97. Hove: Taylor & Francis, 2005.

Guyton, Glen. "One Small Step for Mennonite Church USA." *The Mennonite* (February 8, 2017). https://themennonite.org/one-small-step-mennonite-church-usa/.

Hackman, Heather. "Addressing Shame As White Racial Justice Advocates." (July 8, 2013). http://hackmanconsultinggroup.org/blog/addressing-shame-as-white-racial-justice-advocates/.

Hansson, Sven Ove. "Ethical Criteria of Risk Acceptance." *An International Journal of Analytic Philosophy* 59 (2003) 291–309.

———. *The Ethics of Risk: Ethical Analysis in an Uncertain World*. New York: Palgrave Macmillan, 2013.

———. "Extended Antipaternalism." *Journal of Medical Ethics* 31 (2005) 97–100.

———. "Social Decisions about Risk and Risk-Taking." *Social Choice and Welfare* 29 (2007) 649–63.

Harder, Lydia Neufeld. "Biblical Interpretation: A Praxis of Discipleship?" *CGR* 10 (1992) 17–32.

———. "Naming Myself a Theological Scholar." In *Minding the Church: Scholarship in the Anabaptist Tradition*, edited by David Weaver-Zercher, 193–207. Scottdale, PA: Herald, 2002.

———. *Obedience, Suspicion and the Gospel of Mark: A Mennonite-Feminist Exploration of Biblical Authority*. Waterloo, ON: Wilfrid Laurier, 1998.

———. "Postmodern Suspicion and Imagination: Therapy for Mennonite Hermeneutic Communities." *MQR* 71 (1997) 267–83.

———. "Power and Authority in Mennonite Theological Development." In *Power, Authority, and the Anabaptist Tradition*, edited by Benjamin W. Redekop and Calvin W. Redekop, 73–94. Baltimore: Johns Hopkins, 2001.

Harris, Judith Rich. *The Nurture Assumption: Why Children Turn Out the Way They Do*. New York: Free, 1998.

Hart, Drew. "A Peacemaking God?" *The Mennonite* (September 6, 2016). https://the mennonite.org/a-peacemaking-god/.

Hartsock, Nancy. "The Feminist Standpoint: Developing the Ground for a Specifically Feminist Historical Materialism." In *Discovering Reality,* edited by Sandra Harding and Merrill B.P. Hintikka, 283–310. Boston: D. Reidel, 1983.

Hauerwas, Stanley. *A Community of Character.* Louisville: Notre Dame, IN: University of Notre Dame Press, 1993.

———. *Why Narrative? Readings in Narrative Theology.* Eugene, OR: Wipf & Stock, 1997.

Hawthorne, Gerald F. *The Presence and the Power.* Dallas: Word, 2003.

Hege, Nathan B. *Beyond Our Prayers: Anabaptist Church Growth in Ethiopia, 1948–1998.* Scottdale, PA: Herald, 1998.

Heidemanns, Katja. "Missiology of Risk? Explorations in Mission Theology from a German Feminist Perspective." *International Review of Mission* 93 (2004) 105–11.

Heifetz, Ronald, et al. *The Practice of Adaptive Leadership: Tools and Tactics for Changing Your Organization and the World.* Boston: Harvard Business, 2009.

Heinzekehr, Hannah. "On Neo-Anabaptism and Other Likeminded 'Movements.'" *The Femonite* (November 6, 2013). http://www.femonite.com/2013/11/06/on-neo-ana baptism-and-other-like-minded-movements/.

———. "On Women, Theology, and Mennonite Church USA." *The Femonite* (October 28, 2013). http://www.femonite.com/2013/10/28/on-women-theology-and-men nonite-church-usa/.

Hershberger, Michele. "Reading the Bible through a Missional Lens." In *Fully Engaged: Missional Church in an Anabaptist Voice,* edited by Stanley W. Green and James R. Krabill, 179–89. Harrisonburg, VA: Herald, 2015.

Hicks, Donna. *Dignity.* New Haven, CT: Yale University Press, 2011.

Hiebert, Frances F. "The Atonement in Anabaptist Theology." *Direction* 30 (2001) 129–31.

Horsch, John. "The Rise and Fall of the Anabaptists in Muenster (I)." *MQR* 9 (1935) 92–103.

———. "The Rise and Fall of the Anabaptists in Muenster (II)." *MQR* 9 (1935) 129–43.

Hostetler, Beulah Stauffer. "Nonresistance and Social Responsibility: Mennonites and Mainline Peace Emphasis, Ca. 1950 to 1985." *MQR* 64 (1990) 49–73.

Houser, Gordon. "MJ Sharp: the Witness of 'a Kind Soul.'" *The Mennonite* (March 3, 2017). https://themennonite.org/daily-news/mj-sharp-witness-kind-soul/.

Huber, Tim. "Lancaster Conference to Leave Mennonite Church USA." *MWR* (November 20, 2015). http://mennoworld.org/2015/11/20/news/lancaster-confer ence-to-leave-mennonite-church-usa/.

Huebner, Chris K. "Mennonites and Narrative Theology: The Case of John Howard Yoder." *CGR* 16 (1998), 15–38. https://uwaterloo.ca/grebel/publications/conrad-grebel-review/issues/spring-1998/mennonites-and-narrative-theology-case-john-howard-yoder.

Hybets, Myk. *The Anointed Son: A Trinitarian Spirit Christology.* Eugene, OR: Pickwick, 2010.

Isasi-Díaz, Ada María. *En La Lucha: In the Struggle.* Minneapolis: Fortress, 1993.

———. "Kin-dom of God: a *Mujerista* Proposal." In *In Our Own Voices: Latino/a Renditions of Theology,* edited by Benjamin Valentin, 171–89. Maryknoll, NY: Orbis, 2010.

Jacobs, Donald R. *Pilgrimage in Mission*. Scottdale, PA: Herald, 1983.

Jenkins, Philip. *The Next Christendom: The Coming of Global Christianity*. Oxford: Oxford University Press, 2011.

Johns, Cheryl Bridges. "Grieving, Brooding, and Transforming." *Journal of Pentecostal Theology* 23 (2014) 141–53.

Johnson, Elizabeth A. "For God so Loved the Cosmos: When the Word Became Flesh, All Creation Was Drawn into the Divine Embrace." *U.S. Catholic* 75 (2010) 18–21.

———. "Redeeming the Name of Christ." In *Freeing Theology: The Essentials of Theology in Feminist Perspective*, edited by Catherine Mowry LaCugna, 115–37. San Francisco: HarperSanFrancisco, 1993.

———. *She Who Is: The Mystery of God in Feminist Theological Discourse*. New York: Crossroad, 1992.

Kanagy, Conrad L. *Road Signs for the Journey: A Profile of Mennonite Church USA*. Scottdale, PA: Herald, 2007.

Kasdorf, Hans. "The Anabaptist Approach to Mission." In *Anabaptism and Mission*, edited by Wilbert R. Shenk, 51–69. Scottdale, PA: Herald, 1984.

———. "Towards an Anabaptist Missiology for the 1990s: a Missiologist's Perspective." In *Anabaptist Visions for the Next Millennium*, edited by Dale Schrag and James C. Juhnke, 3–18. Scottdale, PA: Herald, 2000.

Kaufman, Gordon D. *In Face of Mystery: A Constructive Theology*. Cambridge, MA: Harvard University Press, 1995.

———. "Religious Diversity, Historical Consciousness, and Christian Theology." In *The Myth of Christian Uniqueness: Toward a Pluralistic Theology of Religions*, edited by John Hick and Paul F. Knitter, 3–15. Maryknoll, NY: Orbis, 1987.

Keller, Catherine. *Apocalypse Now and Then: A Feminist Guide to the End of the World*. Boston: Beacon, 2005.

———. "Scoop up the Water and the Moon is in Your Hands: On Feminist Theology and Dynamic Self-Emptying." In *The Emptying God: A Buddhist-Jewish-Christian Conversation*, edited by John B. Cobb et al., 102–15. Maryknoll, NY: Orbis, 1990.

Kidane, Beyene. "Holy Spirit Empowerment." In *Fully Engaged: Missional Church in an Anabaptist Voice*, edited by Stanley W. Green and James R. Krabill, 89–95. Harrisonburg, VA: Herald, 2015.

Kim, Grace Ji-Sun. *Colonialism, Han, and the Transformative Spirit*. New York: Palgrave Macmillan, 2013.

———. *Embracing the Other: The Transformative Spirit of Love*. Grand Rapids: Eerdmans, 2015.

———. "A Global Understanding of the Spirit." *Dialogue and Alliance* 21 (2007) 17–31.

———. *The Holy Spirit, Chi, and the Other: A Model of Global and Intercultural Pneumatology*. New York: Palgrave Macmillan, 2011.

———. "In Search of a Pneumatology: Chi and Spirit." *Feminist Theology* 18 (2009) 117–32.

King, Martin Luther. "Experiment in Love." In *A Testament of Hope: The Essential Writings of Martin Luther King, Jr.*, edited by James M. Washington, 16–20. New York: HarperCollins, 1991.

———. "I Have a Dream." In *A Testament of Hope: The Essential Writings of Martin Luther King, Jr*, edited by James M. Washington, 217–20. New York: HarperCollins, 1991.

———. *Where Do We Go from Here: Chaos or Community?* Boston: Beacon, 1967.

Klaassen, Walter. *Anabaptism: Neither Catholic nor Protestant.* Kitchener, ON: Pandora, 2001.

———. "Keeping Salvation Ethical." *JMS* 16 (1998) 241–45.

———. "The Quest for Anabaptist Identity." In *Anabaptist-Mennonite Identities in Ferment*, edited by Leo Driedger and Leland Harder, 13–26. Elkhart, IN: IMS, 1990.

Klassen, William. "Anabaptist Hermeneutics: The Letter and the Spirit." *MQR* 40 (1966) 83–96.

Koch, Roy S., and Martha Koch, eds. *My Personal Pentecost.* Scottdale, PA: Herald, 1977.

Koontz, Gayle Gerber. "The Liberation of Atonement." *MQR* 63 (1989) 171–92.

———. "The Trajectory of Scripture and Feminist Conviction." *CGR* 5 (1987) 201–20.

Koop, Karl. "Anabaptist and Mennonite Identity: Permeable Boundaries and Expanding Definitions." *Religion Compass* 6 (2014) 199–207.

Krabill, James R. *Does Your Church Smell Like Mission? Reflections on Becoming a Missional Church.* Elkhart, IN: MMN, 2003.

———. "God's Shalom Project: Why Peace and Mission are Inseparable." In *Fully Engaged: Missional Church in an Anabaptist Voice*, edited by Stanley W. Green and James R. Krabill, 57–66. Harrisonburg, VA: Herald, 2015.

———. *Is it Insensitive to Share Your Faith?* Intercourse, PA: Good, 2005.

Krall, Ruth. "The Mennonite Church and John Howard Yoder: Collected Essays." In *The Elephant in God's Living Room*, vol 3. http://ruthkrall.com/downloadable-books/volume-three-the-mennonite-church-and-john-howard-yoder-collected-essays/.

Kraus, C. Norman. "American Mennonites and the Bible, 1750–1950." In *Essays on Biblical Interpretation: Anabaptist-Mennonite Perspectives*, edited by Willard Swartley, 131–50. Elkhart, IN: IMS, 1984.

———. *The Community of the Spirit: How the Church Is in the World.* Scottdale, PA: Herald, 1993.

———. *An Intrusive Gospel?: Christian Mission in the Postmodern World.* Downers Grove, IL: InterVarsity, 1998.

———. "Shifting Mennonite Theological Orientations." In *Anabaptist-Mennonite Identities in Ferment*, edited by Leo Driedger and Leland Harder, 32–49. Elkhart, IN: IMS, 1990.

———. "A Theological Analysis of Mennonite Statements of Mission." In *A Relevant Anabaptist Missiology for the 1990s*, edited by Calvin E. Shenk, 19–24. Elkhart, IN: Council of International Ministries, 1990.

Kraybill, Donald B. *The Upside Down Kingdom.* Scottdale, PA: Herald, 2003.

Krehbiel, Stephanie. "Staying Alive: How Martyrdom Made Me a Warrior." *Mennonite Life* 61. https://ml.bethelks.edu/issue/vol-61-no-4/article/staying-alive-how-martyrdom-made-me-a-warrior/.

Kreider, Alan. "Tongue Screws and Testimony." *Missio Dei* 16. Elkhart, IN: MMN, 2008.

———. "West Europe in Missional Perspective: Themes from Mennonite Mission, 1950–2004." In *Evangelical, Ecumenical, and Anabaptist Missiologies in Conversation: Essays in Honor of Wilbert R. Shenk*, edited by James R. Krabill et al., 206–15. Maryknoll, NY: Orbis, 2006.

Kreider, Alan, and Eleanor Kreider. *Worship and Mission After Christendom.* Scottdale, PA: Herald, 2011.

Kreider, Alan, et al. *A Culture of Peace: God's Vision for the Church.* Intercourse, PA: Good, 2005.

Kuiper, Frits. "The Pre-Eminence of the Bible in Mennonite History." In *Essays on Biblical Interpretation: Anabaptist-Mennonite Perspectives,* edited by Willard Swartley, 115–30. Elkhart, IN: IMS, 1984.

Kuitse, Roelf S. "Holy Spirit: Source of Messianic Mission." In *The Transfiguration of Mission: Biblical, Theological and Historical Foundations,* edited by Wilbert R. Shenk, 106–29. Scottdale, PA: Herald, 1993.

Kulkarni, Chaya. "Attachment vs. Attachment Parenting." (August 30, 2012). https://youtu.be/QHto6X7neXk.

Kwok, Pui Lan. *Introducing Asian Feminist Theology.* Sheffield: Sheffield Academic, 2000.

———. *Postcolonial Imagination and Feminist Theology.* Louisville: Westminster John Knox, 2005.

LaCugna, Catherine Mowry. "Baptism, Feminists, and Trinitarian Theology." *Ecumenical Trends* 17 (1988) 65–68.

———. "The Baptismal Formula, Feminist Objections, and Trinitarian Theology." *Journal of Ecumenical Studies* 26 (1989) 235–50.

———. *God for Us: The Trinity and Christian Life.* San Francisco: HarperSanFrancisco, 1991.

———. "God in Communion with Us: The Trinity." In *Freeing Theology: The Essentials of Theology in Feminist Perspective,* edited by Catherine Mowry LaCugna, 83–114. San Francisco: HarperCollins, 1993.

———. "Philosophers and Theologians on the Trinity." *Modern Theology* 2 (1986) 169–81.

———. "The Practical Trinity." *The Christian Century* 109 (1992) 678–82.

———. "Re-Conceiving the Trinity as the Mystery of Salvation." *Scottish Journal of Theology* 38 (1985) 1–23.

———. "The Relational God: Aquinas and Beyond." *Theological Studies* 46 (1985) 647–63.

———. "The Trinitarian Mystery of God." In *Systematic Theology: Roman Catholic Perspectives,* edited by Catherine Mowry LaCugna, 149–92. Minneapolis: Fortress, 1991).

LaCugna, Catherine Mowry, and Killian McDonnell. "Returning from 'The Far Country:' Theses for a Contemporary Trinitarian Theology." *Scottish Journal of Theology* 41 (1988) 191–215.

Lampe, G.W.H. *God as Spirit.* Oxford: Clarendon, 1977.

Lindbeck, George. *The Nature of Doctrine: Religion and Theology in a Postliberal Age.* Louisville: Westminster John Knox, 1984.

———. "The Story-Shaped Church: Critical Exegesis and Theological Interpretation." In *Scriptural Authority and Narrative Interpretation,* edited by Garrett Green, 161–78. Philadelphia: Fortress, 1987.

Loewen, Howard John. "The Mission of Theology." In *Explorations of Systematic Theology from Mennonite Perspectives,* edited by Willard Swartley, 83–111. Elkhart, IN: IMS, 1984.

MacMaster, Richard K., and Donald R. Jacobs. *A Gentle Wind of God: The Influence of the East Africa Revival.* Scottdale, PA: Herald, 2006.

Maltz, Wendy. *The Sexual Healing Journey: A Guide for Survivors of Sexual Abuse.* New York: HarperCollins, 1991.

Manohar, Christina. "Spirit Christology: an Indian Christian Perspective." PhD diss., University of Gloucestershire, 2007.

———. "The Spirit in Mission." In *Foundations for Mission*, edited by Emma Wild-Wood and Peniel Rajkumar, 138–53. Eugene, OR: Wipf & Stock, 2013.

Marshall, Christopher. "Atonement, Violence and the Will of God: A Sympathetic Response to J. Denny Weaver's *The Nonviolent Atonement*." *MQR* 77 (2003) 69–92.

Martell-Otero, Loida I. "From *Satas* to *Santas*: *Sobrajas* No More: Salvation in the Spaces of the Everyday." In *Latina Evangélicas: A Theological Survey from the Margins*, 33–51. Eugene, OR: Cascade, 2013.

———. "Introduction: *Abuelita* Theologies." In *Latina Evangélicas: A Theological Survey from the Margins*, 1–13. Eugene, OR: Cascade, 2013.

———. "Neither 'Left Behind' Not Deciphering Secret Codes: An *Evangélicas* Understanding of Eschatology." In *Latina Evangélicas: A Theological Survey from the Margins*, 108–27. Eugene, OR: Cascade, 2013.

Martell-Otero, Loida I., et al. "Dancing with the Wild Child: *Evangélicas* and the Holy Spirit." In *Latina Evangélicas: A Theological Survey from the Margins*, 14–32. Eugene, OR: Cascade, 2013.

Martens, Peter. "The Quest for an Anabaptist Atonement: Violence and Nonviolence in J. Denny Weaver's *The Nonviolent Atonement*." *MQR* 82 (2008) 281–311.

Martin, Maurice. "The Pure Church: the Burden of Anabaptism." *CGR* 1 (1983) 29–41.

McClendon, James. *Doctrine*. Nashville: Abingdon, 1994.

———. *Ethics*. Nashville: Abingdon, 1986.

McFague, Sallie. *Models of God: Theology for an Ecological, Nuclear Age*. Philadelphia: Fortress, 1987.

Meihuizen, H.W. "The Missionary Zeal of the Early Anabaptists." In *Anabaptism and Mission*, edited by Wilbert R. Shenk, 88–96. Scottdale, PA: Herald, 1984.

The Mennonite. "Mennonite Church USA Releases Report, Makes Recommendations in Sexual Abuse Case." *The Mennonite* (January 23, 2017). https://themennonite.org/daily-news/mennonite-church-usa-releases-report-makes-recommendations-sexual-abuse-case/.

Mennonite Church. "Proceedings." Eighth Mennonite Church General Assembly (1985).

———. "Vision 95: a Summary Report." Mennonite Church 12th Churchwide Convention and General Assembly (1995) 32–35.

Mennonite Church USA. "Church Structure." http://mennoniteusa.org/who-we-are/structure/.

———. *Confession of Faith in a Mennonite Perspective*. Scottdale, PA: Herald, 1995.

———. "John Howard Yoder Digest: Recent Articles About Sexual Abuse and Discernment." http://mennoniteusa.org/menno-snapshots/john-howard-yoder-digest-recent-articles-about-sexual-abuse-and-discernment-2/.

———. "Mennonite Spiritual Directors Network." http://mennoniteusa.org/tag/mennonite-spiritual-directors-network/.

Mennonite World Conference. "About MWC." http://mwc-cmm.org/content/about-mwc.

———. "World Directory." http://mwc-cmm.org/article/world-directory.

Miller, John. *Biblical Faith and Fathering: In Defense of Monotheistic Father Religion*. New York: Paulist, 1990.

Minuchin, Salvador. "Where Is the Family in Narrative Family Therapy?" *Journal of Marital and Family Therapy* 24 (1998) 397–403.

Miriam Webster Learners Dictionary. "Risk-taking." http://www.learnersdictionary.com/definition/risk%E2%80%93taking.

Mitchell, Beverly, et al. "Mission from the Margins." *International Review of Mission* 101 (2012) 153–69.

Moltmann, Jürgen. *The Coming of God*. London: SCM, 2005.

Mosaic Mennonite Conference. "Intercultural." https://mosaicmennonites.org/intercultural/.

Murray, Stuart. *Biblical Interpretation in the Anabaptist Tradition*. Kitchener, ON: Pandora, 1999.

———. *Church After Christendom: Church and Mission in a Strange New World*. Colorado Springs, CO: Paternoster, 2004.

———. *Church Planting: Laying Foundations*. Scottdale, PA: Herald, 2001.

———. *The Naked Anabaptist: The Bare Essentials of a Radical Faith*. Scottdale, PA: Herald, 2010.

———. "Spirit, Discipleship, Community: The Contemporary Significance of Anabaptist Hermeneutics." PhD diss., The Whitefield Institute, 1992.

Navone, John J. *A Theology of Failure*. New York: Paulist, 1974.

Neufeld, Alfred. *What We Believe Together: Exploring the "Shared Convictions" of Anabaptist Related Churches*. Intercourse, PA: Good, 2007.

Niemandt, Cornelius J. P. "Trends in Missional Ecclesiology." *Theological Studies* 68 (2012). http://dx.doi.org/10.4102/hts.v68i1.1198.

Nussbaum, Sarah. "Ascension Day in Amish Country." *Lehman's Country Life* (May 4, 2016). https://www.lehmans.com/blog/ascension-day-in-amish-country/.

Oduyoye, Mercy Amba. *Introducing African Women's Theology*. Cleveland, OH: A. & C. Black, 2001.

Ollenburger, Ben C. "The Hermeneutics of Obedience: Reflections on Anabaptist Hermeneutics." In *Essays on Biblical Interpretation: Anabaptist-Mennonite Perspectives*, edited by Willard Swartley, 45–61. Elkhart, IN: IMS, 1984.

Oxford Dictionary. "Risk." http://www.oxforddictionaries.com/us/definition/american_english/risk.

Pelkey-Landes, Craig. "Purpose-Driven Mennonites." *Missio Dei* 6. Elkhart, IN: MMN, 2004.

Penner, Todd. "Madness in the Method? The Acts of the Apostles in Current Study." *Currents in Biblical Research* 2 (2004) 223–93.

Peppiatt, Lucy. "Spirit Christology and Mission." PhD diss., University of Otago, 2010.

Picirilli, Robert E. "An Arminian Response to John Sanders's *The God Who Risks: A Theology of Providence*." *Journal of the Evangelical Theological Society* 44 (2001) 467–91.

Pinnock, Clark H. *Flame of Love: A Theology of the Holy Spirit*. Downers Grove, IL: InterVarsity, 1996.

Plaskow, Judith. "Feminist Anti-Judaism and the Christian God." In *The Strength of Her Witness: Jesus Christ in the Global Voices of Women*, edited by Elizabeth A. Johnson, 86–99. Maryknoll, NY: Orbis, 2016.

Rahner, Karl. *The Trinity*. Translated by Joseph Donceel. New York: Herder and Herder, 1970.

Raith, Charles D. "*Ressourcing* the Fathers? A Critical Analysis of Catherine Mowry LaCugna's Appropriation of the Trinitarian Theology of the Cappadocian Fathers." *International Journal of Systematic Theology* 10 (2008) 267–84.

Ralph, Emily. "Baptized Again." In *Tongue Screws and Testimonies,* edited by Kirsten Beachy, 239–43. Scottdale, PA: Herald, 2010.

———. "God's Dream on Earth: New Narratives for the Intercultural Church." MA thesis, Eastern Mennonite Seminary, 2013.

Ralph Servant, Emily. "The Gentrification of the Margins." *MQR* 92 (2018) 404–22.

Ramseyer, Robert L. "The Anabaptist Vision and Our World Mission (I)." In *Anabaptism and Mission,* edited by Wilbert R. Shenk, 178–87. Scottdale, PA: Herald, 1984.

Ray, Darby Kathleen. *Deceiving the Devil: Atonement, Abuse, and Ransom.* Cleveland: Pilgrim, 1998.

———. *Incarnation and Imagination: a Christian Ethic of Ingenuity.* Minneapolis: Fortress, 2008.

Reimer, James. *Mennonites and Classical Theology: Dogmatic Foundations for Christian Ethics.* Kitchener, ON: Pandora, 2001.

Rempel, John. "Spirituality in Recent Mennonite Writing." *MQR* 71 (1997) 594–602.

Reynolds, Thomas. *Vulnerable Communion: A Theology of Disability and Hospitality.* Grand Rapids: Brazos, 2008.

Ritchie, Nelly. "Women and Christology." In *Through Her Eyes: Women's Theology from Latin America,* edited by Elsa Tamez, 81–95. Eugene, OR: Wipf & Stock, 1989.

Ross, Jamie, and Andre Gingerich Stoner. "What Anabaptists Bring to the Interchurch Table." In *Fully Engaged: Missional Church in an Anabaptist Voice,* edited by Stanley W. Green and James R. Krabill, 257–61. Harrisonburg, VA: Herald, 2015.

Roth, John D. "Anabaptist Missions and the Critique of Christendom." In *Practicing Truth: Confident Witness in Our Pluralistic World,* edited by David W. Shenk and Linford Stutzman, 82–101. Scottdale, PA: Herald, 1999.

———. *Practices: Mennonite Worship and Witness.* Scottdale, PA: Herald, 2009.

Rothbaum, Fred, and Gilda Morelli. "Attachment and Culture: Bridging Relativism and Universalism." In *Culture and Human Development: The Importance of Cross-Cultural Research for the Social Sciences,* edited by Wolfgang Friedlmeier et al., 99–123. Hove: Taylor & Francis, 2005.

Ruether, Rosemary Radford. "Eschatology and Feminism." In *Lift Every Voice: Constructing Christian Theologies from the Underside,* edited by Susan B. Thistlethwaite, 109–24. Maryknoll, NY: Orbis, 2007.

———. "Feminist Interpretation: A Method of Correlation." In *Feminist Interpretation of the Bible,* edited by Letty M. Russell, 111–24. Philadelphia: Westminster, 1985.

———. *Sexism and God-Talk: Towards a Feminist Theology.* London: SCM, 1983.

———. *To Change the World: Christology and Cultural Criticism.* Eugene, OR: Wipf & Stock, 2001.

Runco, Mark. *Creativity: Theories and Themes: Research, Development, and Practice.* Amsterdam: Elsevier Science, 2014.

Russell, Letty M. *Human Liberation in a Feminist Perspective: A Theology.* Philadelphia: Westminster, 1977.

Ruth, John. *Maintaining the Right Fellowship.* Scottdale, PA: Herald, 1984.

Rutschman, LaVerne A. "Anabaptism and Liberation Theology." In *Freedom and Discipleship: Liberation Theology in an Anabaptist Perspective,* edited by Daniel S. Schipani, 51–65. Maryknoll, NY: Orbis, 1989.

Rutter, Jon. "Lancaster Mennonites OK Female Ordination." *Lancaster Online* (June 29, 2008). http://lancasteronline.com/news/lancaster-mennonites-ok-female-ordination/article_e2af6dfd-b4c6-515f-a600-0aae490241dd.html.

Sanchez, Danilo. "Hope for the Future: The Church I Want to Belong to." Mennonite Church USA (February 22, 2017). http://mennoniteusa.org/menno-snapshots/hope-future-church-want-belong/.

Sanders, John, ed. *Atonement and Violence: A Theological Conversation*. Nashville: Abingdon, 2006.

———. *The God Who Risks: A Theology of Divine Providence*. Downers Grove, IL: IVP Academic, 2009.

Sawyer, R. Keith. *Explaining Creativity: The Science of Human Innovation*. New York: Oxford University Press, 2012.

Say, Elizabeth A. "Many Voices, Many Visions: Toward a Feminist Methodology for Narrative Theology and Ethics." *Janus Head* 1 (1998). http://www.janushead.org/jhfall98/elizsay.cfm.

Schäufele, Wolfgang. "The Missionary Vision and Activity of the Anabaptist Laity." In *Anabaptism and Mission*, edited by Wilbert R. Shenk, 70–87. Scottdale, PA: Herald, 1984.

Schipani, Daniel S., ed. *Freedom and Discipleship: Liberation Theology in an Anabaptist Perspective*. Maryknoll, NY: Orbis, 1989.

Schirmer, Will. *Reaching Beyond the Mennonite Comfort Zone: Exploring from the Inside Out*. Telford, PA: Cascadia, 2003.

Schlabach, Theron F. *Gospel Versus Gospel: Mission and the Mennonite Church, 1863–1944*. Scottdale, PA: Herald, 1980.

Schmidt, Melvin D. "Tax Refusal as Conscientious Objection to War." *MQR* 43 (1969) 234–46.

Schrag, Paul. "Year in Review: Sexuality Issues Test Unity." *MWR* (December 22, 2014). http://mennoworld.org/2014/12/22/news/year-in-review-sexuality-issues-test-unity/.

Session, Irie L. *Murdered Souls, Resurrected Lives: Postmodern Womanist Thought in Ministry with Women Prostituted and Marginalized by Commercial Sexual Exploitation*. Scotts Valley, CA: CreateSpace, 2015.

Shank, David A. "Anabaptists and Mission." In *Anabaptism and Mission*, edited by Wilbert R. Shenk, 202–26. Scottdale, PA: Herald, 1984.

———. "Jesus the Messiah: Messianic Foundation of Mission." In *The Transfiguration of Mission: Biblical, Theological and Historical Foundations*, edited by Wilbert R. Shenk, 37–82. Scottdale, PA: Herald, 1993.

Shenk, Calvin E. "Essential Themes for an Anabaptist Missiology." In *A Relevant Anabaptist Missiology for the 1990s*, edited by Calvin E. Shenk, 63–92. Elkhart, IN: Council of International Ministries, 1990.

———. "The Gospel and Religions." In *Practicing Truth: Confident Witness in Our Pluralistic World*, edited by David W. Shenk and Linford Stutzman, 171–86. Scottdale, PA: Herald, 1999.

Shenk, David W. *Christian, Muslim, Friend: Twelve Paths to Real Relationship*. Harrisonburg, VA: Herald, 2014.

———. *Global Gods: Exploring the Role of Religions in Modern Societies*. Scottdale, PA: Herald, 1995.

———. *God's Call to Mission*. Scottdale, PA: Herald, 1994.

Shenk, David W., and Ervin Stutzman. *Creating Communities of the Kingdom*. Scottdale, PA: Herald, 1988.

Shenk, Joanna. "Becoming an Anablacktavist." *MWR* (May 12, 2014). http://mennoworld.org/2014/05/12/columns/becoming-an-anablacktivist/.

Shenk, Wilbert R. *By Faith They Went Out: Mennonite Missions, 1850–1999*. Elkhart, IN: IMS, 2000.

———. *Changing Frontiers of Mission*. Maryknoll, NY: Orbis, 1999.

———. *The Church in Mission*. Scottdale, PA: Herald, 1984.

———. "A Developing Missiological Vision for Anabaptists." In *A Relevant Anabaptist Missiology for the 1990s*, edited by Calvin E. Shenk, 43–61. Elkhart, IN: Council of International Ministries, 1990.

———. "The Relevance of a Messianic Missiology for Mission Today." In *The Transfiguration of Mission: Biblical, Theological and Historical Foundations*, edited by Wilbert R. Shenk, 17–36. Scottdale, PA: Herald, 1993.

———. *Write the Vision: The Church Renewed*. Harrisburg, PA: Trinity, 1995.

Sider, Ron J. "A Critique of J. Denny Weaver's *Nonviolent Atonement*." *Brethren in Christ History and Life* 35 (2012) 214–41.

Sider, Ron J., and Heidi Rolland Unruh. "Keeping Good News and Good Works Together." In *Fully Engaged: Missional Church in an Anabaptist Voice*, edited by Stanley W. Green and James R. Krabill, 47–56. Harrisonburg, VA: Herald, 2015.

Silverman, Ellie, et al. "'They tried to kill my child to shut her up,' Heather Heyer's Mother Mourns at Funeral for Woman Killed during Nazi Protest in Charlottesville." *The Washington Post* (August 16, 2017). http://wapo.st/2fJ4EEf?tid=ss_tw&utm_term=.4a872e484ae1.

Simons, Menno. "A Fundamental Doctrine from the Word of the Lord, of the New Birth." In *The Complete Works of Menno Simons*, 1:167–76. Translated by John Funk. Elkhart, IN: John F. Funk & Brother, 1871.

———. "The Reason Why Menno Simon Does Not Cease Teaching and Writing." In *The Complete Works of Menno Simons*, 2:235–55. Translated by John Funk. Elkhart, IN: John F. Funk & Brother, 1871.

———. "Reply to a Publication of Gellius Faber." In *The Complete Works of Menno Simons*, 2:7–105. Translated by John Funk. Elkhart, IN: John F. Funk & Brother, 1871.

Sine, Tom. "Joining the Anabaptist Conspirators." *The Mennonite* (June 3, 2008). https://themennonite.org/feature/joining-anabaptist-conspirators/.

Smucker, Marcus G. "Spiritual Direction and Spiritual Formation." *GAMEO* (1989). http://gameo.org/index.php?title=Spiritual_Direction_and_Spiritual_Formation&oldid=110211.

So, Damon W.K. "Christianity and Trinity in Mission." In *Foundations for Mission*, edited by Emma Wild-Wood and Peniel Rajkumar, 123–37. Eugene, OR: Wipf & Stock, 2013.

———. *The Forgotten Jesus and the Trinity You Never Knew*. Eugene, OR: Wipf & Stock, 2010.

Sparks, Paul, et al. *The New Parish: How Neighborhood Churches are Transforming Mission, Discipleship and Community*. Downers Grove, IL: InterVarsity, 2014.

Stayer, James M., et al. "From Monogenesis to Polygenesis: The Historical Discussion of Anabaptist Origins." *MQR* 49 (1975) 83–121.

Stenger, Mary Ann and Ronald H. Stone. *Dialogues of Paul Tillich.* Macon, GA: Mercer University Press, 2002.

Stoner, Andre Gingerich. "Our Victim Mentality." *MWR* (May 28, 2012). http://www.mennoworld.org/archived/2012/5/28/our-victim-mentality/.

Stuhr, John. *Pragmatism, Postmodernism, and the Future of Philosophy.* New York: Routledge, 2003.

Stutzman, Ervin R. *From Nonresistance to Justice: The Transformation of Mennonite Church Peace Rhetoric, 1908–2008.* Scottdale, PA: Herald, 2011.

Stutzman, Linford. *With Jesus in the World.* Scottdale, PA: Herald, 1992.

Swartley, Willard M., ed. *Essays on Biblical Interpretation: Anabaptist-Mennonite Perspectives.* Elkhart, IN: IMS, 1984.

———, ed. *Explorations of Systematic Theology from Mennonite Perspectives.* Elkhart, IN: IMS, 1984.

———. *Slavery, Sabbath, War, and Women: Case Issues in Biblical Interpretation.* Scottdale, PA: Herald, 1983.

Synan, H. Vinson. *The Century of the Holy Spirit: 100 Years of Pentecostal and Charismatic Renewal, 1901–2001.* Nashville: Thomas Nelson, 2001.

Thiessen Nation, Mark. "The Naked Anabaptist or Particular Anabaptist?" *Anabaptist Nation* (September 1, 2012). http://emu.edu/now/anabaptist-nation/2012/09/01/the-naked-anabaptist-or-particular-anabaptists/.

———. "'Who Has Believed What We Have Heard?': A Response to Denny Weaver's *The Nonviolent Atonement.*" *CGR* 27 (2009) 17–30.

Thomas, Linda E. "Anthropology, Mission, and the African Woman." In *Mission and Culture,* edited by Stephen B. Bevans, 119–32. Maryknoll, NY: Orbis, 2012.

———. "Womanist Theology, Epistemology, and a New Anthropological Paradigm." *Cross Currents* 48 (1998–1999) 488–99.

Tillich, Paul. *Biblical Religion and the Search for Ultimate Reality.* Chicago: University of Chicago Press, 1955.

———. *Systematic Theology, Vol 1.* Chicago: University of Chicago Press, 1951.

Toews, Paul. *Mennonites in American Society, 1930–1970.* Scottdale, PA: Herald, 1996.

Townes, Emilie M. "Living in the New Jerusalem." In *A Troubling in My Soul: Womanist Perspectives on Evil and Suffering,* edited by Emilie M. Townes, 78–91. Maryknoll, NY: Orbis, 1993.

Tracy, David. *Blessed Rage for Order.* Minneapolis: Seabury, 1975.

———. "Foundations of Practical Theology." In *Practical Theology,* edited by Don Browning, 61–82. San Francisco: Harper & Row, 1983.

Tucker, Gene. "Creation and the Limits of the World: Nature and History in the Old Testament." *Horizons in Biblical Theology* 15 (1993) 105–18.

Tutu Foundation. http://www.tutufoundationuk.org/ubuntu/.

van der Zijpp, Nanne. "From Anabaptist Missionary Congregation to Mennonite Seclusion." In *Anabaptism and Mission,* edited by Wilbert R. Shenk, 118–36. Scottdale, PA: Herald, 1984.

———. "Maeyken Wens (d. 1573)." *GAMEO* (1957). http://gameo.org/index.php?title=Maeyken_Wens_(d._1573).

van der Zijpp, Nanne, et al. "Martyrs' Mirror." *GAMEO* (2014). http://gameo.org/index.php?title=Martyrs%27_Mirror.

Van Steenwyk, Mark. *The UnKingdom of God: Embracing the Subversive Power of Repentance.* Downers Grove, IL: IVP, 2013.

Vanstone, W.H. *The Risk of Love*. New York: Oxford University Press, 1978.

Villegas, Isaac S. "Fruit of the Vine." *The Mennonite* (August 1, 2010). https://themennonite.org/opinion/fruitvine/.

Weaver, Alain Epp, and Gerald J. Mast, eds. *The Work of Jesus Christ in Anabaptist Perspective: Essays in Honor of J. Denny Weaver*. Scottdale, PA: Herald, 2008.

Weaver, J. Denny. *Anabaptist Theology in Face of Postmodernity: A Proposal for the Third Millennium*. Scottdale, PA: Herald, 2000.

———. "Atonement for the Nonconstantinian Church." *Modern Theology* (1990) 307–23.

———. "*Christus Victor*, Ecclesiology, and Christology." *MQR* 68 (1994) 277–90.

———. "Forgiveness and (Non)violence: The Atonement Connections." *MQR* 83 (2009) 319–47.

———. *Keeping Salvation Ethical: Mennonite and Amish Atonement Theology in the Late 19th Century*. Scottdale, PA: Herald, 1997.

———. "Narrative Christus Victor: the Answer to Anselmian Atonement Violence." In *Atonement and Violence: A Theological Conversation*, edited by John Sanders, 1–29. Nashville: Abingdon, 2006.

———. "Narrative Theology in an Anabaptist-Mennonite Context." *CGR* 12 (1994) 171–88.

———. *The Nonviolent Atonement*. 1st ed. Grand Rapids: Eerdmans, 2001.

———. *The Nonviolent God*. Grand Rapids: Eerdmans, 2013.

———. "The Quickening of Soteriology: Atonement from Christian Burkholder to Daniel Kauffman." *MQR* 61 (1987) 5–45.

———. "Response." In *Anabaptist-Mennonite Identities in Ferment*, edited by Leo Driedger and Leland Harder, 27–31. Elkhart, IN: IMS, 1990.

———. "Response to Hans Boersma." In *Atonement and Violence: A Theological Conversation*, edited by John Sanders, 73–79. Nashville: Abingdon, 2006.

———. "Response to Peter Martens, 'The Quest for an Anabaptist Atonement.'" *MQR* 82 (2008) 313–20.

———. "Response to Reflections on *The Nonviolent Atonement*." *CGR* 27 (2009) 39–49.

———. "Response to T. Scott Daniels." In *Atonement and Violence: A Theological Conversation*, edited by John Sanders, 151–53. Nashville: Abingdon, 2006.

———. "Theological Implications of *Christus Victor*." *MQR* 68 (1994) 433–576.

———. "Violence in Christian Theology." *Cross Currents* 51 (2001) 150–76.

Webster, Alan. "Obituary: Canon Bill Vanstone." *The Independent* (March 11, 1999). https://www.independent.co.uk/arts-entertainment/obituary-canon-bill-vanstone-1079750.html.

Weisner, Thomas S. "The Socialization of Trust: Plural Caregiving and Diverse Pathways in Human Development across Cultures." In *Different Faces of Attachment: Cultural Variations on a Universal Human Need*, edited by Hiltred Otto et al., 263–77. New York: Cambridge University Press, 2014.

Welch, Susan D. *Communities of Resistance and Solidarity: a Feminist Theology of Liberation*. Maryknoll, NY: Orbis, 1985.

———. *A Feminist Ethic of Risk*. Minneapolis: Fortress, 1990.

Wenger, J.C., et al. "Apocalypticism." GAMEO (1989). http://gameo.org/index.php?title=Apocalypticism&oldid=120886.

White, Michael, and David Epston. *Narrative Means to Therapeutic Ends*. New York: W. W. Norton, 1990.

Wild-Wood, Emma. "Common Witness 'in Christ': Peregrinations through Mission and Migration." *Mission Studies* 30 (2013) 43–63.

———. "Mission, Ecclesiology, and Migration." In *Mission on the Road to Emmaus: Constants, Context, and Prophetic Dialogue*, edited by Cathy Ross and Stephen B. Bevans, 51–66. Maryknoll, NY: Orbis, 2015.

Williams, George H., ed. *Spiritual and Anabaptist Writers: Documents Illustrative of the Radical Reformation*. Philadelphia: Westminster, 1977.

Woodley, Randy. "Early Dialogue in the Community of Creation." In *Buffalo Shout, Salmon Cry*, edited by Steve Heinrichs, 92–103. Harrisonburg, VA: Herald, 2013.

———. *Shalom and the Community of Creation*. Grand Rapids: Eerdmans, 2012.

Wright, N. T. "Israel's Scriptures in Paul's Narrative Theology." *Theology* 115 (2012) 323–29.

———. "Narrative Theology: The Evangelists' Use of the Old Testament as an Implicit Overarching Narrative." In *Biblical Interpretation and Method: Essays in Honour of John Barton*, edited by Katherine J. Dell and Paul M. Joyce, 189–200. Oxford: Oxford University Press, 2013.

Yamasaki, Gary. "Shalom for Shepherds: An Audience-oriented Critical Analysis." In *Beautiful upon the Mountains: Biblical Essays on Mission, Peace, and the Reign of God*, edited by Mary H. Schertz and Ivan Friesen, 146–60. Scottdale, PA: Herald, 2003.

Yoder, John Howard. "As You Go." In *Theology of Mission: A Believers Church Perspective*, 399–421. Downers Grove, IL: IVP Academic, 2014.

———. "Marginalia." *Concern for Christian Renewal* 15 (1967).

———, ed. "Schleitheim Confession." Scottdale, PA: Herald, 1977.

———. *Theology of Mission: A Believers Church Perspective*. Downers Grove, IL: IVP Academic, 2014.

Yoder Neufeld, Tom. "Weaver and Nonviolent Atonement: A Response." *CGR* 27 (2009) 31–38.

Yong, Amos. *The Spirit Poured out on All Flesh: Pentecostalism and the Possibility of Global Theology*. Grand Rapids: Baker Academic, 2005.

Zizioulas, John D. *Being as Communion: Studies in Personhood and the Church*. London: Darton, Longman & Todd, 1985.

Index

☆ p. 135 Goal of theology is not Knowledge but relationship

150 Distant immutable God

p. 18 F. Hiebert

p. 36 Marginalizing the marginalized.

37 Discipleship, community, non violence (Bender)

49 Using Herder's method of obedience, suspicion, imagination

50-1 Formed like Christ

61 First step, vulnerability, p. 65

70 failure

74 can't predict outcomes

77 Ethic of control vs ethic of love

79 Vs. self vs other

93 Hard wired to over-estimate risk

99 Risk vs. Martyr's Mirror

☆ 100 Risk of purity vs risk of closeness

☆ 102 The problem in churches
   - need to be for something
   - how serve is against ?! ☆

104 The Church is God's mission.

108 Summary

124 Jesus death as staying w/humans

127 Churches loving at a distance

?! 130 equation of Spirit with Chi., vs. p. 132'.

What is risk-taking?

Left out power or positive goal.

Love is not only vulnerable - it is powerful & strong (p. 115)

☆ God does not reject power! Foucault

Ontology of violence
Milbank

CPSIA information can be obtained
at www.ICGtesting.com
Printed in the USA
FSHW020123260321
79794FS

Cf p. 156
- negative view of power

9 781725 260047